D0223721

Complicit Fictions

Twentieth-Century Japan:
The Emergence of a World Power

Irwin Scheiner, Editor

1. *Labor and Imperial Democracy in Prewar Japan*, by Andrew Gordon
2. *Complicit Fictions: The Subject in the Modern Japanese Prose Narrative*, by James A. Fujii

Complicit Fictions

The Subject in the Modern Japanese Prose Narrative

JAMES A. FUJII

UNIVERSITY OF CALIFORNIA PRESS
Berkeley Los Angeles Oxford

University of California Press
Berkeley and Los Angeles, California

University of California Press, Ltd.
Oxford, England

Library of Congress Cataloging-in-Publication Data

Fujii, James A.
Complicit fictions : the subject in the modern Japanese prose narrative / James A. Fujii.
p. cm. — (Twentieth-century Japan: the emergence of a world power)
Includes bibliographical references (p.) and index.
ISBN 0-520-07757-1 (cloth : alk. paper). — ISBN 0-520-07770-9 (paper : alk. paper)
1. Japanese fiction—1868- —History and criticism. I. Title. II. Series: Twentieth-century Japan.
PL777.55.F85 1993
895.6'3409—dc20
91-42884
CIP

Printed in the United States of America
9 8 7 6 5 4 3 2 1

The paper used in this publication meets the minimum requirements of American National Standard for Information Sciences—Permanence of Paper for Printed Library Materials, ANSI Z39.48-1984.

To My Parents

Contents

In a work entitled *Tristram Shandy*, Sterne wrote that there is no other writing more closely informed by the will of God than his. . . . Appealing to His grace, he simply held the pen and let it take its course. Apparently, the writer is free from all responsibility. . . . Sterne not only denied responsibility, he thrust it in the hands of the Lord. But I, who have no God to assume the burden, finally tossed it into a roadside ditch.

Natsume Sōseki, *Kusamakura*

In setting aside biographical and psychological references, one has already called back into question the absolute character and founding role of the subject. . . . Perhaps one must return to this question, not in order to re-establish the theme of the originating subject, but to grasp the subject's points of insertion, modes of functioning, and system of dependencies. . . . In short, it is a matter of depriving the subject (or its substitute) of its role as originator, and of analyzing the subject as a variable and complex function of discourse.

Michel Foucault, "What Is an Author?"

No matter how theoretically necessary the dismantling of the subject might be, theory embarks on such a course as its peril, for the hypostatized center of domination that the abstract individual represents is also in many cases the last form of resistance to domination available.

Vincent Pecora, *Self and Form in Modern Narrative*

Preface

For reasons that are deeply embedded in the history of Japan's encounters with the Western world, modern Japanese literature has been and continues to be assessed largely through European realist textual conventions by Westerners and Japanese alike. The most distinctive and commanding feature of such realist practices—the centrality of an individual whose thoughts, feelings, and actions merit close attention—has established itself as the most important measure of prose narration in post-Restoration (1868) Japan. This realist subject has decisively determined the trajectory of modern Japanese literature (*kindai bungaku*) by serving as both the ostensible object of appropriation for modern Japanese writers and the standard by which critics in both the West and Japan have evaluated this literature. The purpose of this study is to challenge this overdetermination, first by specifying the limitations and problems of literary criticism rooted in realist subjectivism, then by rereading selected Japanese texts, *not* as efforts to emulate European realism but as narrative acts inscribed with historical particulars very much their own. Recent critical endeavors have provided us with both compelling reasons and the means to rethink existing empiricist or positivist views of literature that insist upon the priority of the "individual" or the subject. As a prelude to this extended interrogation of the modern Japanese prose narrative (*kindai shōsetsu*), I wish to illustrate how the necessity of problematizing the essentialized subject and, more specifically, of reconceiving it as discursive creation and hence as an issue of agency are directly relevant to our own historical moment.

During a recent visit to Los Angeles, I became acutely and unexpectedly aware of the issues of subjects and agency. Branded with the image of urban sprawl without an organic center from which to unfold, Los Angeles remains to many, in spite of itself, the quintessential postmodern American city. I never thought to question this received truth about L.A. as a megalopolis with no central city, a nexus of dispersed clusters of businesses, neighborhoods, and shopping malls linked haphazardly by freeways, car phones, and fax machines—until I drove through its downtown section around five o'clock on a Sunday afternoon. What I witnessed was one of the liveliest downtown shopping scenes I have ever seen in an American city. This vibrant inner city activity was undeniably real to that crowd consisting mostly of Hispanic people shopping and walking the grids of downtown L.A. that day, as they do every weekend. Apparently, class and color establish (or, more precisely, the dominant group determines) the "realities" we choose to embrace as collectively held beliefs. The characterization of Los Angeles as an urban cluster with no center may have widespread currency, but clearly it speaks a partisan "fact." Realities and truths, then, do not bespeak "objective" conditions so much as they alert us to the question of *who* speaks, observes, and pronounces. Such politics of subject positions continue largely to be ignored in both society at large and, more germane for our purposes (and pointedly egregious an omission in view of the cross-cultural nature of the practice), in the interpretation of modern Japanese literary texts.

The kindred value of questioning positive subjects, be they in premodern or contemporary Japan, was for me powerfully linked to lived life in a recent talk by Ryūsawa Takeshi, chief editor of a large Japanese publishing house.[1] A century after Nietzsche's declaration of the death of God and decades after structuralist trends inaugurated a sustained assault on the notion of the individual, late twentieth-century Japan has been repeatedly represented as the vanguard of the postmodern, a term used in this connection to designate an absence of any unified and whole center of meaning, be it deity, subject, or system. Ryūsawa's study testifies to a process that seems to have wrested agency from the subject. As part of his presentation, he compiled a list of selected Japanese general circulation magazines inaugurated in 1989 (including those targeted at men, those covering women's fashion, etc.). Comparing initial publication figures to circulation figures of two to four months later,

1. Ryūsawa's untitled paper was presented at a conference called "Representations of Otherness: Japan and the United States," held at the Humanities Research Institute at the University of California, Irvine, on June 1, 1990.

he found that in every case the number of magazines printed and sold had declined sharply. For example, *Shūkan teimisu* went from 600,000 copies to 170,000, *Elle Japon* from 250,000 to 83,000, and *Gekkan asahi* from 625,000 to 190,000; virtually all of them had ceased publication well within a year. But the publishers of these magazines typically repeated the same cycle the following year, starting a magazine, only to have it fold in a very short time. Why did these publishers persist in repeating decisions that led to these cycles, which could be counted on to last no more than a few months or so? As one might suspect, advertising revenues made these ventures highly profitable. Interestingly, advertisers seemed little concerned about either the longevity of these magazines or the inevitable drop in circulation.[2] Typically, these magazines are little more than a series of glossy ads, between which are sandwiched narrow strips of texts written by social critics and intellectuals, such as Yoshimoto Ryūmei and Karatani Kōjin, who enjoy celebrity status. While advertising revenue has always played a significant role in magazine publication, in the cases cited here it seems to have completely displaced all content.

In such a cycle of publication, where is that vaunted reader, reclaimed so prominently by recent literary criticism in the West and in Japan? If there is a subject in this cycle, it is not a reader but rather a buyer, who purchases a magazine for its use value rather than as written text or even for its illustrations. (Ryūsawa noted that it is the wholesale paper distributor rather than either the publishers or the advertisers who benefit most from this arrangement.[3]) It is my guess that many of these publications find their way directly to hair salon waiting rooms and other enterprises interested in their value as signifiers of glitz and high-tech design. Clearly the roles of writer and reader still operative in the production of many books are suspect in this pro-

2. While it has been suggested to me that tax write-offs make such expenditure profitable for the advertising companies, I cannot confirm or deny this.

3. Global deforestation and the contemporary "subject" are linked in a pernicious cycle that seems helplessly removed from subject agents making willful and informed decisions about reading and writing. Ryūsawa goes on to conclude that reader profiles are no longer possible to construct and that, in such a cycle of reproduction, only a kind of ersatz subject can be found in the shape of the corporation.

duction loop. In those rare instances in which the buyer maintains his or her status as reader, it is the *buyer function* that perpetuates this cycle. Agency rests with the person as buyer, not as reader. It is even difficult to locate subjects as traditionally defined; instead, they are unwitting participants in a process that succeeds merely in enriching a select few at the expense of sound ecology and global health. Ryūsawa's presentation points to one variant of subjecthood or, more correctly, to its displacement by faceless corporations that defy conventional conceptions of the subject.

The scenarios described above emphatically suggest the inadequacy of conceiving subjects in positivist terms, not because the moment represented belongs to what might be designated as the postmodern but because, regardless of the era in question, essentialized conceptions eschew their own historicity. By historicizing the very processes that account for subjects as they take shape (or resist assuming certain forms), we can begin to see a modern Japanese literary history rather different from that narrativized and overdetermined according to standards imposed from afar. These excurses into modern-day experience point to the always tenuous, discursively constructed, constantly changing nature of what we call subjects and underscore the necessity of localizing the subjects of any study. If we are to study a phenomenon such as the subject in "modern Japanese prose narrative," we must account for that subject in terms that do not simply replicate a form fixed and given to us from regions far removed in both geographic and cultural space.

Before we begin this critical engagement with the *kindai shōsetsu,* one other matter compels comment: the absence of women writers in this book. The omission of texts by women from this study in large measure reflects both their exclusion from the *grand récit* of the modern Japanese prose narrative and the gendered construction of its central concept—the (largely male) subject. Yet, if relegation to the periphery were to dictate the condition of dismissal from the present study, Origuchi's text would not have been chosen. His inclusion marks a particular critical path, notably the conjuncture of performance and antiquity, that allowed me to confront crucial issues for this study. In the end, I chose to address the problems I could more forcefully engage at the expense of signaling my own marginal relationship to feminist thought, leaving for this study more dispersed and oblique attention to questions regarding gender (except in my discussion of Tokuda Shūsei's prose, where it figures more prominently).[4] Feminist concerns cannot be reduced to a matter of women writers, and I felt I could more effectively confront some feminist issues in terms of marginalization conceived in other ways.

Romanized transcription of the original Japanese has been provided only when I felt it was integral to the point being made. This book is a substantial revision of my dissertation "The Subject in Meiji Prose Narrative," which first began to take shape during a year of research and study with the late Maeda Ai in 1983–84. While it has taken some unexpected turns since that time, to him I owe a great debt of gratitude—for guiding me with his unerring sense of the important, for giving generously of his time, and for encouraging me and indeed a whole new generation of students of modern Japanese literature to see the theory in the texts. Among those he influenced is Komori Yōichi of Seijō University, to whom I am grateful for unselfishly sharing ideas and materials with me. I have also benefited from the thoughts and suggestions of Kamei Hideo of Hokkaidō University, Mitani Kuniaki's advice on Origuchi, and the collegiality of Seki Reiko and Taneda Wakako, who remain good friends from our seminar days at Rikkyō University. Higurashi Masa has served as a touchstone for a finely tuned literary sensibility that I myself lack, and to Ryūsawa Takeshi I am deeply indebted for many hours of discussion and valuable advice.

My deepest debts are to my teachers and friends who taught

4. While Gayatri Spivak rightly reminds us that "you cannot consider all other subjects and . . . you should look at your own subjective investment in the narrative that is being produced," when the missing subject position is one that consistently has been ignored, dismissed, and disempowered, one can hardly rationalize its absence by invoking her words so lightly. Here, I must simply admit to ambivalence that arises from personal uneasiness in situating myself within the discourse of feminist theory as it is often structured and practiced in the academy. The seriousness with which I consider this issue of positioning has been displaced to the issue of examining my "own subjective investment." The quotation is from Spivak, "The Post-Modern Condition: The End of Politics?", in *The Post-Colonial Critic: Interviews, Strategies, Dialogues*, ed. Sarah Harasym (New York: Routledge, 1990), 29.

at the University of Chicago: I would have been unable to complete my graduate studies (after a decade-long hiatus in the "real world") without the encouragement and erudite instruction of Bill Sibley; Harry Harootunian inspired me to see problems and issues beyond the established borders of my field; and Masao Miyoshi showed me not only how to challenge and to question but to fuse academic labor to committed beliefs. Tetsuo Najita's rigorous critical thinking challenged us all, while to Norma Field I owe gratitude for providing perceptive comments on my work throughout the years. Ted Fowler has been the best of colleagues, reading substantial portions of the manuscript and providing critical suggestions and advice at various points along the book-making process. To Leslie Pincus I have turned often for thoughtful criticism and supportive friendship, and Stefan Tanaka has encouraged and helped me along the way. I am deeply indebted to Naoki Sakai, who read the manuscript in its entirety and offered valuable criticism and support. Among my close friends and associates I am fortunate to count Bill Haver; my many debts to him include his suggestion to examine the status of knowledge in *Kokoro*. I have benefited from Richard Okada's critical acumen, particularly in the form of helpful suggestions for the chapter on Origuchi. Chungmoo Choi's intellectual energy and humanity provided inspiration close at hand during my years at the University of California, Santa Barbara. And, as friend and supportive colleague, Miriam Silverberg read multiple drafts of the entire manuscript and has always been there to show me the strengths as well as the limitations of my own thinking and work.

At the dissertation stage, a Fulbright-Hays grant provided an opportunity to conduct research in Japan in 1983–84. Generous support from the Social Science Research Council and the University of California, Santa Barbara (Faculty Career Development Grant), enabled me to devote the 1989–90 academic year to writing the manuscript; the Japan Foundation provided funds to complete the research. Work was made easier by support offered by the staffs of East Asia libraries at the University of California at both Berkeley and Santa Barbara and at the University of Chicago, where Kuki Yōko and Okuizumi Eizaburō were particularly helpful. Only as my manuscript was going to press was I able to get a copy of the thought-provoking dissertation on Tokuda Shūsei's work by Richard Torrance, who was gracious enough to send me a copy in a very short time. Excepting the McClellan translation of *Kokoro,* all translations are my own. Chapter 4 appeared as "Contesting the Meiji Subject: Sōseki's *Neko* Reconsidered" in *The Harvard Journal of Asiatic Studies* of December 1989.

At the University of California Press, special thanks go to Eileen McWilliam, Betsey Scheiner, and David Severtson. Finally, I wish to thank Ellen Radovic, my wife and intellectual companion, who shared in the sacrifices that attend a labor such as this and provided useful comments as that rare person who almost never reads a work such as this—a general reader.

1
INTRODUCTION

In Japan, a nation persistently and misleadingly characterized by foreigners and Japanese alike as a society where "group" (family) displaces "self," Western (particularly Romantic) conceptions of the individual continue to be embraced with considerable fanfare. Naturalized by over a century of sustained rumination, individualism has been adopted as a powerfully attractive ideal, whether it finds popular expression as an insistent and revealing emphasis on *kosei* (individuality) or when it appears repeatedly as the subject of scholarly discourse. In literature, we cannot but be impressed by the tenacity with which over the years Japanese writers and intellectuals have worked to appropriate the private self. Celebrated as a virtual synecdoche for the West and modernity, the concept of a private, emancipated individual worthy of self-reflection reached Japanese writers in the form of the nineteenth-century European realist novel. The individual has achieved privileged status in modern Japanese literature, illustrated by the autobiographical *shishōsetsu* (I-novel) form that saw only a brief flowering in the Taishō era (1912–26) but that continues to occupy a central place in Japanese letters.[1]

In the middle decades of Meiji (1868–1912) Japanese writers and critics eagerly accepted these realist-mimeticist conventions, which rely upon the notion of the individuated subject as the originary source of meaning in literature, and ever since realism has dominated as arbiter of a literature produced an ocean away in circumstances very much their own. In the decades following

1. If anything, its valorization as the quintessential modern Japanese prose narrative form, despite its relatively limited appeal to the reading public, suggests the powerful attraction of the individual as a signifier in Japanese intellectual circles.

the Meiji Restoration, fabulation of credible, individuated subjects was pursued according to the dictates of Western humanist constructions of the individuated self, but the resulting works were neither similar nor dissimilar to their avowed models in some reductive, categorical way. Moreover, among the literary texts written in an era commonly designated modern (historical convention marks its beginning point as the imperial Restoration of 1868, literary convention from around the 1890s with the emergence of prose narratives modeled on Western conventions of verisimilitude), there were many that deviated from what has been canonized as mainstream modern literature (*kindai bungaku*). Nonetheless, overwhelming consensus views "modern Japanese literature" as an extended attempt to appropriate conventions of the nineteenth-century European realist novel,[2] particularly the novel built around an individuated subject. Ironically, Japanese literature will continue to be secn as distant and exotic or somehow deficient as long as nineteenth-century Western realist standards persist in dictating its literary worth.

THE FICTION OF LITERARY REALISM

Wide and often unbridgeable disagreements separate disparate strands of recent critical theories, be they structuralist, post-structuralist, Marxist, or feminist, but they converge in their singular concern of questioning the positive, empiricist, and commonsensical conception of the subject that has anchored the Western humanist tradition and expressed itself through realist literary conventions. The present study pursues an opening provided by such interrogations of the subject in order to reconsider the trajectory of "modern Japanese literature." Challenging depictions of this literature as it has been overdetermined by a realist discourse that insists on the priority of the

2. In the United States, Masao Miyoshi has insistently argued against the practice of equating the novel with the *shōsetsu*. See, for example, "Against the Native Grain: The Japanese Novel and the 'Postmodern' West," *South Atlantic Quarterly* 87 (Summer 1988): 525–50, and "Reading the Japanese Novel in America," in *Critical Issues in East Asian Literature: Report on an International Conference on East Asian Literature* (Seoul: International Cultural Society of Korea, 1983): 221–48.

individuated self, this study critiques such a positing of an essentialist subject and recasts in narrative terms the discussion of modern Japanese prose. Once subjects are viewed as arising from a network of differential relations (see discussion below), we can directly address what essentialized-subject readings of Japanese literary texts have effectively suppressed—the politics of representation inherent in the transfer of Western realism to a foreign literature and the contest and struggle that mark the contingencies of subject expression in post-Restoration Japanese literature. Most important, taking account of the complex mediating forms (for example, industrialization, urban growth, reworked European conceptions of self and society characteristic of the "complex historical geography" constituting modernity) that shape the relationship between an imperial, modern nation-state and its subjects lets us see how subjects are never just innocent victims of the nation-state.[3] It should not surprise us to discover that, viewed as effects created through "interested" narrative acts, subjects reveal themselves to be the sites of deeply divided competing interests. For example, the proliferation of such documents as imperial edicts, the Rescript on Education (1890), and the Meiji Civil Code (1898) attests to state interests in shaping the contours of subjecthood according to its view of an obedient citizenry.

If the "modern" signals the compression of worldly events into a short time period, the almost forty-year span covered by the texts examined in this study (from Tōson's *Kyūshujin* in 1901 to Origuchi's *Shisha no sho* in 1939) cannot be properly captured as a particular historical moment; as milestones are conventionally designated, the first four decades of twentieth-century Japan are riddled with many. The texts of Shimazaki Tōson (1872–1943), Natsume Sōseki (1867–1916), Tokuda Shūsei (1871–1943), and Origuchi Shinobu (1887–1953) selected for reading in this study are inscribed with the contemporaneous situations marking Japan during this period. Most notably, from about the turn of the century, Japan sought to escape the fate of other Asian nations under virtual or actual colonized status

3. A succinct delineation of modernity can be found in David Harvey, *The Condition of Postmodernity* (Cambridge: Basil Blackwell, 1990).

and in turn achieved the status of an imperialist nation as part of a strategy to fend off colonization.[4] Mary Layoun's view of the Western realist novel as a kind of textual ambassador of European imperialist behavior affirms the hegemonic role played by a mode of expression that powerfully contributed to the narrative practices of non-Western writers. Where Layoun's book focuses on Western oppression of non-Western cultures, we must not overlook the fact that at the same time Japan was spinning its imperialist designs on the eastern perimeter of Asia and beyond.[5] The present study examines these contingencies naturalized on native soil along with other strictly domestic effects on the production of modern Japanese narratives. Every bit as important to these readings are the conceptions of tradition and history at variance with and in terms of which the texts of these Japanese writers were written. Their efforts to embrace Western realism with its privileged subject must be viewed in relation to these worldly conditions, which could not help but powerfully determine the contours of life lived under these tensions. In short, the present study attempts to rethink the category called *kindai shōsetsu* and its relationship to the discourse of Japanese modernity.

Against positivistically informed practices that lead to the recuperation of timelessness and universality in a text or the recovery of a writer's "original vision," the present study is conceived as a set of readings in which the task is creative engagement with texts that will yield explanations and meanings tied to the reader's interpretive environment (her/his own historical moment) and to the very conditions that occasion the texts. These readings of selected Japanese texts (some have contributed to the canon, others have been excluded from it, while yet another—Origuchi's—has actively challenged it) are preceded by self-reflection often ignored by the prevailing

4. Two recent books attend to these issues, Mary Layoun's study of narrative, *Travels of a Genre: The Modern Novel and Ideology* (Princeton: Princeton University Press, 1990), and, less directly, Alan Wolfe's *Suicidal Narrative in Modern Japan: The Case of Dazai Osamu* (Princeton: Princeton University Press, 1990).

5. Layoun's essay on Ōe Kenzaburō does in fact emphasize this aggressor role. See Layoun, *Travels of a Genre*, 209–42.

approaches to textual studies of Japan (under which I subsume modernization-based historiography and Western realist literary studies). In the remainder of this introduction, after further situating my own assumptions, I examine the current discursive situation that authorizes the reigning views on modern Japanese prose narration. A brief look at Bakhtin suggests an alternative way of conceptualizing subjects, and the introductory chapter ends by considering the work of Komori Yōichi, whose revisionist criticism signals a contemporary discursive strain that merits attention by readers of modern Japanese texts outside of Japan.

A sustained critique of positivist subjectivism is central to the revisionist readings in this study, as its principal aim—to interrogate the grand narrative of the modern Japanese prose narrative (*kindai shōsetsu*)—must be realized through a method that permits reflexive conceptualization of the issue. The implicit standard against which the Japanese prose narratives under discussion continue to be evaluated is the adequacy with which subjects mimic their European counterparts. According to reigning (realist) literary assessments, the writers chosen for this study, Tōson, Sōseki, Shūsei, and Origuchi, occupy disparate positions on this canonical grid. The first two effectively define the course of Japan's modern literature as the pursuit of individuated subjectivity; Shūsei represents the distinctly Japanese realization of it; and Origuchi stands entirely outside of this trajectory. Distinctions based upon schools of writing have linked Tōson and Shūsei as naturalist, whereas their statuses as major figures of the Meiji era whose work confronted the contradictions of a modernizing society likewise have framed Sōseki and Tōson as similar. Such realist readings, however, merely reify the relationships among text, author, and the master narrative of the *kindai shōsetsu* as currently conceived.

The present study discloses and challenges this network of relations, providing meanings that are grounded in the texts' own historical coordinates and in the interests that coalesce in the vantage point from which the texts are read (the late twentieth-century United States). Difference rather than similarity dictated the selection of writers and texts chosen for this study, one that identifies realist subjectivism as a field of ideological contest that mediated the relationship of narrative practice to the modern Japanese state. Chapter 2 identifies in the first-person narrative strategy in Tōson's *Kyūshujin* contradictions that reveal a personal *ressentiment* speaking to the emperor system; both the emperor system and this *ressentiment* in turn link the short story to *Hakai*. Tōson's attempt at novelistic narration and closure in *Hakai* reveals a profound discomfort with the centralized authority of post-Restoration Japan; at the same time, the text captures its historical moment by figurating a shift from a vertical hierarchic schema (favored by the Tokugawa authorities) to metaphors cast in spatial terms (e.g., urban–rural).[6] Chapter 4 traces the life of Sōseki's famous cat wending its way through the verdant textuality of *Wagahai wa neko de aru*, a piece that challenges the Western-influenced valorization of the private self and the standardization of colloquially based narrative conventions (the *genbun'itchi* novel) deeply implicated in the construction of the modern subject. The discussion of Sōseki's *Kokoro* in chapter 5 views the text as a response to an era in which a nation's history had been abruptly rendered irrelevant. This reading examines the requirements for what would become one of the central works of the modern Japanese literary canon—to suppress the signs of Japanese imperialism that were everywhere present in the first decades of the twentieth century. Chapters 6 and 7 take as their points of departure the standard attribution to Shūsei of "the purest naturalist writer" and consider the stakes at issue in elevating *aru ga mama* (exactly as things are) to its prominence among the requirements of "naturalist" (*shizenshugi*) writing. Shūsei's extended serialized texts (among them *Kabi*, *Arajotai*, and *Arakure* are discussed here) show how growing urban areas enabled quickly formed and easily replaceable affiliative relations to expand the limits of subjectivity, particularly for women, in prewar Japan. Finally, Origuchi's *Shisha no sho* allows us to rethink realist subjectivism against a project that attempts to recuperate perfor-

6. For a discussion of shifting conceptions of social ordering, see H. D. Harootunian, *Things Seen and Unseen: Discourse and Ideology in Tokugawa Nativism* (Chicago: University of Chicago Press, 1988).

mance as an absent cause of the *kindai shōsetsu*, thereby revealing all the more clearly the process of establishing a dominant narrative discourse (designated the *kindai shōsetsu*) in modern Japan.

MODERN JAPANESE LITERATURE AS OBJECT OF STUDY

Ever since the Meiji Restoration of 1868 made Western material and cultural achievements the keystone for nation building, Japan has been represented and self-represented in terms of by now all too familiar notions of sameness and difference. Unities of language, customs, and cultural expressions and a narrative history affirming wholeness have been invoked to spell out in advance an unbridgeable gap between Japan and the West. Rooted in the particular historical circumstances of Japan's renewed contact with superior Western military might, the terms for understanding and representing Japan have come in the form of a series of binary categories that reflect these inequalities.[7] Over the years, the West-versus-Japan dichotomy has been recast in such recurring oppositions as modern–traditional, individual–group, and pragmatic–esthetic. On the other side, practitioners of *nihonjinron* (who tout Japan's superiority primarily on the grounds of its timeless cultural achievements) have responded with pairs reversing the direction of privilege: spiritual–materialistic, pure–mixed, stable–unstable.[8] The very circumstances of the initial encounter between Japan and the West have undoubtedly contributed to the persistence of conceptualizing Japan both from within and without in contrast to this hegemonic other.

From the inception of Japan studies in the West, dichotomous

7. The problem of binary oppositions that concerns us here is how almost inevitably they are structured to privilege one of the terms over the other. Helene Cixous, for example, enumerates some familiar pairs that underwrite patriarchy: father/mother, sun/moon, culture/nature, head/emotions, logos/pathos. See Toril Moi, *Sexual, Textual Politics* (London: Methuen, 1985), 104.

8. The use of such oppositions in the discourse of *nihonjinron* is discussed at some length in Peter Dale, *The Myth of Japanese Uniqueness* (New York: St. Martin's Press, 1986), 38–55.

thinking has operated effectively to guarantee the status of modern Japanese literature either as being derivative—hence, always lesser than the "originals"—or as being exotically different. The prescience of poststructuralist and Marxist critiques of Eurocentrism only recently have been reflected in a commonplace questioning of Euro-America as the center of an increasingly global economy, as the realities of a spirited dispersion of economic vitality have compelled Americans to resituate their own country in a rapidly changing world. Even a quick glance at recorded history ought to ratify the certainty that fortunes of any nation will change over time. The world of academic discourse, in contrast, remains stubbornly static, acting as if one can continue to reproduce a reality whose very familiarity brings comfort and validation. Thus, in spite of the persuasive call for critical self-evaluation in texts such as Edward Said's *Orientalism* (which appeared in 1978) and Japan's meteoric rise in the world economy—both of which point to rapidly changing socioeconomic relations—vast sectors of humanistic academic inquiry remain tightly wedded to the authorities of enduring Western shibboleths.

Despite validation that has come from the repeated use of such a binary approach to the study of post-Restoration Japan, it is hardly a disinterested, neutral "method." This is not surprising when one recalls that in the United States, "serious" study of Japan began only with the advent of the Pacific War. In the years to follow, Japanese studies would be institutionalized and configured by the dynamics of an adversarial and unequal relationship between the two countries and by the politics of the cold war.[9] Subsequently, a generation of historians, both Japanese and American, has alerted us to the fact that such employment of postwar Japanese history reflected the agenda of cold war politics to appropriate a positive example (Japan) for other non-Western nations to emulate. The overdetermined view of Japan as a model of industrial development for non-

9. See "E. H. Norman, Japan and the Uses of History," the introduction to John W. Dower, ed. *Origins of the Modern Japanese State: Selected Writings of E. H. Norman* (New York: Pantheon Books, 1975), 3–102. Also useful is the discussion of modernization theory in Wolfe, *Suicidal Narrative in Modern Japan*, especially 23–36.

Western nations and a society indebted to Western culture and thought finds expression in the persistent academic practice of viewing Japan as the site of raw material to be subjected to the superior mnemonic procedures of the Western world. In a discussion of the Subaltern Study Group, Gayatri Spivak differentiates the "great narrative of the modes of production and, by uneasy implication, within the narrative of the transition from feudalism to capitalism" from Subaltern groups that plot histories as confrontations rather than as transitions.[10] In order to avoid the practice of inserting Japan within this grand narrative of modernization, we must take Spivak's hint and attempt to locate the sites of confrontation in the narrativization of modern Japanese literature. The texts selected for this study permit us to observe contestatory engagements with Western realism; far from simple mimicking or capitulation, modern Japanese prose narratives offer themselves up (through these readings) as plentifully inscribed with such confrontation.

Within this field of contest, nothing provoked and pressured modern Japanese writers as did the discourse of national consolidation. It entered and suffused daily life by assuming a wide array of forms; for writers of literature, it was most provocative and far-reaching in its effects as a movement to establish a modern, colloquially based, standardized writing (*genbun'itchi*). As the conjuncture of everyday life, a sense of wholeness and unity, and a newly reconceived view of the private subject, *genbun'itchi* stands inscribed with matters central to a nation-state interested in suppressing heterologies so that it might more effectively consolidate the populace. Such a narrative of unity was bound to engender contest and resistance. As we shall see, Japanese writers had to confront the state as represented in a broad array of filiative and authoritative discourses seeking to claim the subject in post-Restoration society. Their efforts to rescript Japanese literature in accordance with conventions underlying the

10. Gayatri Spivak, "Subaltern Studies: Deconstructing Historiography," in *In Other Worlds: Essays in Cultural Politics* (New York: Routledge, 1988), 197. In the Japan field, H. D. Harootunian's work has eloquently challenged the modernization narrative of transition. See, for example, "Ideology as Conflict," in *Conflict in Modern Japanese History: The Neglected Tradition*, ed. Tetsuo Najita and J. Victor Koschmann (Princeton: Princeton University Press, 1982), 25–61.

nineteenth-century European novel simultaneously echoed and contested the problem of fixing the private citizen in the revamped social structure of post-Restoration Japan.

The resulting strategies of narrativizing subjects reveal in turn resistance and capitulation to, uneasiness and complicity with, the discourses of national consolidation and modernity, which discourses mediated the relationship of writer to state in early twentieth-century Japanese literature. For example, modernity expresses itself in a dizzying array of ways, obtruding on the human figure as a growing urban landscape with its accelerated rhythms (pronounced in Shūsei's work) and marking itself by a shift in the way subjects are narrated, from primarily filial (temporal) to increasingly affiliative (spatial) terms (Tōson, Sōseki, and Shūsei). The effect of such forces mediating the experience of modernity and their effects in shaping subjectivities are the primary concern of this book.

In order to avoid the common practice of transposing a Euro-American historical moment onto Japan, I attempt to show how Japanese writers' concerns with "new" subjects lay at the heart of localized efforts to engage with, shape, and reshape Japanese experiences of modernity. Japanese modernity, one must remember, did not simply replicate its predecessors in various European nations. Just as importantly, where modernism was largely a reaction to enduring cultural forms in Europe, for Japan it was simultaneously a confrontation with a foreign culture. If we choose not to ignore moments of change synchronically, we are more likely to grasp the interanimation of differences, plural expressions, changes, and more change as a diversified cluster of self-reflective and other-directed acts and reactions that lead to the creation of the new and the different. (We shall take a more extended look at how Bakhtin's theorizing of the novel as dialogic permits a way to grasp the confrontation of difference in a politically informed way.) Modernism surely took altered form when transplanted to an island removed from its birthplace, but as Miriam Silverberg's studies of popular culture of the Taishō and early Shōwa years suggest, the dynamics of radical and productive change characterize Japan's encounter with the West far more convincingly than "influence–imitation" models, whose very repetition and familiarity have misleadingly conferred credibility where it should not exist.[11] Just as we might be better served by abandoning a static model of binary influence in favor of a view that accounts for what was and is a dynamic process of often self-reflective engagement with otherness, it is incumbent upon us not to dismiss contemporary Japanese engagements with their own literature as we confront it, inevitably from a position of difference.

THE SUBJECT AND THE RISE OF *KINDAI BUNGAKU*

Before we examine the limits of realist subjectivism, particularly the way its use promotes the erasure of cultural and historical specificity, let us take a brief look at the literary scene in post-Restoration Japan. The first milestone marking Japanese efforts to textualize the Western realist subject is generally held to be the Meiji critic-writer Tsubouchi Shōyō's essay "Shōsetsu shinzui" (The Essence of the Novel, 1885).[12] Shōyō's landmark manifesto trumpeting the conventions of Western realism is seen as inaugurating the era of "modern" Japanese letters. Reacting to the discursive, episodic, and often fantastic legacy of *gesaku* still flourishing almost two decades after the promising change of guard signified by the Restoration, Shōyō hoped to upgrade the status of fiction in Japan by encouraging writers to adopt Western realist conventions, which seemed to underwrite the higher status accorded creative writing and fiction in the West. Shōyō's tract emphatically stresses two imperatives—to portray human

11. The influence-binarism approach is challenged by Silverberg, who provides a model based upon production. See Miriam Silverberg, *Changing Song: The Marxist Manifestos of Nakano Shigeharu* (Princeton: Princeton University Press, 1990). See also the essays in *Recreating Japanese Women, 1600–1945*, ed. Gail Lee Bernstein (Berkeley: University of California Press, 1991).

12. The process, of course, is a far more dispersed and incremental one; for example, this characterization ignores the scores of translations (from European languages to Japanese) that, in their own ways, wrestled with issues of the self and form. See Yanabu Akira's studies of translation in modern Japan: *Hon'yakugo seiritsu jijō* (Iwanami shinsho, 1982) and *Hon'yaku no shisō* (Heibonsha sensho, 1977). Unless otherwise indicated, all Japanese-language books were published in Tokyo.

For an English language discussion of Shōyō's essay, see Marleigh Grayer Ryan's preface in *Japan's First Modern Novel: Ukigumo of Futabatei Shimei* (New York: Columbia University Press, 1967).

emotions skillfully and to develop a written language adequate to the task of presenting these feelings in a realistic manner. The story line of modern Japanese letters is henceforth drawn by standard literary histories as the shared mission of writers and critics alike to fulfill these requirements of the Western novel. But read another way, the history of an extended effort to domesticate what has eluded easy appropriation among Japanese writers (the romantic, humanist self) raises questions about the naturalness and the common sense we attribute to this form. As noted above, far from being universal or longstanding, this relationship of self to literary form (the novel) represents a local practice that attained its now familiar form of the "realist novel" only in nineteenth-century Europe. This is not to argue the absence of subjective individuation in pre-Restoration Japan, whether it be conceived of in positivist or discursive terms. The insistent attribution of the group (in place of the individual) given to Japanese society as a whole notwithstanding, even premodern Japanese literatures attest to clear, if often decidedly different, expressions of subjective agency.[13]

As we stop to consider the path of Japanese literature after it leaves *gesaku* behind, we cannot help but notice the dominance of what comes to be known as the *kindai shōsetsu* (prose narrative form). When Mary Layoun problematizes the modern Western novel and traces its transplantation to foreign cultures, she rightly restores the inequality of nations engaged in colonizer–colonized relationships, which inequality is surely inscribed in the migration of a genre of a cultural form (here the novel) from one country to another.[14] Conventions of the Western realist novel found a receptive audience in post-Restoration Japan. Over the next century this development promoted the com-

13. See Norma Field's discussion of distinguishable narrative voices in *The Splendor of Longing in the "Tale of Genji"* (Princeton: Princeton University Press, 1987). Naoki Sakai's study of Tokugawa narrative, "Voices of the Past: The Discourse on Language in Eighteenth-Century Japan," (Ph.D. diss., the University of Chicago, 1983), also affirms the contours of subjectivity in premodern Japan. Yet another recent rigorous investigation of subject agency is Richard Okada's *Figures of Resistance: Poetry, Narrating, and the Politics of Fiction in "The Tale of Genji" and Other Mid-Heian Texts* (Durham, N.C.: Duke University Press, 1991).

14. See Layoun, *Travels of a Genre*, 8–20.

forting view (from a Western perspective) that modern Japanese literature is best viewed in terms of the influence wrought by this literary form. What mediates this migration of a genre from one cultural arena ("West") to another (Japan)—and we can think only provisionally in terms of "migration," as if the one and self-same form moved from one place to another, when in fact as Miyoshi's examination of the "novel" makes clear the *shōsetsu* does not equal the novel[15]—is the power and the variety of narrative strategy that give shape to subject positions. My readings of selected Japanese texts repeatedly demonstrate (against the tendency of realist perspectives, which presume their own universalism) how specific contingencies govern the production of something called the modern Japanese prose narrative, compelling us to abandon the implicit claims of omniscience or objectivity, claims that have authorized the hegemonic position of realist approaches to textual studies.

While the production of prose narratives in the Meiji period cannot be referred to in the same declamatory terms appropriate for describing the explosion of *gesaku* in the late Tokugawa period, as mentioned above, it would be fair to say that the *shōsetsu* was clearly the preferred form during the decades following the Meiji Restoration.[16] Stimulated by the confluence of a lively urban culture, a print technology permitting rapid dissemination of cheap reading matter, and a rise in literacy, the late Tokugawa period witnessed a lively efflorescence of writing. Popular writing meant to entertain the masses, *gesaku* works might well have been dismissed as frivolous light fare from any vantage point. But it seems worth noting that its development within an official discourse of Confucian austerity in part explains the institutionalization of views dismissing *gesaku*. In addition, as criticism directed against Ozaki Kōyō's *Ken'yūsha*

15. The argument runs throughout Masao Miyoshi's work. See particularly "Against the Native Grain."

16. The enduring production of the random essay (*zuihitsu*) and diary (*nikki*) and the ascendance of criticism (*hihyō*) in mid-Meiji (not to mention other literary genres such as poetry and drama) attest to the heterogeneous constitution of *kindai bungaku*. While the *kindai shōsetsu* may rightly be singled out as the preeminent textual form in twentieth-century Japan, its dominance also speaks to its relationship to the discursive network called Japanese modernity.

(Friends of the Inkstone) in early Meiji suggests, the negative assessment of *gesaku* is also a product of retroactive judgment from an era (Meiji) that embraced the sobering task of incorporating a broad range of Western practices. Framed by the righteous narratives of statist Confucianism and patriotic duty to appropriate the best of the West, *gesaku* was an easy target to belittle. In contrast, Meiji prose narrative informed by Western literary imperatives would be seen as a literature constructed to signify modernity, truth, seriousness, the West, and even wholeness as a nation. We might fruitfully take as a point of departure Hayden White's view of narration and narrativity as "the instruments with which the conflicting claims of the imaginary and the real are mediated, arbitrated, or resolved in a discourse."[17] To a literary heritage inherited from China privileging histories and biographies over base fiction, modern Japan added its own reasons for revalorizing the *shōsetsu* form as the nation entered a new era of international intercourse.[18]

As the gap between the "modern novel" and the *kindai shōsetsu* reveals, the *kindai shōsetsu* is not simply the modern European novel transplanted to Japan. In Japan, the word *shōsetsu* has come to designate virtually all that is not verse. Unlike its English-language "equivalent," the novel, the *shōsetsu* is not bound by requirements to be of a certain length, nor to be marked clearly as fiction, and the boundary that separates it from other genres such as essays, meditations, diaries, and biographies is much less defined than it commonly is in the West. The term *shōsetsu* is closer in meaning to the English "prose narrative," or even "prose" (without the requirement for telos denoted by the word "narrative"), than it is to the commonly used equivalent, the novel. It must not be the inclusiveness of the word that explains the preponderance of the *shōsetsu* in post-Meiji Restoration Japan, for the much more restricted word

17. White, "The Value of Narrativity in the Representation of Reality," in *The Content of the Form: Narrative Discourse and Historical Representation* (Baltimore: The Johns Hopkins University Press, 1987), 4.

18. As it pertains to Japanese literature, work tracing the ties between literature and nation has only just begun. Miyoshi's studies of the *shōsetsu* and Layoun's *Travels of a Genre* are the only existing ones. For discussion unrelated to Japan, see Timothy Brennan, "The National Longing for Form," in *Nation and Narration*, ed. by Homi K. Bhabha (New York: Routledge, 1990), 44–70.

"novel" has enjoyed a similar privilege in European and American letters over the last century and a half. The ascendance of prose or prose narrative might be better understood on the one hand by examining the prominence of verse in earlier eras (in both Japan and in Western nations) and on the other hand by paying close attention to the steep rise in recent years in the popularity of tightly framed visual media (comics, video, and other screened forms)—an undertaking that is beyond the scope of the current text. I am nonetheless interested in the dominance of prose that marks Japan's "modern" era, the years following the rapid introduction of Western material artifacts and ideas.

By a number of separate measures—the documented priority of oral literary-performative genres, be they religious incantations, ritual chanting, various forms of poetic expression, or the place accorded verse in Heian and pre-Heian recorded life—Japan's early history is marked by the presence of versification (direct vestiges of orality) in a way that the modern Japanese landscape is not. As Gary Ebersole puts it, "the early Japanese did not differentiate religion, politics, and literature in the ways we do, for poetry/song participated immediately in these other dimensions of social life to a far greater extent than is now generally recognized. Verse forms were at once part of an intellectual discourse and a social practice."[19] In the way that visual media have moved aside textual presentation, especially in places like Japan and the United States, a discernible ascendance of prose can be seen in the Tokugawa period and again with renewed energy and in altered form in the decades following the Meiji Restoration. This is not to deny the significance of poetry as the site of language reform, or *genbun'itchi* (Shimazaki Tōson and Masaoka Shiki) and social transformation (Ishikawa Takuboku, Yosano Akiko, Nakano Shigeharu), nor to ignore the continuing hold that poets such as Miyazawa Kenji and Hagiwara Sakutarō have had on generations of Japanese readers. But as if to parallel in other Western countries the fall in poetry's popularity, once competing performative entertain-

19. Gary Ebersole, *Ritual Poetry and the Politics of Death in Early Japan* (Princeton: Princeton University Press, 1989), 17.

ment not integrally tied to poetry emerges, the period of Japan's "opening up" to the West is singularly marked by the rise of prose narratives. To explain the phenomenon as replicating the rise of the Western realist novel and its celebration of the concept of individualism (anchored in the workings of capitalism) is to universalize Western experience.

The present study provides what can be at best a partial and provisional response to the question of the *shōsetsu*'s dominance. Framed by this problematic and the particulars of modern Japan, we will explore the relationship between textuality and renewed social contest over the status of the subject in a society that had newly restored the emperor and urgently needed new social arrangements to secure and manage its populace. Undoubtedly, social and economic developments similar to those that governed the European scene helped ensure the priority given to the *shōsetsu* form in turn-of-the-century Japan, but we must move beyond the characterization of sameness supported by generalities and begin to identify concrete forms, processes, and interrelations that mediate and thus help explain the particulars that govern subject creation in "modern" Japan. Among the several important mediations, such as the new colloquially based language (*genbun'itchi*) and the rapid expansion of urban areas and concomitant reformulations of the countryside, none figure as prominently in the process of subject creation as the state.

In twentieth-century Japan, subjects were narrativized never free of an oppressive mediating presence of the state determined to have a direct hand in constructing and managing its citizen subjects. Among the narratives treated in this study, all but Origuchi's *Shisha no sho* (1939) appeared in the first two decades of the century, a period in which the achievement of a modern Japanese nation-state called for the production of civic-minded citizens.

> The words *kokka* and *kokumin* were suddenly everywhere in the late eighties. . . . National spirit, national thought, national doctrine, national essence, nationality—this outburst of nation-mindedness included explorations of national character, reassertions of indigenous ways, and projections of Japan into the world order as the nineteenth-century West defined it. . . . The invocations of nation included, more and more pressingly, the effort to draw all the

> people into the state, to have them thinking national thoughts, to make *kokumin* of them.[20]

By the turn of the century, the invocation of national consolidation was not enough to contain the pressures for social change that found a voice in socialist movements, in regional agricultural unrest, and in worker discontent in these rocky times. The wars with China and Russia exacerbated the problems of a materially poor country, though they also laid the groundwork for rapid industrial development. Oka Yoshitake sees the years after the war with Russia marked by an "unprecedented degree of individual self-awareness." This heightened attention to self, he says, took a disturbing turn: Where success and careerism (*risshin shusse*) in preceding generations had been associated with the elevation of one's family and home town, the new youth imbued it with the goal of *seikō*, a more privatized conception of success. The desire to serve one's country through government service was displaced by hopes for acquiring wealth. While the new youth appeared more hedonistic, according to Oka, they were also being "swallowed up by skepticism and despair in the course of their search for meaning in life."[21]

Late Meiji represents the confluence of a recuperated emperor system, increasing social dislocation, and what Oka calls "the emergence of individualism . . . closely related to the expansion and diffusion of capitalist culture and ideology."[22] But the inward turn taken by Kitamura Tōkoku in the 1890s, and by the later *shishōsetsu* writers through the 1920s, reveals the limits placed upon the exercise of the individual, while social movements that began in the second half of Meiji point to the grim reality that promises of political enfranchisement held out by the Restoration were not being kept. In Harootunian's words,

20. Carol Gluck, *Japan's Modern Myths: Ideology in the Late Meiji Period* (Princeton: Princeton University Press, 1986), 23.

21. Oka Yoshitake, "Generational Conflict after the Russo-Japanese War," in *Conflict in Modern Japanese History: The Neglected Tradition*, ed. Tetsuo Najita and J. Victor Koschmann (Princeton: Princeton University Press, 1982), 197, 199, 200. See also Earl Kinmonth, *The Self-Made Man in Meiji Japanese Thought* (Berkeley: University of California Press, 1981), 9–80, for an extended discussion of the pursuit of selfhood and social position by Japanese youth in Meiji Japan.

22. Oka, "Generational Conflict after the Russo-Japanese War," 202.

> The structure of late Meiji social life is well known. . . . The government reinstated communal (*kyōdōteki*) arrangements patterned after the relationships found in the family because these were known to be non-political. Thus, the non-political and non-public character of late Meiji reforms found expression in the form of a "family-state" (*kazoku kokka*). . . . Men either became public in their demeanor and sought to satisfy publicly sanctioned goals, such as the pursuit of "success and careerism" (*risshin shusse*) or, as contemporary literature began to dramatize, they became entirely private, removed (like Futabatei Shimei's anti-hero Bunzō or Natsume Sōseki's artist in the "Grass Pillow" (*Kusamakura*), from all external associations.[23]

The failed promises of political participation helped determine the shape of Japanese narrative expression in subsequent years, but we must note that the distribution of power and its absence did not split neatly between state and (writing) subjects. The texts we examine in this study show the displacements of subject position by state authority and power on the one hand and by the protean strategies of narrativized confrontation with the state on the other hand—each affecting the other in sometimes unpredictable and often unintended ways. Most important, writing, like other spheres of human expression, would show the signs of its belonging to the currents of flux and change wrought by the industrialization and urbanization of twentieth-century Japan. There is wide variation in the narration of subjects that appear in a literature at such a time. A study such as this one, which explores the possibilities as well as the limits of subject expression, must also confront the effects of nation building, especially its concomitant, imperialism, which this literature does not simply refract but in turn also helps shape.[24]

It is perhaps the very plasticity of the *shōsetsu* form—used by

23. H. D. Harootunian, "Between Politics and Culture: Authority and the Ambiguities of Intellectual Choice in Imperial Japan," in *Japan in Crisis: Essays on Taisho Democracy*, ed. Bernard S. Silberman and H. D. Harootunian (Princeton: Princeton University Press, 1974), 114.

24. The simplistic view of literature reflecting real life was convincingly displaced by Bakhtin's notion that a text *refracts* the milieu of which literature is a part: Like light that is altered when passing through a prism, literature takes from other spheres and shapes it variously, in the process altering the very material conditions (society) that it takes from.

the state in its myriad expressions, at the same time serving as a forum for writers to question, challenge, and even refuse a unity based upon the ideology of the modern nation-state—that accounts for the rise of the *shōsetsu* in post-Restoration Japan. Before we examine such relations as they are played out in textual form, let us take a closer look at the essentialized realist subject, whose continued centrality in the study of Japanese literature demands our critical attention.

AGAINST THE TRANSCENDENTAL SUBJECT

In a study critically affirming Western realism, Auerbach argued that virtually the whole of European letters was built upon a realist tradition,[25] but what we today still commonly associate with the realist novel are conventions that became institutionalized in eighteenth-century Europe. By now its features have been reiterated with numbing frequency: markers suggesting beginning and end, a narrative of chronological sequence, emplotment tracing events or characters' thoughts that occur in the fabric of everyday life, and credibility that suggests depiction of real life, to name a prominent few. Among the traits that define the realist novel, none gives it the distinction nor so clearly marks it as a product of its own social historical moment more than the primacy of the private self. The realist novel centers the experience of an individuated self through a narrative conceived as referential—that is, a work that *refers* to an outside reality that it depicts in the same way that a camera might produce an image of reality. The focus of such a narrative is on the private individual, whose psychology and actions constitute the object or the content of narration. In the Western realist novel, *form* exists to express a *content* (the simulation of an individual who is defined according to the dictates of "what seems credible"). Unfortunately, through the use of a binarism that clearly favors content, the ways in which a text produces meaning and how it participates in its own circumstances become lost to the transcendental meaning of the stated content.

25. See Erich Auerbach, *Mimesis: The Representation of Reality in Western Literature* (Princeton: Princeton University Press, 1953).

The centrality of the private subject rightly has been linked to the socioeconomic conditions of industrial capitalism, which demands it both as its source of production and its primary unit of consumption. Validated over the years across a broad spectrum of Western discourses—be they Christianity, constitutions and other state declarations, documents propounding democratic rule, or expressions in popular culture—the sovereignty of the private self continues to enjoy a highly privileged position in Western societies. So natural has become this valorization of the individuated subject that even "common sense" attests to its status as a verity beyond question.[26] Common sense marks the thoroughness with which the thing so designated has been overdetermined. The close association of common sense with the individual subject points to the latter as a construct built upon convention and agreement. Just as common sense often fails to cross national borders, specific concepts of the subject are similarly bound to specific times and places. That the private individual should be the subject and organizing center of literature, especially in the Western world, appeals to our common sense as appropriate and natural.[27] Both here and in Japan, the novel is seen as tracing the life of a character, the narrator, or the author, whose escapades or thoughts and feelings are artfully transcribed in the text as a simulation of "real life."

As one of the critical voices perhaps most familiar to us, Wayne Booth illustrates a practice that appeals to our common sense when he claims "a unified, coherent, and transcendental subjectivity . . . behind the text."[28] His notion of the implied author is critiqued by Fredric Jameson this way: "Booth's book is a defense of the omniscient narrator, the implied author or reliable commentator, who unobtrusively but strategically makes his presence between reader and characters felt in such a way that the former is provided with the standards by which

26. See especially Catherine Belsey, *Critical Practice* (London: Methuen, 1980), 1–36.

27. In her critique of the realist novel, Belsey reiterates Saussure's questioning of common sense: "the 'obvious' and the 'natural' are not *given* but *produced* in a specific society by the ways in which that society talks and thinks about itself and its experience" (Belsey, *Critical Practice*, 3).

28. The phrase is from Cheryl Walker, "Feminist Literary Criticism and the Author," *Critical Inquiry* 16 (Spring 1990): 551–71.

to judge the latter appropriately."[29] Booth's assumption appears so natural to the study of literature because it is congruent with the system of which we are and have been part of since the entrenchment of industrial capitalism. Jameson most tellingly concludes his assessment of Booth's theorizing with these words: "The implied or reliable narrator described by Booth is possible only in a situation of relative class homogeneity."[30] In separating out one subject position from another (the author from an implied author, also different from a narrator), Booth, to use the language of the social critic Mikhail Bakhtin, has imposed a monologic organizing center, another transcendental figure looming over the other voices of a text.

Closer to home for critics of modern Japanese texts, Janet Walker conferred special privilege on the individual in her extended treatment of the modern Japanese novel. For her, the Japanese novel is distinctive from earlier literate forms by virtue of its focus on the "ideal of individualism." In her words, "of the literary forms of this time, only the novel, with its concern for the individual as a moral being involved in action and growth in time, provides a coherent vision of the individual."[31] Walker's study weds social history to literary form in a cogent discussion of the concept of the individual in Meiji literature. Without diminishing her significant achievement, it is important to note that her discussion is firmly rooted in a realist tradition that treats writing as an instrument, something that transparently expresses the author's "personal convictions in literary form."[32] In light of more recent critical theories, her assessment of Tōson's *Hakai* illustrates the limits of such an unambiguous ratification of the individual:

29. Fredric Jameson, *Marxism and Form* (Princeton: Princeton University Press, 1971), 356.

30. Jameson, *Marxism and Form*, 357.

31. Janet Walker, *The Japanese Novel of the Meiji Period and the Ideal of Individualism* (Princeton: Princeton University Press, 1979), ix. Janet Walker's work, written over a decade ago, still stands as a notable contribution to Japan studies in America. Her subsequent work suggests some inclination to rethink the realist assumptions of this study. See, for example, "On the Applicability of the Term 'Novel' to Modern Non-Western Long Fiction," *Yearbook of Comparative and General Literature* 37 (1988): 47–68.

32. Walker, *The Japanese Novel of the Meiji Period*, 52.

> *Hakai* . . . was for Tōson . . . both a personal victory of self-expression and a mature statement of his views of the individual and his inner life.
>
> *Hakai,* then, even more than *Ukigumo* or *Futon,* is the first novel of the inner life in modern Japanese literature. The hero of *Hakai,* because he is a reflection of the Tōson of those years, is the first hero of modern Japanese fiction to become conscious of and take responsibility for his selfhood.[33]

Her belletristic concern for the individual as a transcultural and eternally given entity effectively suppresses the cultural and historical circumstances of Japan within which writers such as Tōson labored to narrate subject positions.

In her critical appraisal of Western realism, Catherine Belsey characterizes its requirements this way: "The artist must both represent (*re*-present) faithfully the objects portrayed and express the thoughts and feelings they evoke in him or her."[34] What anchors realist conventions is the anteriority of a person (usually an author or a protagonist) whose story is there simply to be told. While this romantic valuation of the individuated self as the source of truth, meaning, and worthiness (of a text) has continued to assume a strong hold, particularly in the Anglo-American traditions of textuality, the limitations of empiricist subjects have been eloquently argued from many quarters,[35]

33. Walker, *The Japanese Novel of the Meiji Period,* 157; 193.

34. Belsey, *Critical Practice,* 8.

35. One can say that criticizing these realist assumptions represents the enabling condition, the point of departure for the otherwise often disparate narratives of Western Marxism, deconstruction, semiotics, feminism, and other textualist critical discourses. Here we confine our examination of positively conceived notions of the subject to a brief look at Foucault's interrogation of the "author" in "What Is an Author?", in *Textual Strategies,* ed. Joshua Harari (Ithaca: Cornell University Press, 1979), 141–60. It should be noted that the work of Roland Barthes, including "The Death of the Author," in *Image, Music, Text,* trans. Stephen Heath (New York: Hill and Wang, 1977), 142–48; the corpus of Jacques Derrida's assault on a broad spectrum of Western epistemologies; structuralism, which gave focused energy to destabilizing the private subject by giving priority to systems; Mikhail Bakhtin's theory of dialogism, which displaced positivities with relationality and difference; and many other bodies of inquiry have contributed to a radical critique of positively conceived notions of the subject.

and here I provide but a sharply attenuated critique of the Western realist subject.

Foucault's attack on the "author" in his widely quoted essay "What Is an Author?" challenges the commonplace view of writing as a transparent vehicle that merely articulates the author's thoughts. His designation of "author-function" rests on the perspective that, far from being "given," an author is a social construct. "There was a time when the texts that we today call 'literary' (narratives, stories, epics, tragedies, comedies) were accepted, put into circulation, and valorized without any question about the identity of their author."[36] In his account of the ebb and flow of authorship, Foucault cites several historical periods, such as when certain religious texts were identified as heretical, that suddenly elevated the hitherto inconsequential attribution of authorship to a position of importance. When examined in light of these historically specific "author-moments," the author loses the essentiality we commonly attribute to it. Over the course of history, the very notion of author will be given quite different form, social standing, and meanings determined by a large array of socially established practices, forces, and conventions.

Authors (like other subjects) are not sources of creation but are themselves discursively created. While it may be possible to identify an author (the case of Shakespeare, by no means a case unto itself, makes even attribution suspect), the narrative product is far more fruitfully considered the site of many often competing voices inscribed with particular interests and desires. Thus, in place of the notion of "influence," which suffers from the problem of privileging the person or work "influenced" and also fails to account for more than naive unidirectional effects, textualist critics insist on an intertextual view of narrative as productive—creating something new from the collision of differences. Subject to a broad range of forces impinging on any given moment, a text is best conceived not as the simple expression of a given person's thoughts, ideas, and views; more compellingly, it is the product of a multitude of historically prior events (genre conventions, specific earlier texts, the absence of

36. Foucault, "What Is an Author?," 149.

certain texts) and contemporaneous events, both narrative and other. In contrast to the notion of "influence," which posits simple appropriation of an outside source by the influenced subject, the notion of intertextuality draws attention to the plural, often contradictory positions inscribed in subject statement or position. An author or an individual (e.g., characters) ought not be seen as a static, given, unproblematic center from which meaning issues or viewed as a figure that confers meaning to narratives. As a socially produced construct, subjects are profoundly determined by the ever-changing *conditions* within which they participate in narrative acts.

The consequence of textualist demystification of realism's positivist assumptions results in a radical inversion: Narrative acts create subjects. Subject expressions, be they authors, characters, or politicians, are thoroughly contingent upon their moments of occurrence and the intertextual effects that bear on those moments. No longer the source of ultimate validation, subjects are instead *effects* of discourses, not stable essences that transcend spatial and temporal contingencies. An "author," or, for that matter, a literary work, can be understood only as it is at once determined by and in turn helps shape the often inchoate systems that Foucault calls discourses.[37] Far from spelling the loss of the subject, this change in its status opens the possibility of seriously engaging the very notion that has established itself over the years as an unquestioned first principle of modern Western literature.

The coterminal ascendance of the individuated subject with capitalism and science masks an issue of subjecthood in its own historical coordinates. The subject's rise to primacy comes from the convenient and self-validating fiction that human sciences can be treated similarly to the natural sciences. Where the sub-

37. According to Foucault, "discursive practices are characterized by the delimitation of a field of objects, the definition of a legitimate perspective for the agent of knowledge, and the fixing of norms for the elaboration of concepts and theories. . . . It is usually the case that a discursive practice assembles a number of diverse disciplines or sciences or that it crosses a certain number among them and regroups many of their individual characteristics into a new and occasionally unexpected unity" (*Language, Counter-Memory, Practice: Selected Essays and Interviews by Michel Foucault*, ed. Donald F. Bouchard [Ithaca: Cornell University Press, 1977], 199–200).

ject stands outside of the object of study in the natural sciences, in the humanities it necessarily occupies a place in the field of inquiry itself. In Todorov's words, "the difference in the object is a factual given: the object of the human sciences is a text, in the broad sense of signifying matter. . . . In the natural sciences we seek to know an *object*, but in the human ones, a *subject*."[38] Thus, when we read (literary) texts, subjects are immanent, inscribed in the text through narration, but they are simultaneously and reflectively, as reader/writer/interpreter, the subject of the text.

Left with the dilemma that such reflections on textuality present, we must find ways of studying subjectivity, not as something that precedes narrative figuration but as effects of such acts. The replacement of a positivistically conceived individual with the subject permits us to identify the exercise of will, power, and desire far more broadly conceived: Thus, even when we place Japan within the familiar narrative of modernization, the subject can be the state, a collectivity, a government, and so on. The continued use of the Western humanist subject keeps us captive to the "grand narrative of the modes of production":[39] Japan becomes inserted into a trajectory of modernization and all that it signifies, including scientific method, the emancipated individual, and global refiguration of nationhood. Whether the subject is conceived as a nation (in relation to the West and to Asia) or as a smaller unit, agency requires us to attend to those often hidden or "unintended" constructions of (plural) subjects. In other instances, subjects can manifest themselves as voices, expressions of resistance or affirmation, speakers of a particular language, even grammatical or linguistic forms.

By investing subjects with the notion of agency we have foregrounded interest/will and difference—that is, politics that are inevitably inscribed in texts (events). In the maze of conflicting views in the deconstructive theories of the subject, the present study aligns itself with those that see subjects as the effects of agency. The creation of meaning, exercise of intention, and willfulness then lead me to designate as provisional to that specific

38. Tzvetan Todorov, *Mikhail Bakhtin: The Dialogical Principle* (Minneapolis: University of Minnesota Press, 1984), 18.

39. Spivak, "Subaltern Studies," 197.

occurrence of such interestedness the production of a subject.[40] If structuralist and deconstructive theorists called into question the individual or subject as the source of meaning or the center of meaning-producing activities, according to David Carroll they never exceeded the practice of displacing it with another subject.[41] In poststructuralist theories, the subject is most often replaced by language as a determining force. During the short but eventful history of criticism that has refigured the subject in nonessentialist terms, it is the mediation of language studies (seen earlier, for instance, in the studies of Russian formalists Eichenbaum and Schlovsky and in a more self-enclosed form in the work of the "new critics") that has figured most prominently in revealing the subject's "loss of innocence." What has most insistently confounded attempts to theorize critical approaches with deconstruction has been the question of the subject in terms of agency.[42] I cannot cleanly resolve the contradictions raised by the encounter of these theoretical positions; instead, I proceed with analyses of the conditions of a subject's possibility and view subjects as reflections that can claim presence only through the intentions, deeds, or enactment of deeds from which subjects are inferred. This perspective carries with it what many will judge an unfortunate ambiguity regarding the status of the subject and agency. Whatever its shortcomings may be, this approach has the virtue of focusing on the processes that narrativize or create subjects, regardless of what empirical status they may finally have. For it is precisely in the praxis, or the failure to act, the contingencies, and the unfolding of responses to them, not in some finalized image of a subject, that meaning resides. Like events, acts, and moments, texts are visible discursive spaces that give visibility to subjects.

If views prompting attention to the actual environment of a text's occurrence have served to undermine a transcendental

40. For a discussion along similar lines, see Paul Smith, *Discerning the Subject* (Minneapolis: University of Minnesota Press, 1988), 46–55.

41. David Carroll, *The Subject in Question: The Languages of Theory and the Strategies of Fiction* (Chicago: The University of Chicago Press, 1982).

42. Recent critical trends, particularly in the vocabulary of feminist criticism, have looked to agency as a way to mediate the relationship of "deconstructivist" theories with Marxist-oriented approaches. Spivak's work continues to set the standard.

view of such notions as authors, novels, and characters, it is renewed attention to form that inaugurated the possibility for this radical restoration of history to the subject. Taken together, textualist critics have shown that views of literature that suppress the meaning of form—particularly by dismissing it as merely a term opposite to content—are grossly inadequate for textual interpretation. Catherine Belsey acknowledges the value of textualist views as powerful alternatives to referentiality this way: "There is no unmediated experience of the world; knowledge is possible only through the categories and the laws of the symbolic order. Far from expressing a unique perception of the world, authors produce meaning out of the available system of differences, and texts are intelligible in so far as they participate in it."[43]

Arguably, Mikhail Bakhtin did more than any other twentieth-century critic to explore the sign and the production of meaning as it obtains from social relations. Earlier I pointed to the parallel conditions of sociality that define not only the production of texts and texts themselves but the environment of reading (receiving, analyzing, interpreting, and contextualizing) those texts—that is, the conditions that govern the particular reading of these texts. As we prepare for readings of selected modern Japanese literary texts themselves, we must find ways to engage them without suppressing the social contest, tensions, and marks of inequality—in short, questions of agency that are tightly woven into the fabric of Japan's modern prose narratives. There is no theoretical template that can ensure "correct" or more powerful readings and interpretations, but I have found the Russian cultural and literary theorist Mikhail Bakhtin's discussion of the dialogic novel a powerful tool that can at least keep us vigilant in avoiding the overdetermined grooves of positivist-realist perspectives.

RELATING BAKHTIN'S NARRATED SUBJECT

The reclamation of Mikhail Bakhtin's work (1895–1975) by Julia Kristeva and other European critics in the late 1960s and En-

43. Belsey, *Critical Practice*, 45.

glish language translations of his studies in the 1970s and 1980s have helped make Bakhtin one of the most frequently invoked textual theorists of the late twentieth century.[44] The wide and generally enthusiastic reception given Bakhtin reflects such features of his work as its apparent accessibility, the fecundity of dialogism rooted in the familiar academic tradition of Platonic dialogue, special privilege given to the novel, Bakhtin's points of convergence with poststructuralist criticisms, and views of plural voices that accommodate liberal humanistic thought. More specifically, his concrete explication (through the use of literary texts) of dialogics, polyphony, and heteroglossia (the multiplicity of unofficial linguistic practices), explorations of carnival as a parodic subversion of fixed hierarchies, the nuanced consideration of verbal interactions seen in his study of direct and indirect discourse, and detailed discussion of the socialized nature of utterance and rhetoric have provided a rich corpus that critics have appropriated for their own programs.[45] Unfortunately, all too frequently the sharp critical edge inherent in Bakhtin's ruminations on heterogeneous voicings and utterances have been reduced to schemas of civil pluralistic exchange. The tendency to domesticate the critical edge found in Bakhtin takes yet another form, which Ken Hirschkop identifies in an anthology of essays on Bakhtin: "The contributions share an ideological drift, the ultimate effect of which is to evade the most radical aspects of Bakhtin's work in favor of an interpretation that renders him useful in the argument against the recent advances of post-structuralism and recent literary theory

44. A good bibliography of works by and about Bakhtin's work can be found in Ken Hirschkop and David Shepherd, eds., *Bakhtin and Cultural Theory* (Manchester: Manchester University Press, 1989). In addition to the article by Julia Kristeva entitled "Word, Dialogue, and Novel," in *Desire in Language: A Semiotic Approach to Literature and Art* (New York: Columbia University Press, 1980), I have found the following studies to be useful in pursuing the radical implications of his *oeuvre*: Graham Pechey, "Bakhtin, Marxism and Post-Structuralism," in *Literature, Politics, and Theory*, ed. Frances Barker, Peter Hulme, Margaret Iversen, and Diana Loxley (New York: Methuen, 1986), 104–25; Dominick LaCapra, "Bakhtin, Marxism, and the Carnivalesque," in *Rethinking Intellectual History: Texts, Contexts, Language* (Ithaca: Cornell University Press, 1983), 291–324.

45. See Pechey, "Bakhtin, Marxism, and Post-Structuralism," 123.

in general.[46] Aspects of Bakhtin's theory that appear to validate a liberal pluralism frequently have been used to counter the threat of chaos or (one of the deadliest sins of all) relativism thought to characterize contemporary theory.

The present study has been inspired particularly by the radical nature of Bakhtin's sustained examination of the Western novel, at once the subject of his work and the displaced form or mediation by which he was able both to theorize and to mount an attack on his own enunciative moment—Stalinist Russia.[47] Embracing Bakhtin's dialogism as polite encounters of respectful individual differences ignores the aspect of social struggle so central to his criticism. Consider for a moment the gulf that separates the homeless in downtown Santa Barbara and the socialite in Montecito, its wealthy "suburb." To treat their disagreements as differences in perspective is to ignore a vast network of socially structured determinations and contradictions and to recast it in the polite and depoliticized framework of reconcilable differences solvable in "civil society" is, predictably, to yield to precisely the terms dictated by the empowered over the impoverished. The same mentality that suppresses such politics will read Bakhtin's theory of the dialogic novel, written by a man who was banished to the wilds of Kazakhstan for six years, as a theory of polite pluralism.

The hard political edge in Bakhtin's thought is vital to the present study, which examines literary production as it occurred in modern Japanese society and as it became an arena for conceiving and situating the private subject in a society bent on suppressing its heteroglot nature. Bakhtin's theory presents a way of thinking through the complexly reflexive relationships

46. Hirschkop, "A Response to the Forum on Mikhail Bakhtin," in *Bakhtin: Essays and Dialogues on His Work*, ed. Gary Saul Morson (Chicago: University of Chicago Press, 1986), 74. The December 1983 (vol. 10, no. 2) issue of *Critical Inquiry* provided a forum on Bakhtin which, in turn, has intensified the critical debate over the appropriation of Bakhtin's ideas.

47. We are reminded by Timothy Brennan that the object of Bakhtin's attack cannot be restricted to Stalinist Russia. Commenting on Michael Holquist's study of Bakhtin, Brennan states: "As a whole, Holquist has interpreted Bakhtin's assault on the orthodoxies of fixed language to be veiled attacks on Stalinism; but it is much more likely that they were attacks on the belletrism, scientism, and obscurantism of western cultural practice" ("The National Longing for Form," 69).

among subjects, institutions, and various exertions of power in discursive terms. Thus, John Frow is able to locate in Bakhtin's critique of Russian formalism what the latter's thought shares with the object under criticism: "The crucially important thing the Formalists did was to establish the unity of the conceptual level at which extraliterary values and functions become structural moments of a text, and at which, conversely, the 'specifically literary' function acquires an extra-aesthetic dimension."[48] Bakhtin's explorations of textualized dialogics allow one to eschew realist conceptions of language as being merely or at least primarily referential, thereby separating text from context or real life. Opening the way to what today we call discourse analysis, Bakhtin presents a way of understanding texts as socially engaged participants in a contestatory social field. Literature is for him a site of ideological contest in which readings can reveal the often tense relations between dominant and dominated subject positions.[49] Finally, but no less important for the present use of Bakhtin, is the applicability of his theorizing to Japanese texts, in no small measure determined by the orality that is deeply inscribed in and shared by Bakhtinian thought and Japanese literate and performative cultural traditions.[50]

It is through the essays collected in *The Dialogic Imagination* that Bakhtin's theorizing is most explicitly articulated, though works like *Rabelais and His World* and *Problems of Dostoevsky's Poetics* do not merely illustrate but extend his exploration of the

48. John Frow, *Marxism and Literary History* (Cambridge, Mass.: Harvard University Press, 1986), 99.

49. Nicos Poulantzas contends that "the dominant ideology does not simply reflect the conditions of existence of the dominant class, the pure and simple subject, but rather the concrete political relation between the dominant and the dominated classes in a social formation" (*Political Power and Social Classes*, trans. Timothy O'Hagan [London: New Left Books and Sheed and Ward, 1973], 203, quoted in Frow, *Marxism and Literary History*).

50. It is no accident that *skaz*—a "yarn" or a story "in which the manner of telling . . . is as important to the story itself"—was a central concept in Russian formalist criticism, a concept that Bakhtin's work takes as its point of departure. Whether it be a tradition of forms of orally recited literature or unflagging concern for metrics, sounds, and rhythm, Japanese literate expression remains notably marked by the oral. The quotation is from Boris Tomashevsky, "Sterne's *Tristram Shandy*: Stylistic Commentary," in *Russian Formalist Criticism: Four Essays*, ed. Lee T. Lemon and Marion J. Reis (Lincoln: University of Nebraska Press, 1965), 67.

novel form. In "Epic and Novel" he underscores the novel's "special relationship with extraliterary genres, with the genres of everyday life and with ideological genres."[51] Bakhtin's extended views on the novel provide a means for engaging issues of power (implicit in his discussion of relationality) and subject position. That his work, which powerfully critiques existing social configurations of his time, takes the form of textuality (the novel) is no accident, at once showing Bakhtin's remarkable sensitivity to the productive properties of language and his recognition of its power, and reflecting the necessity of masking his socio-critical intent. Like Foucault's work, which Bakhtin's interest in subjects and relations of power anticipates, Bakhtin's study of novelistic discourse has encountered its most serious challenge from those concerned with the issue of agency and intentionality. As we shall see, this is precisely where Bakhtin can help provide at least a provisional strategy for confronting issues of the world, the text, and the subject.

Bakhtin's point of departure is found in his criticism of Ferdinand de Saussure's linguistics as "abstract objectivism," misguided, he says, because Saussure disregarded the individual utterance (*parole*) in favor of language (*langue*).[52] The problems with this are manifold, but here we focus on the following point that troubles Bakhtin: Such positivistic abstract objectivism reifies the language system, conceived in terms of a static, synchronic, unified whole, ignoring the far more important aspect of language—its behavior as a contingent activity that changes with every utterance. His preference for utterance (performance) implicitly questions the conception of a unified, positive subject: "The speech act or, more accurately, its product—the utterance," he says, "cannot under any circumstances be con-

51. Mikhail Bakhtin, *The Dialogic Imagination: Four Essays by M.M. Bakhtin*, ed. Michael Holquist (Austin: University of Texas Press, 1981); *Rabelais and His World*, trans. Helene Iswolsky (Cambridge, Mass.: MIT Press, 1968); *Problems of Dostoevsky's Poetics*, ed. and trans. Caryl Emerson (Minneapolis: University of Minnesota Press, 1984).

52. V.N. Volosinov, *Marxism and the Philosophy of Language*, trans. Ladislav Matejka and I.R. Titunik (New York: Seminar Press, 1973), 60–61. While debate over the identity of the historical figure called Bakhtin continues, I shall follow the convention taken by many and consider studies appearing under Volosinov's name to be the work of Bakhtin.

sidered an individual phenomenon in the precise meaning of the word and cannot be explained in terms of the individual psychological or psychophysiological conditions of the speaker. *The utterance is a social phenomenon.*"[53] On the one hand, his criticism of system in Saussurean linguistics affirms subjects, but it is significant that his focus is on utterance—an act (of relationship) rather than a finished or preexisting individual: "[The] *immediate social situation and the broader social milieu wholly determine—and determine from within, so to speak—the structure of an utterance* [emphasis in original]."[54]

Even though Bakhtin's entire project can be considered a sustained critique of individuated subjectivism, whether we see it in his frontal attack on romanticism and philological studies or in his study of dialogism and the novel, Bakhtin's vocabulary invites criticism from those wary of positivistic conceptions of the subject. Among them is Vincent Pecora, who charges Bakhtin with essentializing the subject.[55] Pecora quotes from one of Bakhtin's later texts, "Discourse in the Novel," to launch his critique: "The living utterance, having taken meaning and shape at a particular historical moment in a socially specific environment, cannot fail to brush up against thousands of living dialogic threads, woven by socio-ideological consciousness around the given object of an utterance; it cannot fail to become an active participant in social dialogue."[56] Just what is this "participant"? In Bakhtin's dialogic schema, there are two categories of language, authoritative discourse (e.g., political, paternal, religious) and what he calls internally persuasive discourse, which "affirm[s] through assimilation, tightly interwoven with 'one's own word.'"[57] Pecora argues that this latter voice, through its capacity to assimilate and to reformulate other voices as its own, reproduces a totalized subject position. His criticism concludes this way:

53. Volosinov, *Marxism and the Philosophy of Language*, 82.
54. Volosinov, *Marxism and the Philosophy of Language*, 86.
55. Vincent Pecora, *Self and Form in Modern Narrative* (Baltimore: The Johns Hopkins University Press, 1989).
56. Quoted from Bakhtin, *The Dialogic Imagination*, 276.
57. Bakhtin, *The Dialogic Imagination*, 345.

> Bakhtin's theory of discursive heteroglossia, for all its "deconstruction" of the indicative surface of the speech act, never really questions the presence of expression, of intentionality. . . . In the end Bakhtin's highly suggestive theory tends to reproduce the bourgeois individual, already implicit in the novel, along with its divided consciousness, contradictory liberalism, and ironic social alienation . . . without ever addressing the degree to which this concept of the autonomous individual is both the foundation of the novel's form and the source of the novel's discontent with itself.[58]

In fact, as I see it, the place given to "intention" in Bakhtin's writing is highly ambiguous, insofar as he frequently tends to confer a provisional subject status to language itself:

> Characteristic for the novel as a genre is not the image of a man in his own right, but a man who is precisely the *image of a language*. . . . If the subject making the novel specifically a novel is defined as a speaking person and his discourse, striving for social significance and a wider general application as one distinctive language in a heteroglot world—then the central problem for a stylistics of the novel may be formulated as the problem of *artistically representing language, the problem of representing the image of a language*.[59]

The importance of Bakhtin's focus on language does not come simply from a meaningful strategy for displacing the individuated subject; by recasting the subject in narrated terms, he is able to address social contradictions inscribed within a text, not in the humanistic vocabulary of irony (which underwrites Pecora's argument) but as the site of ideological contest. Some of the specific terms employed by Bakhtin do indeed come from a liberal-humanist tradition, but his conception of the social in contestatory terms challenges the reification of the subject with an "unfinalizeability" of either the social or the private or, least of all, that very opposition. Bakhtin enables us to approach texts outside of the discursive framework (humanist realism centered by a sovereign subject) within which the object of critical inquiry (the European novel) has been overdetermined. His sustained assault on conceptions of language as referential lead him to

58. Pecora, *Self and Form in Modern Narrative*, 25–26.
59. Bakhtin, *The Dialogic Imagination*, 336.

focus on the material effects and meanings of linguistic form. Textualist critics of the last several decades have eagerly accepted materialist views toward language inaugurated by Saussurean linguistics, and, salutary as these developments might be, we must guard against fetishizing the rediscovered materiality of the signifier. As John Frow reminds us: "The signifier is not material; the signifier is necessarily realized in phonic or graphic material but is not identical with this material. Its 'identity' is that immaterial mode of existence of the trace defined and constituted by a system of differential relations."[60] Bakhtinian studies of language and dialogics prefigured the possibilities of semiotics, giving us a conceptual framework for considering texts in terms of "differential relations." Dialogics contests the discourse of discrete subjects, for the "speaking person [which he does not construe to be a unitary, closed individual] in the novel is always, to one degree or another, an *ideologue*, and his words are always *ideologemes*. A particular language in a novel is always a particular way of viewing the world.[61] When a provisional subject is posited, even that can no longer exist or be expressed in unitary form, for "the intentions of the prose writer are refracted, and refracted *at different angles*, depending on the degree to which the refracted, heteroglot languages he deals with are socio-ideologically alien, already embodied and already objectified."[62] Ken Hirschkop puts it this way: "Bakhtin's purpose was to reintegrate historicity, evaluation, and activity—in short, all that had been excluded as style—into the social reality of language and thereby to develop a concept of linguistic structure which was dynamic rather than ahistorical."[63] As it happens, this conjuncture of what Hirschkop calls historicity,

60. Frow, *Marxism and Literary History*, 45.
61. Bakhtin, *The Dialogic Imagination*, 333.
62. Bakhtin, *The Dialogic Imagination*, 300. Susan Stewart argues that refraction replaces simple reflection theory and shows how it characterizes the ideological sign "by an intersecting of differently oriented social interests within one and the same sign community. . . . Thus various different classes will use one and the same language. As a result, differently oriented accents intersect in every ideological sign. Sign becomes an arena of class struggle" ("Shouts on the Street: Bakhtin's Anti-Linguistics," in *Bakhtin: Essays and Dialogue on His Work*, ed. Gary Saul Morson [Chicago: University of Chicago Press, 1986], 53).
63. Hirschkop, "A Response to the Forum on Mikhail Bakhtin," 77.

evaluation, and activity constitutes the manner in which the subject is conceived in the present study. If Bakhtinian thinking can exceed the problems of essentialist discussions of the subject, it is through a view of relational difference as productive and meaningful.

BAKHTIN CROSSING BORDERS

Bakhtin has found supporters within the Japanese academic scene, to which we must do more than gesture if we are serious about intentions of engaging Japanese texts, for far from being historical artifacts far removed in time and place from us, they continue to be reshaped by ongoing interpretive acts by Japanese scholars, critics, and readers. No one has used Bakhtin as a theoretical touchstone for the study of modern Japanese literature as assiduously and effectively as has Komori Yōichi, who began as a student of Russian literature. His series of essays on Futabatei's *Ukigumo* represents a significant contribution to narratological perspectives on Japan's modern colloquial literature (the so-called *genbun'itchi* narrative). Following the lead of critics such as Maeda Ai, he cites the relationship of dialogue to narration (*jinobun*) as one of the critical issues of early modern Japanese literature. He departs from Maeda's position that Futabatei appropriated the raconteur San'yūtei Enchō's performative delivery to depict charcters, arguing instead that finally it was Futabatei's task to forge a new relationship between writer and character through a new written language (*écriture*).[64]

Like other Japanese critics studying the emergence of *genbun'itchi* narratives, Komori states that the narrator in *Ukigumo* was shaped by the *gesaku* writer Shikitei Sanba's dialogue and the oral art of *rakugo*, but, in addition, Komori has identified the imprint of the Russian short story writer Gogol in Futabatei's text. Gogol's pieces are alive, he says, not because of their plots but because of their narrative qualities. A Gogol-like emphasis on each character's idiosyncrasies expressed through variation in the representation of speech permitted Futabatei to write a dialogic

64. Komori Yōichi, "Ukigumo no ji no bun: kotoba no bottō to shite no buntai," *Kokugo kokubun kenkyū* 62 (August 1979): 14. Also in *Kōzō to shite no katari* (Shinyōsha, 1988).

text in which several subject voices collide. Komori is especially effective when he teases out the voices presented as straight narration (as Bakhtin does in many of his studies), tracking *Ukigumo*'s narrator, who in the beginning can stand apart from and comment ironically on the inept and straight-laced Bunzō but by part 3 becomes fused to the protagonist.[65] Finally, paralleling his reading of Gogol, Komori sees *Ukigumo* as a *shōsetsu* that can claim our attentions not for its plot but rather for its formal narrative characteristics. Particularly noteworthy in this respect are the marks of orality shared by the literary heritages common to Russia and Japan, a matter that resurfaces with renewed urgency in *genbun'itchi* narrative seeking to renew itself through modern spoken language. The emphasis on orality is fortuitous, not only because Japanese writing as a whole is conspicuously marked by conventions of spoken-intoned language (not unlike the way that similarly marked Slavic languages led to the seminal studies of orality by Albert Lord) but because it allows Komori to see modern Japanese literature as a "people's literature."

Bakhtinian dialogics informs Komori's study of narrative as its constructs refracted subject positions. An essay on Ōgai's *Maihime* (Dancing Girl, 1890) concludes that through an interiorized dialogue between a writing self and a written self, Rintarō the protagonist discovers a new self (*jiga*).[66] In discussing literature of the 1880s and 1890s, Komori tentatively suggests that the *genbun'itchi* narrative reflects a change in social structure from that based on *kyōdōtai* (cooperative system) to one requiring clearer means of articulating self–other distinctions.[67] Komori's attention to seeing and seen subjects, which resonates with the phenomenological project of his mentor Kamei Hideo,[68] is but one of many manifestations of Komori's tendency (rightly, I believe) to view mid-Meiji prose as a sustained effort to separate the "author's voice from those of the characters,

65. Komori, "Ukigumo no ji no bun," 16.

66. Komori, "Ketsumatsu kara no monogatari: *Maihime* ni okeru ichininshō," in *Buntai to shite no monogatari* (Chikuma shobō, 1988), 166.

67. Komori, "Ninshō-teki sekai no seiritsu: Ōgai doitsu sanbu saku ni okeru buntai to kōsei," in *Buntai to shite no monogatari* (Chikuma shobō, 1988), 196.

68. See Kamei Hideo, *Kansei no henkaku* (Kōdansha, 1983), and *Shintai: kono fushigi naru mono no bungaku* (Renga shobō, 1984).

which makes narrative possible."[69] Komori's dialogism focuses on the myriad permutations of otherness (*tasha*) present in Meiji literature—subject positions of the reader and writer, the gazing narrator, objects of vision, speaking subjects, shifts in perspective, changing diacritics as a device for differentiating subject positions.

As my abbreviated representation of his work suggests, Komori's narratological analyses, particularly in his earlier essays, tend to posit subjects within the fixed categories of author, narrator, character, and so on, even when he identifies multiple accents in a single utterance or interiorized dialogue. The various "voices" in any sentence are always given to a subject identified in those boundaries that traditionally define subjecthood. For example, when the narrator in *Ukigumo* states something in his own words but utters the feelings or thoughts of Bunzō, the parts of the "whole" utterance are always viewed in terms of those fixed whole "persons." I would suggest that in part Komori's practice is dictated by an environment that still finds even the humanist view of the individual or self to be problematic. At the same time that his theoretical inclinations lead him to reject essentialized subjects, he must affirm something (the individuated subject) that has been characterized as absent from Japanese society.

Echoing widespread interest in Japanese critical circles, Komori focuses on Meiji writers' attempts to forge a narrator distinct from characters, readers, and other voices. His sensitivity to relationality is also expressed in one of his primary concerns, also shared by many of his contemporaries: the relationship between writer and reader.[70] In the context of Japanese literary criticism, discussions of this relationship often revolve around the assumption that by its nature the Japanese language is listener- (reader-) oriented. These matters of language and attention to reader are related, of course. The problem of estab-

69. The quotation is from Hirschkop describing an essay by Cesare Segre on Bakhtin's polyphony. Hirschkop, "A Response to the Forum on Mikhail Bakhtin," 11.

70. Shinoda Kōichirō, Karatani Kōjin, Maeda Ai, Kamei Hideo, Hasumi Shigehiko, among critics of modern Japanese literature, have shown interest in the reader.

lishing appropriate levels of address, vantage points, or positions of narration—a kind of "neutral" narrative point, for instance—is concerned with the narrator's stance toward the reader, an integral member of the relationality inscribed in these questions of inflectionless neutral narration. Komori notes that Ōgai's *Maihime* first-person *genbun'itchi* narration, strongly determined by the interlocutor-other, together with the framework of reminiscence (two temporalities) permits a separation of observing self from observed self, and this separation sets the text in motion.[71] The text, which he says shows the process of the writing self progressively losing itself to the written, observed self, is also an illustration of the strong other-directedness (to the second person) inherent in *genbun'itchi* writing. In its particular first-person narrative scheme, Ōgai's text replicates the relationship of writer to reader that we may infer Komori sees to be a central condition of modern Japanese texts.

While Komori's readings may seem to presume essentialist views of Japanese language, at other moments he very deliberately challenges such tendencies by treating language as itself a discursive effect. For example, he argues that Sōseki's early pieces such as *Wagahai wa neko de aru* (1905), *Botchan* (1906), *Kusamakura* (1906), and *Yōkyoshū* (1906) were narrated in the first person as Sōseki struggled to forge a literature to meet the demands of a new kind of literature: a literature intended for circulation through moveable type printing (*katsuji insatsu*) to a large, anonymous, and dispersed audience.[72] (As I will argue later in my discussion of Tōson's *Kyūshujin* [1902], these first-person works mediated the creation of a writing [*genbun'itchi*] that, by demanding new relationships among writer, reader, and character, shaped the very contours of these subjects.) It is well known that *Neko* was written for reading aloud to Masaoka Shiki's salon gathering, duplicating in effect the performative space of *rakugo*. Komori suggests that much of transitional modern Japanese literature (from *gesaku* and *monogatari* to *shōsetsu*, consciously modeled after European novels) is best viewed as an effort to produce a written language that catered to a new set

71. Komori, *Buntai*, 225–26.

72. Komori, "Shōsetsu gensetsu no seiritsu: Kindai-teki 'katari' no hassei," in *Kōzō to shite no katari*, 56.

of social conditions. The most significant of these were changes in writer–reader relationships reshaped by a technology of mechanical reproduction, which among other things displaced oral communication with a more anonymous print-mediated relationship.

For our present purposes, Komori's far-ranging work is most effective when it is turned to what many Japanese critics, particularly those who work in premodern literature, acknowledge to be a central issue: the inscription of orality in Japanese writing. That the title of his two books published in 1988 both prominently feature the term *katari* (variously translatable as narrative, the word, language, and speech, depending on its occurrence) clearly marks its significance to the author.[73] It is at once obfuscatory and revelatory that the commonly used equivalent for the English term "narrative" in Japanese (*katari*) subsumes various aspects of spokenness. And it is in his explorations of the multiple refractions that *katari* holds in modern Japanese letters that Komori's work is most convincing.

This distillation of some of Komori's topics and approaches to modern Japanese literature illustrates an important discursive strain that too often remains ignored entirely or is relegated to footnotes meant to signify the exercise of scholarly responsibility. The same things happen to other contemporary Japanese critics whose work I will address in subsequent chapters. Like Western critical theories currently in circulation, histories of modern Japan, secondary studies of Japanese literature, and Japanese–U.S. relations, ongoing revisionist Japanese readings of their own literature form a vital element in the discursive field that students of Japan, no matter who they are and where they are situated, must engage. As critics foreign to Japan, we are particularly well positioned to see the unfamiliar in what to the Japanese has become natural. Thus, while recent critical interest in "narration" by Western critics might tempt us to see a parallel increase in interest given *katari* by Japanese scholars and view the two as the same, as suggested above, it would be wrong to equate the two without noting the problems in doing

73. In one title *katari* occurs as a discrete word, while in the other it is part of another word, *monogatari*. The two books, already cited earlier, are *Kōzō to shite no katari* and *Buntai to shite no monogatari*.

so. Attention to the work of our Japanese counterparts (such as Komori) can help us identify such slippages, the gaps in perspective that help open paths of critical inquiry not captive (at least in the same ways) to the reigning (realist) practices of textual analysis. Open to the heterologies that define our contemporary moment, we can read the inscription of social relations of voice, power, and discourse in Japanese texts in ways that allow us to conceptualize our own situation as students of Japan in the West in relation to those in Japan who examine their own cultural expressions.

POSITIONS

The present study affirms the view that as critics we must engage literature mindful of the too often suppressed recognition that (to borrow Edward Said's phrase) texts, like other constituents of life, are worldly.[74] My claim is that texts constitute history no less than do people, events, and other cultural forces. They lend themselves to careful scrutiny by their direct participation in the general circulation of thoughts, beliefs, ideas, and values that inform the events of any particular moment. Thus, they help constitute social life and must be studied as part of the issue of the form and distribution of power and its absence. When we talk of Japan from after the Russo-Japanese War (1904–5) through the decades leading up to the Second World War we must account for its status as both aggressor and victim in a discourse of imperialism, and, insofar as the very conditions of being are inescapably shot through with relationality, subject expressions on more localized levels (whether they be as narrators, voices, characters in a text, or historical figures) will be similarly implicated in a network of (unequal) power positions. In the profoundest sense, the humanities trace the arrangements of social organization to see how subjects are continually created, shaped, empowered, subjected, suppressed, and used. It is in the interest of those in positions of power and entitlement to suppress any awareness of existing conditions that at any

74. See Edward Said, *The World, the Text, and the Critic* (Cambridge, Mass.: Harvard University Press, 1983).

given time are built upon a complicated nexus of haves and have nots, of the empowered and powerless, the mainstream and the marginalized. The texts read here (prose narratives by Tōson, Sōseki, Shūsei, and Origuchi) must be considered in light of the present interpretive moment, as the relationship between that moment and our texts will necessarily help determine the networks of tension and struggle that inscribe the texts and the time and place of their examination. Once we recognize even as a provisional first principle the thoroughly relational nature of society, it is no longer possible to assume the mantle of objective and scholarly remove that has served to validate academic inquiry.

These conditions make reading, like virtually any other activity (insofar as it is inscribed with the social), an unmistakably political deed. That is, reading is performed by an agent with particular vested interests and tied to the rest of the world in ways that will condition the exercise of that agency. That reader engages a text equally caught in a network of filiations and affiliations—in this instance, across a vast spatial and somewhat smaller temporal distance. To borrow Edward Said's words again, there is "no vantage *outside* the actuality of relationships between cultures, between unequal imperial and nonimperial powers . . . a vantage point that might allow one the epistemological privilege of somehow judging, evaluating, and interpreting free of the encumbering interests, emotions, and engagements of the ongoing relationships themselves."[75] We reader-interpreters occupy subject positions along with other subjects (characters, narrators, discrete voices) of a text. If the present study is to effectively and conscientiously challenge the sustained fiction of objectivity claimed by that scholarly tradition, it must proceed by articulating its own biases and theoretical assumptions.

Let me bring the confrontation inherent in this set of readings into more immediate focus. This book is marked by an author's name that invokes neither a privileged transfer of authentic native information nor the promise of seamless rigor

75. Said, "Representing the Colonized: Anthropology's Interlocutors," *Critical Inquiry* 15 (Winter 1989): 216–17.

conventionally assured by a signature of white male identity; it may also be subject to the reader's presumption that this author writes from a position of nostalgic yearning for lost roots and the recovery of personal identity. Thus, in some senses, this text cannot escape a designation such as "Japanese-American," a rubric whose seeming absurdity is overturned by the politics of exclusion that has stamped the field of Japanology as surely, if not as viciously, as race has restricted the lives of blacks in this country. This book is additionally marked by a critical stance, shared by several recent studies, against a solidly entrenched genealogy of Western Japanology.[76] I have been encouraged to align my own work with theirs, which affirms the importance of destabilizing what are unmistakably interested and statically institutionalized perspectives.

Although my own effort is not as ambitious, it too faces a situation not unlike that confronting Henry Louis Gates, who has sought to give voice to a poetics of black literature amidst the overdetermined dominant discourses of unequal power:

> Naming the black tradition's own theory of itself is to echo and rename other theories of literary criticism. Our task is not to reinvent our traditions as if they bore no relation to that tradition created and borne, in the main, by white men. Our writers used that impressive tradition to define themselves, both with and against their concept of received order. We must do the same, with or against the Western critical canon.[77]

The ingrained habit of relating modern Japanese literature to the Western realist tradition should be accompanied by a similar sensitivity that neither rejects nor blindly embraces the respective genealogies. Modern Japanese literature is best conceived as the site on which native narrative practices encounter Western realism as both object of appropriation and as method of self-evaluation. Japanese willingness to embrace Western approaches to literature has been reinforced and mirrored by an

76. I have included as part of my acknowledgments those practitioners' works that have inspired my own work from such an angle.

77. Henry Louis Gates, Jr., *The Signifying Monkey: A Theory of African-American Literary Criticism* (New York: Oxford University Press, 1988), xxiii.

equally unyielding proclivity among Western scholars to domesticate Japanese textual expressions. Modern Japanese prose narratives cannot be properly understood by wrenching theory from practice or text from its moment of enunciation.

We would merely repeat the blindness to agency practiced by Japan specialists who have assumed an artless objectivity in their representations of Japan were we to undertake another study of modern Japanese literature without engaging our own enunciative moment. Most important, it would have to include current efforts of Japanese critics who have sought to reassess their own literature through judicious use of Western critical theories as a way out of the essentially Eurocentric standards inscribed in nineteenth-century European mimeticism. Here we are faced with the conundrum of lapsing into a facile binarism (are not these Japanese practitioners of Continental theories merely reassessing their literature with the latest imported method?), which, as I indicated earlier in this chapter, has dominated Japan studies in America. Over the years there have been many countertrends and voices contesting the primacy given to Western realism.[78] Today, the socio-historic conditions may be different, and the terms used to assess texts may have changed (largely to European critical perspectives that deconstruct the grounds of privilege accorded the humanist-realist tradition), but, fueled by a confidence born of unprecedented economic health, contemporary Japanese critics have participated in a spirited revisionist effort to reexamine and in many instances rewrite the legacy of intellectual indebtedness to the West.[79] I suspect that much of contemporary Japanese theorizing is mo-

78. Takayama Chōgyū's cry for a national literature, the Kokusui-ha, and the prose of such writers as Izumi Kyōka, Tanizaki Jun'ichirō, and the Nihon Roman-ha in one form or another all express dissent from Western realist practices.

79. The invocation of contemporary European critical procedures by Japanese critics often serves to reproduce a strident call for native traditions. The speed with which Continental criticism finds its way into Japanese translations and circulates through academe and bookstores suggests the distinctive significations given to it in that environment. See, for example, Marilyn Ivy, "Critical Texts, Mass Artifacts: The Consumption of Knowledge in Postmodern Japan," *South Atlantic Quarterly* 87 (Summer 1988): 419–44.

tivated by a conservative inclination (passing as progressive) to claim an essentially deconstructive heritage predating European expressions by centuries and, relatedly, to affirm a native literary tradition along similar lines. I will incorporate in my discussion of texts those theoretical discussions that I believe attempt instead to truly radicalize the study of Japanese literature.

2

NARRATING RESENTMENT THROUGH URBAN–RURAL TENSION

Shimazaki Tōson's *Kyūshujin*

Despite the fact that neither of Shimazaki Tōson's two texts chosen for discussion in this study closely conform to what would later be called Japanese naturalism (*shizenshugi*), these two early works tend to be placed within this category. Here, instead of providing yet another reading that affirms their place in the narrative of *shizenshugi-shishōsetsu* (naturalism and the I-novel), I track their participation in the Meiji-era discourse of nation building. Over the years, both government authorities and social critics-historians would promote the belief that a vertically conceived social order (Tokugawa) had been replaced by a horizontally cast egalitarian (spatial) society. In Tōson's early texts that were critical of the imperial state, such as *Kyūshujin* and *Hakai*, we can see how the new metaphor of horizontality merely masked enduring conditions of social inequality. In an era when accelerated industrialization would change the demographics of Japan, *Kyūshujin* and *Hakai* show how conceptions of the urban and rural were closely tied to the contingencies of national consolidation.

TŌSON'S *KYŪSHUJIN* AND *KINDAI BUNGAKU*

The place of Shimazaki Tōson (1872–1943) in modern Japanese letters is secure. Known best as a "naturalist" writer whose self-revelatory texts would point the way to the confessional *shishōsetsu* of the Taishō era, his early novel *Hakai* (The Broken Commandment, 1906) remains canonized as a pivotal text among early modern Japanese prose narratives. To many Japanese, his standing comes from the massive tome that many consider his masterpiece, *Yoakemae* (Before the Dawn, 1929–35), the sweeping historical drama that captures the tensions in Japan as it turns outward in the direction of the West.[1] What is often overlooked is Tōson's start in letters as a poet of *shintaishi* (new-form poetry). His poetry anthology called *Wakanashū* (Seedlings, 1897), which enjoyed immediate popularity in its time, was written mostly in a traditional florid style and established 5-7 metrics,[2] but, along with other poets associated with the movement, Tōson saw this new poetry as a vehicle for expressing privately felt emotions in a straightforward manner. A similar imperative, based on the reception of Western realist standards, to present the truth or reality, was to dictate the shape of Japanese prose narrative writing in the modern era.

Poetry has been long considered the repository of the Japanese soul, the form to which literary tradition demanded one turn when seized with a desire for self-expression. Within a few decades after Japan turned to the West, the European realist novel was to become the form that Japanese prose narrative writers were to emulate, replacing poetry as the standard form for self-expression. The ascendance of the prose narrative form (*shōsetsu*) in post-Restoration Japanese letters was accompanied by a similar claim for the *shōsetsu* as a vehicle for expressing personal feelings; but insofar as the *shōsetsu* was inspired by the Western realist novel, this "genre" subscribed to the view that "truth can be discovered by the individual through his senses."[3] The skill with which truth could be depicted in credible fashion would quickly become the most important determinant of good literature.

1. For an account of the attention given to *Yoakemae*, see the introduction to the English language translation of the text by William Naff: *Before the Dawn* (Honolulu: University of Hawaii Press, 1987), xi.

2. Tōson would not turn to the use of everyday language until he began writing prose. See Itō Sei, "Tōson no hassō to sutairu," in *Shimazaki Tōson zenshū bekkan* (Chikuma shobō, 1983), 39.

3. Ian Watt, *The Rise of the Novel* (Berkeley: University of California Press, 1957), 12.

Across a broad spectrum of writing—from poetry to sketches and to the *shōsetsu*—Tōson's work has claimed "truth" realized in distinctive ways. His poetry proclaimed "truthfulness" for its direct expression of genuinely and personally held feelings. A penchant for dispassionate expression marking his early "prose poem" exercises that would come to be associated with Masaoki Shiki's "sketching" (*shasei*) would result in *Chikumagawa no suketchi* (Sketches from the Chikuma River), published in 1913 but begun over a decade earlier. Here, truthfulness was signified by writing conceived as purely transcriptive. The place given to truth in prose narrative was promoted by and in turn engendered such Tōson texts as *Haru* (Spring, 1908), *Ie* (The Family, 1910–11), and *Shinsei* (A New Life, 1918–19). He would establish himself as a progenitor of so-called naturalism and the later *shishōsetsu* by drawing directly from his own life and presenting it as if subjective perception were absent.

We have in effect followed the widely accepted version (*teisetsu*) in this abbreviated account of Tōson's literary turns. The present study focuses on a virtually neglected piece, *Kyūshujin*, that subverts the standard representations of Tōson as a figure who inaugurates the mainstays of realist convention, truth and reality, and on *Hakai*, a highly acclaimed text linked to the first through its inscription of the emperor system. Written around the turn of the century when Tōson lived in the Shinshū mountains are two short pieces that represent his initial attempts at fiction, *Kyūshujin* (Former Master, 1902) and *Warazōri* (Straw Sandals, 1902). Dismissed as early efforts no more than a prelude to Tōson's *Hakai* and subsequent *shizenshugi* texts, *Kyūshujin* is important because it demarcates the moment when *gesaku*-like demands to entertain an audience collide with a new elevated and paradoxical fictional imperative to pursue the truth. I have chosen to read *Kyūshujin* adjacent to *Hakai* because taken together they show so clearly the trajectory of Tōson's efforts to narrativize subjects. The resistances and leaps required in the movement from the narrative strategy in the first text to the second play out one of the key issues of Meiji prose narration—textualizing subject positions. And it is here in the conventionally overlooked gap that we find, revealed with the clarity that comes from the contradictions of an era not quite able to present itself as seamless and finished, the strategies that Tōson used in his attempts to narrativize "modern" subjects.

Well before writers in the middle decades of Meiji began to engage Western realist conventions, there was a firmly established literary heritage that revolved around the creator of a literary work. It is well known that Japan has had a long and rich tradition of diary literature and discursive essays (*zuihitsu*)—writing that is unified not by Western novelistic organizing devices, be they plot, causal reasoning, or temporality, but by its writer. Novelization as practiced in the West brought a different set of requirements for expressing the subject. Where subjective, impressionistic narratives such as diaries (*nikki*) and random essays (*zuihitsu*) rest on the recognition of their writers, the emphasis on objectivity, detachment, and reality in the *shōsetsu* draws attention to the narrative "content." Such a valorization cannot help but be present in the appropriation of Western ideas in post-Restoration Japan, when the discourse of science and Western thought enjoyed a privilege that to this day remains undiminished. Japanese literature has always had to confront the issue of fiction, fabrication, or falseness as a tag of denigration. The association of literature with verisimilitude in Western realism represented a sign that modern Japanese writers could invoke in carving out legitimacy for their own work. *Shizenshugi-shishōsetsu* assumed a privileged place in modern Japanese literature, in good measure as a response to the continuing imperative to legitimate the work of writers of fiction. The consequence of a literature represented by both Japanese writers and critics and by Western critics alike as an extended effort to rewrite itself along nineteenth-century European realist terms has been a literature continually misrecognized as inadequately mimeticist.

Any literary text is a site inscribed with intertextual relating, a place in which the formal conventions of earlier texts meet with new standards to engender yet newer forms and in which the text explicitly and obliquely addresses former and existing narratives. In the present readings of *Kyūshujin* and *Hakai*, what emerges are two texts that engage the problem of subject expression by reworking the critical role of the narrator—that entity mediating "form to content" (revealing in the process the spuriousness of such an opposition). In *Kyūshujin* Tōson wrestles with the issue of representation at a formal level, opting to skirt the problems associated with forging a style of transparent reference by creating a first-person narrative. *Kyūshujin* is both about narration ("content") and an experiment in figurating a fictive subject in the emerging space of "serious" (non-*gesaku*) prose narration. In *Hakai* Tōson thematizes the problem in the figure of the protagonist, Segawa Ushimatsu. Taken together, the texts allow us to trace one of the central concerns of literary production in turn-of-the-century Japan: the search for adequate forms for presenting subject positions.

In the introduction we saw how realist criticism assumes an essentialized view of subjects. This chapter examines how in Tōson's texts the subject is a figurative expression of authenticity, a value that exceeded the status given to the citizen-subject during the middle Meiji years. In what might best be conceived as a series of links and displacements, the privilege granted authenticity as a guiding principle of literary composition is inextricably tied to conceptions of authority in Meiji Japan. While quite different in appearance, both *Kyūshujin* and *Hakai* reflect the two imperatives that defined the environment of turn-of-the-century prose writing in Japan—authority and authenticity. Reinscribed within the demands for modernity, the prose narrative in the decades following the Restoration was distinguished more than ever by the necessity of integrating these two requirements. (By the latter part of the Meiji period, the necessity of informing one's writing with attention to these notions was sublated into a depoliticized literary form insisting upon sincerity as its mark of validation.) *Kyūshujin* and *Hakai* negotiate these requirements of narrating subjects against the hegemonic discourse of national consolidation—in these texts expressed in the figure of the emperor.

Most important for my purposes is the way in which both texts engage the statist discourse of centralization. I hope to show through these readings how they unwittingly participated in the construction of an image, eagerly adopted by the authorities, that would represent reordered social relations by a new metaphor of the center (versus the periphery). In contrast to the vision of vertical hierarchy commonly ascribed to Tokugawa society, the reordered terrain appeared to promise the possibility, if in most cases not the reality, of advance and social change. Tōson's texts show us how new conceptions of the social in truth spelled severe restrictions on the ways subjects could be narrativized in Meiji Japan.

Western belletristic standards may find *Kyūshujin* wanting, and even on native soil it is generally ignored as being an immature early experiment. But far from being a simple exercise in "sketching" (*shasei*) that enjoyed a vogue in the salons of Masaoka Shiki and other poets, *Kyūshujin* is significant in the storyline of post-Restoration writers coming to grips with the task of narrativizing the individuated subject. Tōson's early prose narratives do not employ an omniscient narrator, the narrating device closely associated with new realist standards of prose literature adopted with missionary zeal by the emergent literary establishment. In *Kyūshujin* Tōson opts to address the demands placed upon the Meiji writer of appealing to a mass unknown readership by creating an emotive first-person narrator (a far cry from later *shishōsetsu* writers who wrote laconic sentences for an audience of fellow writers). *Kyūshujin* represents a narrative that predates the authority of the *shishōsetsu*, and it similarly appears before the conventionalized use of an omniscient narrator. When he writes *Hakai* a few years later, Tōson installs what appears to be an effaced, third-person narrator, but, as we shall see, it frequently lapses into emotional commentary that is reminiscent of the narrator-maid in *Kyūshujin*. In both texts, the narrator function plays a key role in establishing subject positions. Let us examine the narrative strategies of these two works, beginning with *Kyūshujin*.

From the time they first appeared in print, *Warazōri* and *Kyūshujin* were seen as companion pieces, the former expressing the spirit of rural life and the latter rooted in city life.[4] Janet

4. *Warazōri* is a short story about a young man who in anger over the outcome of a horse race in his village unwittingly injures his wife. The questions concerning narrative that I felt directly relevant to this study led me to omit this tale from my discussion. It appears in Yamada Akira, ed., *Shimazaki Tōson shū I*, vol. 13 of *Nihon kindai bungaku taikei* (Kadokawa shoten, 1971), 463. The text for both *Hakai* and *Kyūshujin* discussed in this book come from this edition, henceforth abbreviated *STS*.

Walker's appraisal of the latter text eloquently mirrors the prevailing critical consensus:

> During the years Tōson was experimenting with *shasei* he was also trying his hand at several short stories in the Western realist-naturalist vein. In 1901 . . . he wrote the short story *Kyūshujin*, a work that, inspired by *Madame Bovary* but based on details in the lives of people he knew in Komoro, told the story of a citified woman who, unhappily married to a man much older than herself and dissatisfied with country life, has an affair with a local dentist. . . . The fiction Tōson wrote at this point in his career (before *Hakai*) is not typical of his later fiction, in that it presents a Zolaesque view of man as a creature of instinct. It is for this reason that I consider it only in a footnote.[5]

The view of these works as "naturalistic" is echoed by such critics as Takahashi Kuniko, who noted that the twin naturalistic pieces revealed Tōson's view that animal instinct dictated human actions.[6] A variant of this theme is forwarded by Senuma Shigeki, who saw in *Kyūshujin* the contradictory views of woman as an emancipated individual, intrinsically untrustworthy, licentious, and unable to properly fulfill the duties of a housewife.[7] In an essay entitled "Shinsan to kanbi" (The Bitter and the Sweet), the writer and critic Takeda Taijun characterizes *Kyūshujin* as a text in which the simple rusticity of the country is depicted favorably in relation to the gaudy trappings of city life. He suggests that contemporary Japanese writers (Taijun's article appeared in 1949) might look to some of these early Tōson prose narratives as models that would allow them to steer clear of producing *shishōsetsu*.[8] Taijun's observation is interesting because unlike the other critics who explain the presence of instinct and animal drive under the rubric of *shizenshugi*, he argues that *Kyūshujin* serves as a model for avoiding the trappings of the *shishōsetsu*.

Overwhelmingly, critical comments directed at *Kyūshujin* borrow the framework of "naturalism." The rubric attests to the tendency of critics to trace the relationship of modern Japanese prose narrative texts to currents of Western literature, a practice

5. Walker, *The Japanese Novel of the Meiji Period*, 165 66.

6. Takahashi Kuniko, "Tōson no *Kyūshujin* to *Warazōri*," in *Shimazaki Tōson*, ed. Nihon bungaku kenkyū shiryō gisho (Yūseidō, 1971), 148.

7. Senuma Shigeki, Foreword to *STS*, 16.

8. In Yamada Akira's annotation to the text in *STS*, 379 n. 6.

that has hindered rather than promoted rigorous critical assessment. As American and Japanese critics have noted, the contours of "naturalism" as it took shape in turn-of-the-century Europe bear little resemblance to its expression in twentieth-century Japan.[9] Particularly interesting for my purposes is the different meaning given to the notion of individual in these different forms of naturalism. As Donald Keene observes, European naturalism "arose as a reaction to the excessive emphasis on the individual in Romantic literature, but in Japan the most salient feature of naturalist writing was the search for the individual."[10] Keene is correct in explaining Meiji writers' interest in naturalism in terms of its association with the Western concept of the private self, but the important dimension of this issue is captured not by asking how Japanese literature succeeds in appropriating a foreign notion but in seeing how it becomes thoroughly reworked on Japanese soil. All too often categories such as "naturalism" are employed as critical explanatory tools when in fact they are descriptive. Naturalism suffers, as other transcendental categories do, from its tendency to displace alternative critical readings. Additionally, it is important to rethink the constellation of other presumptions inherent in the notion of Japanese naturalism: the centering of *kindai jiga*, the significance of the country(side), and the discourse of scientific causality that underwrites this "school."

Before turning to the text of *Kyūshujin*, it is worth noting that this short tale represents a moment in modern Japanese literature not unlike the turning point that Ross Chambers in his study of fictional narratives credits Walter Benjamin with identifying in Western literature:

> the development to which Walter Benjamin refers when he distinguishes between the traditional storyteller as the conveyor of experience and the modern novelistic narrative as posing a question: What is the meaning of existence? . . . Narratorial authority depends on some such shift from the function of transmitting infor-

9. See, for example, William Sibley, "Naturalism in Japanese Literature," *Harvard Journal of Asiatic Studies* 28 (1968): 157–69.

10. Donald Keene, *Dawn to the West: Japanese Literature of the Modern Era* (New York: Holt, Rinehart, and Winston, 1984), 221.

> mation, on the one hand, to an operation, on the other, best described, albeit vaguely, as the arousing of "interest."[11]

Tōson faces the dilemma of a writer who has no established guidelines for writing fiction. If "novelistic narrative" represents a shift in the demands placed on the writer who must now write to meet the imperative of "interest" expected by an anonymous readership, how is Tōson to address such a demand? Takeda Taijun's reference to *Kyūshujin* as a model to avoid relying upon the self for writing material is germane, for Tōson himself was to decide in ensuing years, like other Japanese writers of his time, that arousing reader interest took a back seat to, or at least was taken care of, by returning to personal experience as the site of material for narrativizing. *Kyūshujin* is both a transitional and experimental text in this sense: Tōson has not yet decided how best to address the issue of appealing to an unknown readership or to effectively depict an individuated subject who could hold the interest of those readers.

At the same time, another imperative confronted writers who chose to veer away from Tokugawa-era prose narrative and to establish a written style appropriate to an age that demanded seriousness of purpose. The *teisetsu* has it that sincerity was valued by writers of the *shishōsetsu* seeking a "primary attribute for an authentic voice."[12] *Kyūshujin,* written primarily as a text that would grab the attention of an anonymous readership at a time when a discourse of seriousness and authenticity was beginning to take shape, required a narrator to match the salaciousness of its content if it was to seek legitimation. The requirement for authenticity (a condition of writing for the new era) was addressed in a *gesaku*-like text by the creation of a credible narrator-character. In a subsequent text, *Hakai,* Tōson attempted to create a narrator who could credibly be associated with the tale that is narrated. *Kyūshujin* is explicitly a text *about*

11. Ross Chambers, *Story and Situation: Narrative Seduction and the Power of Fiction* (Minneapolis: University of Minnesota Press, 1984), 11.

12. William L. Andrews, "The Novelization of Voice in Early African American Narrative," *PMLA* 105 (January 1990): 23–34. While I am not suggesting direct parallels between the situations of modern Japanese and early African-American writers, both had to confront issues of empowerment and narrativization.

authenticity (not to be confused with "sincerity") and in which congruence between narrator and narrated story is particularly important. Well into the latter years of the twentieth century, the relationship between the narrator and its narrative would continue to be the site in which the problematic issues of agency and the subject in Japanese literature would most insistently reveal themselves.

Kyūshujin is a personal reminiscence by Osada, who relates to an undisclosed figure many years later her experiences as a maid for Arai, a prosperous local businessman from the Shinshū area. He marries a spoiled young woman from Tokyo, Aya, and sets up house in the small town of Komoro. Out of place and bored with provincial life, Aya begins an affair with a dentist. An impressionable young girl unaccustomed to her *haikara* (a transliteration of "high collar," the term denoted urbanity and the currently fashionable) mistress with fancy Tokyo tastes, Osada is captivated by Aya and defends her against the gossip and criticism of local folk. Aya buys her maid's confidence and loyalty through small gifts and attention but in time comes to feel uneasy about Osada's knowledge of her affair. In order to have her dismissed, Aya lies to her husband that Osada has stolen from her. Angered by Aya's betrayal, Osada tells Arai about his wife's infidelity. The tale ends as Arai catches his wife and her lover locked in an embrace.

In this brief tale that might even be seen as a harbinger of his more explicitly confessional literature, Tōson works through issues of subject placement through the tensions of urban–rural Japan. One of the trademarks of Japanese naturalism is the focus given to the writer's geographic roots in the country. Much has been made of the fact that *shizenshugi* writers thematize the relationship between Tokyo and a "hometown" located at some remove from the city. Not merely a shared biographic quirk, the practice deserves consideration from an angle different from that conventionally employed by critics of this literature. Naturalist readings of texts subsumed under the same rubric often attribute to the writers an enduring nostalgia for the countryside from whence the writers hailed. These critics tell us that *Kyūshujin* and *Hakai* are closely associated with Shinshū, where they were written and wherein the stories take place. Like many of Tōson's texts, the settings are in the mountainous regions of present-day Nagano, where the author had spent his youth and young adulthood. In the present reading of Tōson's texts, place is recast as a chronotope (I borrow the term from Bakhtin, for whom the specific way in which a novel handles space and time is of primary importance), the essential figuration of time and space that writers, regardless of their literary hue, must confront in some form in producing a text.[13] In *Kyūshujin* the chronotope of place splits into a clear opposition pitting countryside against the city (Tokyo). One can understand the use of such an opposition as a way of making sense of city life with its bewildering set of new and different conditions for day-to-day living. In both *Hakai* and *Kyūshujin* the countryside is a figurative means for articulating social change in the country at large. This chronotope of urban–rural conflict marks the texts' own moments of enunciation, echoing the requirements and the strategy of the Meiji authorities for constructing a centralized nation-state concentrating political and economic activity in rapidly growing Tokyo.

Kyūshujin narrativizes its subject, the (narrating) maid, Osada, through the opposition that cleaves the city from the country. Her dual role as narrator and actor in the events is underscored from the first page when she narrates her origins:

> I was born in Kashiwagi Village—yes, just over a mile outside the town of Komoro. The women of these parts have to work outside in the harsh conditions of the region, and work long and hard to help the men in any way they can. It must be partly because they have to work so hard that my aunt and mother are so driven and so resourceful. I began working out in the fields with my mother when I was thirteen.
>
> (350)

For the narrator, hard physical labor, women, and poverty are linked together as the lived experience of country life. Osada

13. See Bakhtin's essay, "Forms of Time and of the Chronotope in the Novel," in *The Dialogic Imagination*, 84–258. Chronotopes, he says, "are the organizing centers for the fundamental narrative events of the novel. . . . Functioning as the primary means for materializing time in space, [they emerge] as a center for concretizing representation as a force giving body to the entire novel" (250).

lapses into sentimentality in her account of her diligent mother, and it becomes clearer that a contrast is being drawn between the impersonal interactions of the city-bred and the touches of humanity that are rooted deeply in the relationships among simple country folk. The rhythms of daily life and the proliferation of tasks, roles, and other demands upon people obviously differ considerably for city life and for life in the countryside. Aya, Osada's mistress and a young bride from Tokyo, has no role to fulfill in the small community of Komoro, where she is the mistress of a small nuclear family. Osada's first impression of her mistress couches difference by using contrasts between city and countryside: "Her refined speech revealed that she was not native to this region. Compared to the whiteness of her hands, my mother's big-boned swarthy hands looked like a man's" (351–52). The differentiation of countryside from urban center by "her refined speech" marks one of the most repeatedly recurring forms of this dichotomy in *shizenshugi* literature. Speech, which immediately places its utterer within the constellation of sharp differences between center and periphery, hints at its own unequal opposition to the ideal of *genbun'itchi*, the sign of power, progress, and central authority. The self-abnegation implied in Osada's comparison of her own mother to her Tokyo-bred mistress is a nervous self-reflection of a text that must claim a form of empowerment through its own privatized gesture of resistance and revenge, which must take the form of a localized and gendered revelation of a scandal.

The contrast between rusticity and polish is prefigured in Osada's recollection of the day she and her mother had walked to the Arai household, when they seemed to cross the boundary from rural to urban life. "The house enclosed by an earthen wall with an overhanging persimmon branch belonged to the Arai family. While the gate was in the Komoro style, once inside it was built in the new latticed architecture, a subdued two-storied residential home" (351). One cannot miss the incongruence of the styles—the stolid heaviness of the gate and the urbanity of the new latticed windows, a style suggestive of Edo architecture. But the distinctions between city and country are not simply a way for the narrating maid to underscore the distance between herself and her mistress. In the narrator's disclosure of tensions between the Arai family and the main family headed by Arai's older brother, we see not only Osada's intention of stressing the urbanity and modernity of her mistress's nuclear household composition but a critical glance at the "traditional" family, disapproval that does not belong to Osada.

> The house where I came to work was called the new branch [*shintaku*]. The main branch employed over ten clerks and servants, while the Arais kept only an old caretaker and myself. . . . Master Arai lived like he had transplanted Tokyo to Komoro, his appearance, his speech a repudiation of the old—a source of constant annoyance to the main family.
>
> (352–53)

In addition to the opposition of city and country that figurates the separation of Osada from her mistress, from time to time an unnamed, shapeless sensibility intrudes, casting a nervous glance at the problems that are reflected in the process of urbanization. Meiji Japan saw Tokyo grow from an already vigorous center of commerce to a city of unprecedented proportions as the center of the Japanese state. As a writer, Tōson faced the changing demographics of a large and unnamed readership, growing beyond what the development of a print industry and a vigorous urban culture in the Edo era could respond to and shape as a literate critical mass.[14] The tense city–countryside binarism expresses the disconcerting conditions of urbanism that give rise to the conditions that sustain writing as a livelihood. (The very appearance just a few years later of writers like Sōseki, who brings respectability to serial narrative publication, and Shūsei, who gives voice to a reemerging mass audience, signals the arrival of new writer–reader relationships.)

KAMEI HIDEO'S *KANSEI* AND PERSPECTIVE

In order to articulate my own interpretive position further and to locate *Kyūshujin* in an important self-reflexive contemporary

14. For a pioneering study of readership and literature in transitional (Tokugawa-Meiji) Japan, see Maeda Ai, "Kindai dokusha no seiritsu," in *Kindai dokusha no seiritsu*, vol. 2 of *Maeda Ai chosaku shū* (Chikuma shobō, 1989), 17–259.

native critical field, let us look briefly at the work of Kamei Hideo, who has explored in some depth the question of perspective and the issue of subject expression in modern Japanese literature.[15] In a book entitled *Kansei no henkaku* (The Transformation of Sensibilities; *kansei* is an elusive term that overlaps such notions as sensitivity, sensual awareness, sensibility, and consciousness), Kamei examines early Meiji literary texts long canonized through the overarching discourses of Westernization and Western realism in particular.[16] Recasting the concept of *jiga* (individual) with a theory of representation, Kamei identifies the locus of focalization in Japanese prose narratives. He notes that whereas conventions of Western realism call for placing the narrating perspective within the field of portrayal, Edo literature tended to employ a narrator who made observations from a position *outside* of the narrated events through the use of *togaki*, reminiscent of stage directions for a play. The continuation of such a strategy, he points out, can be seen in *kanbungesaku* writers of the early Meiji period such as Hattori Bushō and Narushima Ryūhoku. But such writing, Kamei continues, might permit a method of setting the scene but is inadequate for the overall design of a text. "From a detached self-consciousness, it is not possible to create a dramatic textual space."[17] According to Kamei, only when one recognizes the

15. Among the early works of theoretically informed Japanese studies of the subject that remain influential are Maeda Ai, *Toshi kūkan no naka no bungaku* (Chikuma shobō, 1982), Kamei Hideo, *Kansei no henkaku* (Kōdansha, 1983), and Karatani Kōjin, *Nihon kindai bungaku no kigen* (Kōdansha, 1980). Komori Yōichi's narratological essays did not receive wider recognition until their appearance in book form, *Buntai to shite no monogatari* and *Kōzō to shite no katari*, in 1988.

16. In the beginning of chapter 2, Kamei's text clarifies its contestatory position vis-à-vis Kobayashi Hideo's assumptions as they have colored the views on Meiji literature. In the essay "Watakushi-shōsetsu ron," Kobayashi's analysis is premised on the assumption that human understanding, knowledge, and ideas arise and that ways of expressing them follow. (It is likely that these notions echo Kobayashi's critical stance toward Marxist insistence on materialism.) *Kansei* challenges this realist essentialism. In its place, Kamei offers an alternative means of conceptualizing subjectivity. Arguing that the notion of the "individual" is too specific to the West to be directly used for discussing Japanese prose narratives, he develops the notion of *kansei*—an elusive term coined to indicate a locus of perception, awareness, and sensation.

17. Kamei, *Kansei no henkaku*, 45.

separateness of the self's sensibilities (*kansei*) from the idealization of such consciousness (the creating self from the created self) can one capture the process of self-awareness. This was the task that troubled Japanese writers who struggled to establish the conventions for inserting an unobtrusive narrating vantage point within the confines of the narrated text.[18] In a climate wherein the notion of the individuated subject came under protracted scrutiny, it was no longer possible to place an obtrusive commenting narrator outside of the narrated events as had been done in *gesaku*. Positioning the narrator, establishing its relationships to various characters and to the reader, and endowing it with consistency of knowledge that is appropriate to its placement in the text were the tasks that faced writers whose exposure to Western realism made *gesaku* models obsolete. Kamei points to *kanbun fūzoku* texts (novels of manners written in *kanbun*) such as Tōkai Sanshi's *Kajin no kigū* (Chance Encounters with Beautiful Women, 1897) and Yano Ryūkei's *Keikoku bidan* (Inspiring Instances of Statesmanship, 1883) to illustrate the importance of *bōdokutai*, which, in contrast to *yakudokutai*, has neither inflected endings nor any honorific markers that distinguish social stratification among textual subjects. The ability to locate a narrative position minus the markers that would signal relative social standing leads to what Kamei calls an absent narrator (*muninshō no katarite*, literally personless narration). Kamei identifies Tsubouchi Shōyō's *Tōsei shosei katagi* (The Ways of Contemporary Students, 1885) as the work in which the expression of a new *kansei* makes its debut: "At the moment when the rupture between idealization of environment (context) and the sensitivities of the subject is recognized, a new type of novel—one that captures the process of this awareness—is born."[19] But there is a significant break between Shōyō's text and Futabatei's *Ukigumo* (Drifting Clouds, 1886–89): The latter text exhibits for the first time in Japanese literature an absent narrator. As man-

18. Mitani Kuniaki argues that Kamei's *muninshō no katarite* (personless narration) is better seen as the disjunction that results from the attempt to impose upon *genbun'itchi* a prose narrative tradition to employ a past tense (*shōsetsu keishiki no kako*). See Mitani Kuniaki, "Kindai shōsetsu no gensetsu joshō: shōsetsu no 'jikan' to gabuntai aruiwa Kamei Hideo 'Kansei no henkaku' o yomu," *Nihon bungaku* 33 (July 1984): 49.

19. Kamei, *Kansei no henkaku*, 46.

ifest in *Ukigumo*, this narrator does not appear in the text as a character yet makes self-reflecting comments to the reader ("let's join Bunzō in his room upstairs") and cannot quite freely adopt varying vantage points in a text as might an omniscient narrator frequently found in Western realist texts, instead being limited to the externalized, visible aspects of a character. More significantly, this narrator is distinguished by its desire to "experience the same interests and sensibilities as that of the reader."[20]

In contrast to the absent narrator identified by Kamei, Western realism requires a text to present its characters without markers that foreground the artifice of textual expression (early Western realist texts such as Henry Fielding's *Tom Jones* employ a shamelessly chatty and self-referring narrator). Characters are presented to the reader by a narrator who avoids the signs of judgment, of subjectivity. Omniscience is one outgrowth of this imperative not to interrupt the realist contract to present a text as if it were presenting itself as real or true. This, by convention, has become the accepted condition of the realist novel, which depicts individualized subjects without the contamination of narrators (necessary to present the text) or their intrusive comments. The narrator Kamei designates the absent narrator cannot quite hide itself, in part because the interlocutor-directed nature of the Japanese language discourages it[21] and in part because the tradition on which is based Japanese writers' attempts to forge such an absent narrator—the stage direction-like *togaki* in *gesaku*—makes use of emotive, judgmental, or otherwise intrusive narration. Kamei's revisionist views still rightly focus on the subject as central to modern Japanese letters, which is driven by the impulse to locate one's own image in a literary

20. Mitani questions the status of the personless narration that Kamei attributes to Futabatei's *Ukigumo*, arguing that its narrator is no different from the *togaki* found in *kokkeibon* and *ninjōbon*. Kamei is quoted in Mitani, "Kindai shōsetsu no gensetsu joshō," 48.

21. For a discussion of Japanese language as other-directed, see Edward Fowler, *The Rhetoric of Confession: Shishōsetsu in Early Twentieth-Century Japanese Fiction* (Berkeley: University of California Press, 1988), and Barbara Mito Reed's applications of linguistic theory to Japanese narrative in "Language, Narrative, Structure, and the 'Shōsetsu'" (Ph.D. diss., Princeton University, 1985).

text. The result, he says, is the creation of an idealized provisional subject (viz., political novels of turn-of-the-century Japan). In his discussion of Tōkai Sanshi's *Kajin no kigū*, Kamei observes how it took the mediation of a radical other—an idealized Western woman—to produce an image of a worthy, interesting author, thinly disguised as the protagonist. The process of reflecting upon oneself, its idealized presentation in prose form, and, most important, the resulting dissolution of such an idealized subject (the dissolution coming from a recognition of its idealized state), says Kamei, lead to what would come to be known as pure literature, or *jun bungaku*.[22] Ōgai's *Maihime* (Dancing Girl) is cited as an early example of such a text.

Kamei's separation of an idealized self and a self that recognizes the image of oneself as idealized presumes the "self" to be an arbitrary and socially constructed entity and at the same time recognizes the utility of *not* observing the practice of assuming congruence between a person and subjectivity. Kamei runs the risk of essentializing a different subject that is defined not so much in terms of flesh and bone as the locus of perception and sensibilities. Yet, by relativizing subject positions, he manages to provide a way out of some problems associated with positivist conceptions of the individual. Insofar as the subject is conceived as an entity that exists as it takes shape in specific narratives, these subjects take on meaning that rests not so much in the hands of an author but in the field of interplay of which they are a part. This allows Kamei to see the development of polyphony in the modern Japanese novel. Yano Ryūkei's *kanbun gesaku* text, he says, was the first in which the views of different characters were clearly differentiated. In earlier fiction, once a narrator fixed a character with certain descriptions—for example, "X could not be trusted to keep such a secret"—all the other characters in the text would woodenly respond to X as if he were untrustworthy. Ryūkei allowed characters to respond individually to each other, as if they were endowed with their own *kansei*.[23] Subjecthood came not in a finished and unchanging form but was produced in the encounters among various

22. Kamei, *Kansei no henkaku*, 43.
23. Kamei, *Kansei no henkaku*, 50.

characters. In *Keikoku bidan* and *Kajin no kigū*, characters were given their own voices and their own sensibilities, which permitted them to act, react, change, and grow within the text. A similar identity through difference can be seen in Kamei's view of Futabatei's depiction of interiority. Kamei notes that *Ukigumo*'s protagonist Bunzō has difficulty expressing himself and that it is this very inarticulateness that engenders (or produces) the depiction of his hidden thoughts.

Kamei has given us some very interesting readings of early Meiji texts; in turn his readings yield some compelling theoretical insights. Despite his confinement of subjectivity to the traditional categories of literary discussion (narrator, protagonist), his readings display a finely honed sensitivity to the material creativity and sensuality of language. His method of analysis reveals the emergence of narrative techniques that show earnest engagement with the problematic of the individuated subject—how it is defined, by whom, and what position it occupies in turn-of-the-century Japan.

NARRATING THE SUBJECT

Tōson's *Kyūshujin* can benefit from discussion of subject narration similar to that proposed by Kamei. The separation of city from country noted earlier provides a way for the narrating maid Osada to order her narrative act of retaliation against her former mistress. The narration is given to Osada, whose sensibilities in turn define a subject through whom we see the events. She is the one who sprinkles the account with epigrammatic comments, who resorts to the conventions of popular Edo culture in relating her tale, and who has reasons of her own to color the narrative. *Kyūshujin* is told by a narrator-maid bent on exacting revenge through the act of revealing her former mistress Aya's infidelity to an unnamed interlocutor. Years after the events depicted in this text have transpired, the first-person narrator recalls her life as a maid in the service of a local businessman and his young bride, who had moved from Tokyo to live with her husband in the provincial town of Komoro. Both as a means of intensifying readerly interest and as an exploration of subject expression, the narrator occupies a central role

in the way meaning is created in the text. The use of such a narrating figure stands in contrast to the classic realist text, which strives to validate itself through the use of language written to efface its "own presence," the use of preterite tense, and other formal conventions.[24] First-person narration by itself does not represent a move away from the kind of novel that attempts to pass itself off as a transparent medium of reality-based events and thoughts, but the choice of an emotive narrator serves to subvert "transparent" writing that is the hallmark of the realist text. In the context of early twentieth-century Japanese prose, *Kyūshujin*'s narrative is meaningful for what it is not—that is, third-person omniscient narration that stands as the sign of realist literature in the West. Tōson effectively evaded those markers that signify *genbun'itchi*—issues of perspective, of access to characters' thoughts, and of transparent writing—by employing first-person narration.

The narrator-maid Osada is a mediating step toward the installation of an effaced narrator in *Hakai*. Osada is separated by class and function from Aya, whose wealth and citified ways cut a high profile in this provincial little town. The two women are directly associated with either Tokyo or the country to intensify their differences and to delineate their respective subjectivities. Whenever Aya walks through the streets, curious women peep through holes in the walls and through windows and gaps in the *shōji* panels. Osada defends her mistress when the former is harshly criticized by the hired hands in the main family. But as the narrator who is reconstructing this account to an undisclosed listener years after the events had transpired, Osada seems a little disingenuous about representing herself as initially a staunch defender of Aya. When the maids from the main family are characterized as sharply critical of her mistress, it sounds suspiciously like the displacement of Osada's own criticisms. Osada details the ways in which Aya stands out in Komoro. It is unheard of in these parts to see a couple (the old businessman and his young *haikara* wife with fancy Tokyo tastes) outside the home strolling hand in hand: "Such a Tokyo de-

24. See Roland Barthes's "Writing and the Novel," in *Writing Degree Zero*, trans. Annette Lavers and Colin Smith (New York: Hill and Wang, 1968), 29–40.

meanor—they had never even dreamed of seeing—the two walking outside the home and displaying such intimacy" (357). The scene is so out of place that the local help jokes how Aya must be blind to be led about by the hand. The narrator defends her mistress against these attacks, but her assertions seem feeble in the context of the depiction of Aya as a figure so visibly out of place.

The first-person narrator is important to this work in a number of ways. We have already seen how, in providing a nuanced and decidedly subjective angle on the events portrayed, Osada becomes a way for the text to work out a proper form of agency. This kind of narrator also allows the reader to see with relative ease the "social situation" of the text. Words are born and shaped by a social context, and they are always directed *to* someone *by* another. Tōson's text begins with Osada recounting events long past to a listener who never appears in the tale but is nonetheless present, as the narrator's words indicate: "Ima de koso watashi mo konna ni futotte orimasu mono no, sono jibun wa yasegisuna kozukuri na onna deshita" (350; As you can see, I am quite heavy now, but in those days I was a trim, small-boned woman). Her polite diction, which is immediately clear in Japanese, at once establishes her relationship both to the listener-reader and to the couple that figure in the narrative. If convention binds her to a narrative style that is on the whole respectful and polite, the nature of her disclosure (the tale itself) is anything but genteel. In a contest of "intentions," *what* the narrator says undercuts the *way* in which it is presented.

This is not surprising, as the only "power" that Osada has as a maid to the young mistress Aya comes from the narrator's intimate knowledge of the couple with whom she lives. She gains such power by eavesdropping and peeping and, at the time that the tale is being recounted, by narrating this story. The tale is not so much about adultery as it is an act of revenge by a maid who years later tells the tale to someone else in order to get back at her former mistress. The meaning of *Kyūshujin* is produced in the relationship between the narrator Osada and her mistress and between the narrator and her audience. Once again, Bakhtin-Volosinov's observations about language in context make this clear: "All intonation is oriented in *two directions*: toward the listener as ally or witness, and toward the topic of the utterance, as if to a third active participant. Intonation abuses, curses, humiliates or extols it. *This dual social orientation determines and gives sense to all aspects of intonation.*"[25] He tells us that language is best understood as a social event, or, to use an expression that over the years has gained currency among linguists and literary critics in describing the nature of Japanese language, it is context-dependent.

Another "consequence" of having a first-person narrating character is a reliance on *gesaku* conventions for gaining access to hidden dimensions of other characters. (The neglect *Kyūshujin* has suffered is explained in part by the overall quality of the work: Clearly, it is not Tōson's best piece. That it was rooted in real-life scandal and was accordingly suppressed by the authorities may or may not have hurt its evaluation as literature.[26] But in large measure the text has been ignored because it employs "premodern" textual conventions.) Limited by the sensibilities and the expressive abilities of an uneducated maid from the countryside, *Kyūshujin* is laced with epigrammatic statements as a way of broadening and enlivening the account. Elaborate descriptions of women's fine garments and accoutrements provide another means for Osada to narrate her own sensibilities. Much as *The Tale of Genji* picture scrolls depict people on the other side of screens, walls, and cut-away ceilings, *gesaku* typically offered glimpses behind the thin walls and papered screens of the brothels in the pleasure quarters by having characters peep through the porous barriers. Maids and other persons with special access to the interior of households, along with the convention of peeping, were widely used by writers to establish perspectives that would allow disclosure of information gen-

25. Volosinov, "Discourse in Life and Discourse in Poetry: Questions of Sociological Poetics," in *Bakhtin School Papers*, ed. Ann Shukman, trans. John Richmond (Oxford: Holdan Books, Ltd., 1983), 16 (emphasis in the original).

26. See discussion in *STS*, 455 n. 63. The often quoted explanation has it that Yamaji Aizan, who was then a reporter for a regional newspaper in Shinshū, was angered by Tōson, who modeled his story on a prominent local couple, and complained to the police. Jay Rubin attributes the banning of the text to both the subject matter and to the personal connections alluded to above. See his *Injurious to Public Morals* (Seattle: University of Washington Press, 1984), 51.

erally hidden from public view. From *gesaku* texts such as Tamenaga Shunsui's *Shunshoku umegoyomi* to Futabatei Shimei's *Aibiki* and *Ukigumo*, the use of both peeping and of (peeping) maids flourished through the 1890s as devices to gain entry to unknown information. The revelation of lives through barriers makes the reader keenly aware of the privateness of the bared scene, and in the case of *gesaku*, the device no doubt had a calculated function of titillating the reader. In juxtaposing the emperor, the revelation of Aya's adultery, and the act of peeping, *Kyūshujin* expresses a critical stance toward the nation-state, and its vigilant efforts shift the loyalties of its subjects from local groupings to the nation; this is another way in which *Kyūshujin* relates to *Hakai*, a text that more overtly confronts state actions to contain the limits of self-expression.

As a writer unsure of how to draw the attention of his readers, Tōson was undoubtedly affected by the effectiveness with which peeping and (later) confession heightened his readers' prurient interests. Tōson took care to invest these sensibilities expressing *gesaku* conventions in the figure of a countrified maid. The entire account and the manner of its presentation is an expression of this narrator-character. Finally, Osada's manner of getting back at her mistress during the course of events as they had taken place years ago is restricted to the staple of *gesaku* texts—peeping (*nozoki*). Soon after she is brought into her mistress's confidence, Osada begins to snoop on Aya. "When I approached her room, they seemed to be discussing something. Not knowing quite what to do, I stood to one side of the sliding door and listened intently while peering into the room" (368). Eavesdropping and peeping soon become a regular practice for the maid, who is driven by curiosity, excitement, and eventually the desire for revenge.

It is telling that a narrator, rather than a character, was to be the figure Tōson endowed with what Kamei would call *kansei*. In the trajectory of Japanese prose narrative, *Kyūshujin*'s narrator stands at that mediating point, looking much like the obtrusive narrators in traditional forms and pointing the way to Kamei's effaced narrator. At this point in his career, Tōson felt it necessary to employ a first-person female narrator, a figure sufficiently distanced from himself. The maid does not possess the sensibility and sense of subject that can engender a narrative to unfold; she is, rather, the vehicle for the telling of a tale. Osada does attain a measure of awareness of her own socio-geographic position (geography does have its own hierarchical connotations), but, for example, she cannot experience her own sensual awakening. Sexuality remains displaced on an other to whom she can only react with disapproval and distaste. Osada remains curiously suspended between the status of a sentient character and an impersonal narrator when it comes to sex, as she can only be captured in the coarser explanatory opposition of country and city. The only "act" that she is capable of is that of telling, of revealing what she had seen. It is in this sense that her subjecthood is more a function of *telling* a tale. It is only when "telling" is combined with acting, behavior, and so forth that narrative or literary history appears to empower women.

When Arai (Aya's husband) shows her an award he has received for service to the community, out of place and unhappy in the countryside, distanced from her husband by age and interests, and possessed with guilt from her ongoing affair, she petulantly tosses it aside. The narrator Osada feels it important to sway our sympathies in her master's direction and to that end provides the following melodramatic account:

> "I just wanted you to appreciate the honor bestowed upon me, but. . . ." A hot tear dropped from my master's eyes and fell into the golden sake cup. . . . He seemed unable to contain his sorrow and anger and he abruptly grasped the award he had received and tore it to shreds. His manly visage was stained with tears. This man who could by himself sustain the economy of Komoro was powerless to control his wife's feelings. . . . He grabbed and pulled at his hair and kicked the floor in anguish before leaving the house.
>
> (370–71)

The next time Osada listens in, she is "all ears" (watashi wa maru de mimi deshita) as she overhears Aya's false accusation that she has stolen from her, spread malicious gossip, and flirted with the milkman. Aya wants to get rid of Osada, with whom she feels increasingly uncomfortable for having confided in her earlier.

Osada's days are now filled with bitterness over Aya's betrayal.

One day there is commotion in the neighborhood caused by the news that a maid (Osada's friend) has thrown herself into the river; speculation is that she took her life because she was mistreated by her mistress. This incident helps focus Osada's own feelings about her mistress:

> Since coming to work here, I had become a changed person. Imperceptibly, I had become accustomed to the flashy life of my mistress. . . . I would steal glances in the mirror, secretly apply a razor blade to unwanted hair, and enjoy the indulgence of long baths, carefully cleansing my body and removing the dirt from under my nails . . . and by the time I had come to think of my friend [who had just died] as a bit rustic, I was even inclined to give little thought to my mother. I was appalled at how I had changed. Were I to thoughtfully consider my work, the troubles, the hard work that I had endured, all that was left was the cold sweat of remorse.
>
> (393–94)

The recognition that she has strayed from the unimpeachable values of country life hits her like cold water, and, after a night of torment, the final reckoning comes as she decides to tell her master about his wife's infidelity. It takes an incident that sharply underscores the differences between herself and her mistress to make her take action. Initially, her retaliatory impulse is limited to eavesdropping and peeping. That being insufficient, she reveals Aya's secret to her master. Finally, years later, she feels compelled to tell the tale again, venting her anger and asserting the rightness of her position and the small victory of a powerless peasant woman over a rich and beautiful city woman.

The narrator's hyperbolic account underscores the subjectivity of the text, revealing the temperament of this woman, thereby providing safe distance between the narrator/tale and the author, Tōson. In reworking a scandal based upon an actual event, Tōson surely did not want to write mere "frivolous" literature (*gesaku*) that still held a secure place with the reading public. He may have felt unsure of how best to depict adultery (what would become an almost obsessive theme in his work) and felt it expedient to give the text over to an uneducated woman who would vent her spleen. There is a clumsiness in *Kyūshujin* in the way *gesaku* conventions are employed next to more recent literary practices, much in the same way that the leader of the *Kenyūsha* coterie Ozaki Kōyō's more modern texts such as *Tajō takon* (Passions and Griefs, 1896) fail to bridge the eras convincingly.

When Osada discloses Aya's unfaithfulness to her husband, Arai admits to having been dimly aware of the state of affairs, but to satisfy his curiosity he asks Osada to arrange things so that he can witness their adultery. The moment arrives, and as he sneaks into the house to spy on his wife and her lover, on the occasion of a local festive event celebrating the emperor, a band begins to play the national anthem in the schoolyard that adjoins the house. Silent gestures between maid and master reveal the location of the lovers, and as Arai tiptoes to the sliding door, Osada follows him to sneak a peek herself. The cinematic finale evokes an overdrawn *gesaku* scene.

> Their burning lips were just about to come together in a kiss. Her breasts were crushed against his chest as she stood on tiptoe, her large toes straining up against the floor; her arms hung limply, her fingers slightly curled up, her shoulders raised, while his hands were nestled under her arms. It seemed as though their bodies had come to a complete standstill, and all the blood in their veins had rushed to their lips like the turbulent waves of the summer sea. My master was immobilized by the spectacle and just stood there gazing at the two from behind, as if he had been nailed to the spot.
>
> "Saikeirei, saikeirei" [profound obeisance], came the cries that floated in from atop the knoll on the ceremonial grounds. . . .
>
> "I'm home" came the voice of the returning guest [Aya's father is a house guest]. "I've just returned." Shocked by the calls of the returning guest, the two turned around, only to discover Mr. Arai silently standing behind them. Having no time to push the man away, Aya could only look away, turning white as a sheet. The dentist, half in shock, pried open her mouth with his left hand and positioned his right hand as if extracting a tooth. . . . At that moment, the sound of blaring trumpets and the thunderous sound of drums flooded into the room. The masses of celebrants outside shouted out in unison, "Long live the emperor, long live the emperor."
>
> (401–2)

The text ends on this note, the maid's revenge complete. The desperate cover-up attempt by the two lovers is comic, adding a measure of satisfaction to the revenge-seeking narrator, and it also strikes a blow at the emperor as institutionalized and celebrated in Meiji society. As critics have often noted, the scene may have been inspired from the Agricultural Development Meeting in chapter 8 of *Madame Bovary*.[27] Although the juxtaposition of the emperor and adultery is the act of the narrator Osada, the informing sensibility that links the disclosure of infidelity to the scene of imperial celebration clearly does *not* belong to the narrator. Another voice has intruded here. (In *Hakai* there is a scene that shows the mistreatment of Shota the *burakumin* boy during the celebration of the emperor's birthday. Tōson's linking of the ridiculous, the ignoble, and the immoral to the emperor casts an unmistakable shadow over the latter and cannot be dismissed as meaningless.) The polyphonic note on which the text ends is left as a harbinger of greater polyphony in *Hakai*.[28] Here it emerges as a final border, placing all that has transpired—the tale itself taking the form of an emotional act of revenge by a peasant maid—in a larger framework of protest that cannot be the maid's.

When we consider *Kyūshujin* in light of narrativized subjects, we are left with several considerations. Within the text, Osada is a woman defined in terms of her reactions to a citified woman. The narrator's vantage point is not simply "rural." Osada has contextualized the opposition, defamiliarizing one against the other. The sensibility of this narrating woman is not only that of a woman older than the Osada depicted in the tale but one whose angle of perception is refracted by the tensions of country and city. As mentioned above, it is significant that this narrator is "self-depicted" as being at some remove from the author Tōson by virtue of gender and the traits and sensibilities she reveals. Why this peasant woman narrator? The tale rests upon conventions of women as jealous creatures and the social code

27. For example, see Yamada Akira, *STS*, 396 n. 3.

28. The notion of polyphony in language and literature is most clearly stated in Bakhtin, *Problems of Dostoevsky's Poetics*. See especially "Dostoevsky's Polyphonic Novel and Its Treatment in Critical Literature," 5–78, and "Discourse in Dostoevsky," 181–269.

that makes infidelity by a wife more scandalous than that by a husband. The frequent peeping by the maid is in fact an appropriate metaphor for the tale as a whole: It appeals to the prurient interests of a readership invited to snoop on this prominent couple. The very "peep-worthiness" of the couple is built upon the division of city and country; an old man from the countryside (Komoro) marries a young, glamorous woman from Tokyo and settles in the countryside. Like "peeping," the construction of the narrative along these tensions of city and rural sectors serves to intensify reader interest in the tale. The distance between Tōson the writer and the female narrator puts in perspective the gendered nature of the gaze. In the confines of the related story, the narrator-character does all the prying, but the frame given to the narrator's tale at the end—that is, the introduction of a sensibility that juxtaposes the emperor and the scandalous scene and that does not belong to the narrator herself—unwittingly controverts Tōson's strategies to distance himself from the text.

One may argue that the insertion of the celebration into the text was a device to heighten the climactic scene of infidelity, making Aya look even worse. The reappearance of such imperial celebration in *Hakai*, where it does not function similarly, casts doubt on such an interpretation. Just as the city–rural split helps define the narrator, a second opposition, that between emperor and private behavior, narrativizes the *status* of the private subject in Meiji Japan. The ever-sharper distinctions between the metropolitan center and outlying regions (*chihō*) represent a political dimension in the tensions between the two realms. The metaphor of Tokugawa verticality has been transformed into a new Meiji metaphor of center and periphery, the emperor placed in the new locus of authority in the city that emphatically signals its own status. The tensions between countryside (*chihō*) and city (Tokyo) sharpen, largely in response to the contradictions accompanying the process of urbanization, but here they also reflect the reformulation of political relations. Osada's narrative of revenge would be difficult to conceive of within a society in which class and social distinctions are cast in a figure of verticality; a figure of center and periphery, however, introduces a new dimension of space that can intervene in human relations and thus engender this type of narrative (one can retreat *or* be banished to the periphery). The shift from a social landscape conceived in hierarchical terms to one that spatializes relations, however much the new vision accords with or departs from its referent (actual conditions), sets the stage for increased incidents of resentment, the intensity of that resentment being directly related to the pretensions to egalitarianism that such a spatialized conception claims. *Kyūshujin* is hardly an openly polemical text, and it does not adopt a mannered political stance, but the resentment that Osada feels toward her city-bred mistress rests upon social agreement that embraces an ostensibly horizontal metaphor.

Here, as in *Hakai*, the division between rural and urban serves as a vocabulary for subject expression. In many of Tōson's works, including the two under discussion, the countryside is the site in which the actual struggle for subject affirmation unfolds, but the imperative to seek such expression is engendered by the very opposition provided by the city. Recent critics have identified the convention of communal voices as a central form of Japanese narrative expression.[29] The social organization around which communal narration is based begins to disintegrate as the reality and fiction of social wholeness is displaced by a landscape rent in two. The realities of increasing fragmentation are manifest in many ways, including the level of governance: "The center had charged the localities with a range of national responsibilities, from electing assemblies and collecting taxes to providing police and teachers and building schools. Since the government decreed, but seldom paid for, many of these requisites of state, seventy to eighty percent of local budgets was devoted to executing national tasks on the local level. . . . But the localities did not comply at once, without cost, or without conflict."[30] As Gluck's account suggests, bureaucratic agrarianist policies resulted in the redefinition of the countryside as a colonized possession of the center. The narrator of

29. An example is Masao Miyoshi, "Reading the Japanese Novel in America." Naoki Sakai's discussion of individuated subjectivity in Tokugawa texts raises new questions about communal narrative. See his "Voices of the Past: The Discourse on Language in Eighteenth-Century Japan."

30. Carol Gluck, *Japan's Modern Myths*, 61–62.

Tōson's *Kyūshujin* plays out a populist version of the tensions between urban and rural Japan, but the voice that ties the maid's tale to the symbol of a centrist ideology belongs neither to the narrator nor to the author. Captive to the coarse net of urban–rural tension, the narrator's status as subject remains unclear.

The issue of agency—"positions" characterized by a self-reflective sense of responsibility and self-affirmation—is not localized in the figure of the narrator-maid.[31] As I have stated above, the degree of politeness in *Kyūshujin* would be a direct function of the listener to whom the narrator is telling the tale, but it will also in part be determined by the persons about whom she is talking, in this case her former mistress and master. Enclosing this event is another frame, of which the reader would not be aware until faced with the juxtaposition of the emperor celebration and the scene of indiscretion at the end. It is not the kind of frame that completely encircles the narrated tale; that is, there is no imposition of a monologic definitive voice that governs *Kyūshujin*. The sensibility behind the "voice" that juxtaposes a celebration of the emperor and the emotive telling of a salacious tale cannot be located in a materially narrated point, be it the narrator, another character, or the author himself. What *Kyūshujin* does illustrate (perhaps inadvertently) is the elusiveness of the very notion of the subject. In this instance, we are left with a subject created in the very relationship between one textual frame and another, as there is no material subject in any traditional sense. In *Kyūshujin*, there is an agency that is lost from sight precisely because it is apparent, or, more correctly, it is created through the relationships among disparate texts. Thus, the subject that is responsible for the oxymoronic juxtaposition of the moment of private absurdity and the

31. Discussion of "agency" as a way of confronting the problems inherent in conceptions of the subject (itself a critique of the "individual") has proliferated in recent years. Alex Callinicos, for example, attempts to restore a sense of class that is rooted in the experience of social-productive-power relations in his attempt to affirm human agency in place of idealist subjects. See his *Making History: Agency, Structure, and Change in Social Theory* (Ithaca: Cornell University Press, 1988). Gayatri Spivak has rigorously confronted the issue directly in a wide range of works. See, for example, "The Post-Modern Condition" and *In Other Worlds*.

celebration of the emperor resides dispersed to two sites—between the frames of *Kyūshujin* and between *Kyūshujin* and *Hakai.*

Early modern Japanese prose narratives were overdetermined by the dual goal of centering an individuated private subject and developing a writing that was appropriate to the articulation of the subject. To paraphrase John Frow's description of Althusserian symptomatic reading, *Kyūshujin* contains the contradictions of a text that has questions it cannot pose nor address (i.e., the subject). In this light, the use of a first-person narrator represents a significant "unsaid"—the problematic status of a speaking subject in early twentieth-century Japan. Tōson's texts offer a "structure of *positions of reading* through which individuals inscribe themselves within the semiotic system."[32] In *Kyūshujin,* the narrating subject must narrate herself within the constraints of the imperatives of realism that define writing in twentieth-century Japanese letters, the restrictions that derive from a moment of narrative strategies in flux, the absence of clearly set conventions, and the marginal space of the feminine that has been reassigned since the days of Heian courtly literature. The rightful insistence on viewing the centrality of "feminine" literary tradition in Japanese literature notwithstanding, it is important to recognize the relegation of women's voices to newly marginalized regions in modern Japan. Far from the image of the Heian woman who "writes herself" as women did through the protocol and chance encounters of courtly activity, Tōson's text takes as its subject a woman who spies on another.[33] *Kyūshujin* is a text that mirrors the marginalized status of its first-person narrator Osada, self-consciously unable or unwilling to do more than look nervously in the direction of what it cannot be, a text inhabiting what will become a discourse of the center, the "serious," *genbun'itchi* novel.

Tracing the outlines of its own storyline, *Kyūshujin* is a text about storytelling (speaking) in an era rapidly giving way to a form of communication and socialization that places writing in the service of centralized, bureaucratic society. At the same time the use of an emoting first-person narrator in *Kyūshujin* shows

32. Frow, *Marxism and Literary History,* 54.

33. For a compelling examination of gender and writing, see Richard Okada, *Figures of Resistance.*

the inability of Tōson to immediately discard the orality that has underwritten Japanese literature for centuries. The tension between orality and script enacts the struggle between center and periphery (city and countryside), essentially a matter of power and control exercised over individual subjects by a centralized (imperial) state. In the words of Cynthia Ward, "it is only with writing that discourse takes on its dictatorial 'discursive universe' aspect, in which words become objects with genealogies, subject to use in the service of establishing power and affirming an oppressive status quo, its coercive power internalized by its 'speakers,' that is, readers and writers."[34] The problem of writing in post-Restoration Japan cannot escape the oppressive mediation of the state, for the writer's will and the exercise of state authority converge in the figure of the subject, which the writer seeks to narrate in her or his own way and the authorities seek to "subject" as loyal, obedient citizens. How *Hakai* negotiates these conditions will be our concern in the following chapter.

34. Cynthia Ward, "What They Told Buchi Emecheta: Oral Subjectivity and the Joys of 'Otherhood,'" *PMLA* 105 (January 1990): 88.

3

CHANGING METAPHORS

From Vertical Hierarchy to Centralization in Tōson's *Hakai*

Tōson began writing *Hakai* during the latter part of his stay in Komoro, and it was completed in Tokyo and published at his own expense in 1906. The novel received immediate critical acclaim, and the copious outpouring of secondary works it has generated since attests to the fecundity of this text. *Hakai* is one of the few turn-of-the-century prose narratives that observes the formal requirements of what modern Japanese literature avowedly set out to emulate, the nineteenth-century European novel. Following the teleological requirements of unfolding action that builds to a climax, *Hakai* ends neatly, albeit clumsily, at the end of the protagonist's tale. A survey of the secondary literature indicates that virtually all of the prominent literary issues of early twentieth-century Japanese letters were present in *Hakai*: "sketching from life" (*shasei*), naturalism, literature as representation of society and its problems, and the exploration of the "self," particularly its role in confessional prose narratives.

Confusion over the title when *Hakai* first appeared in book form prefigures the extended debate over its status as either a highly privatized novel or a socially engaged text that takes on a pressing social issue. Japanese critics have noted that when Tōson's text was published the word *hakai* was generally associated with the transgression of priestly vows.[1] Reviews by Ogawa Bimei and Ōtsuka Kusunoki in a 1907 issue of the journal *Waseda bungaku* contain observations that the title suggested the confessions of a priest. Tōson's use of the word signals his

1. Cited by both Shinoda Kōichirō, *Shisō to shite no Tōkyō* (Kokubunsha, 1978), and Togawa Shunsuke, *Shimazaki Tōson* (Chikuma shobō, 1979).

intent to bring new meaning to a term with an existing, more "traditional" meaning. *Hakai* depicts a pivotal moment in the life of a young schoolteacher, Segawa Ushimatsu, who is caught between a pledge made to his father never to reveal his *burakumin* origins and a desire to confess his secret and leave behind a life of pretense and silent suffering. The humiliation experienced by other *burakumin* figures (such as Senta, one of Ushimatsu's students; Inoko Rentarō, the activist who is eventually murdered for his politics; and a man who is evicted from his lodgings when his *buraku* origins come to light) feeds Ushimatsu's determination to reveal his own identity in spite of his promise to his father, who lives the solitary life of a herdsman. Only after his own father is gored to death by a bull is he finally able to disclose his roots, and in an ending that has invited much criticism, Ushimatsu marries the kind-hearted young woman who remains loyal in spite of his confession and goes off with her to Texas.[2] By the time of *Hakai*'s publication, other works dealing with *burakumin* already had appeared, including Tokuda Shūsei's *Yabukōji* (Spear Flower, 1897) and *Nadeshiko no iro* (The Color Pink, 1904).[3] A "popular novel" that had appeared in the *Ōsaka Asahi shinbun* in 1904, *Nadeshiko* was apparently popular enough to be rewritten as a tearjerker (*onamida chōdai*) play.

Yoshida Seiichi claims that it was not the presence of social problems that distinguished *Hakai* from other texts. In an assessment that today has become the standard view of the *shishōsetsu* (generally regarded as directly descended from such "naturalist" texts as *Hakai*), Yoshida notes that "the sincerity with which individual soul-searching, suffering and ultimate confession was examined marked the work as the starting point of Japanese naturalist literature."[4] Once again we turn to Janet Walker, who clearly presents the orthodox critical view. Walker observes that *Hakai* is an early successful attempt to express the individual in modern Japanese narratives:

2. This sounds improbable to us now, but according to Senuma Shigeki, such emigration was not unheard of in those days. From the Introduction to *STS*, ed. Yamada Akira.

3. Yoshida Seiichi, *Shizenshugi no kenkyū* (Tokyodō, 1955), 2: 80.

4. Yoshida, *Shizenshugi no kenkyū*, 2: 82–83.

> His decision to practice *shasei* rather than devote himself to the Zolaesque social novel implies that he had decided, whether consciously or unconsciously, to depict the individual's inner life in its relation to nature rather than his social self in relation to society. . . . Tōson was concerned with the inner self . . . and often depicted the individual as truly himself only when united with nature. . . . Tōson was merely using the situation of the *eta* as a means of exploring a problem that was much nearer to his heart: the problem of self-definition.[5]

The bulk of discussion on *Hakai* has congealed into arguments that either support its assessment as a "social novel" or that label it as the precursor of the *shishōsetsu*. An essay Tōson himself had written in 1928 appeared to further the latter view:

> I intended to write about the liberation and regeneration of a young educator who had been born a member of the eta class. . . . The main intent of my book was to describe how the hero came to break the solemn vow he made to his father. For this reason, I should like this book to be read essentially as the study of relations between a father and son, even though I have added many other characters and incidents by way of background.[6]

The arguments of the poet-novelist-critic Satō Haruo and of the writer Noma Hiroshi (who once worked for the city of Osaka as an official dealing with *buraku* issues prior to his career as a man of letters) encapsulate the competing claims that divide critical opinion viewing *Hakai* either as a privatized *shishōsetsu* or as a "social novel." Satō, who was generally critical of the self-enclosed nature of the *shinkyō-shōsetsu* (a novel of the inner state), claims that Ushimatsu represents Tōson himself and that the work is best viewed as a grand version of the *shinkyō-shōsetsu*. Noma takes the other side, arguing that *Hakai* turns on the transition of Japanese society from feudalism to modern nation-state. The novel, he says, attacks discrimination in a society that still clings to feudalistic norms.[7] Like Noma, Hirano Ken laments the pronounced tendency among critics to read the text

5. Walker, *The Japanese Novel of the Meiji Period*, 175.
6. From Keene, *Dawn to the West*, 256.
7. From the notes by Yamada Akira in *STS*, 442–43.

as a struggle of individual consciousness, and Nakamura Mitsuo's *Fūzoku shōsetsu ron* follows Hirano's lead by identifying *Hakai* as an aberration in modern Japanese literature because of its adoption of a broad social perspective similar to that found in European realistic novels.[8] Critics on both sides of this argument come together, however, in attributing literary progressiveness and modernity to this prose narrative. On the one hand Yoshida Seiichi argues that this virtual extended soliloquy expressing personal struggle was a sign of contemporaneity, whereas the proponents of the "social novel" see its focus on a social problem (*hisabetsu buraku*) as an attack on feudal society, thereby representing an advance over literature that did not challenge those values of premodernity.

Itō Sei's assessment of Tōson's text belongs to the discursive framework of Western mimeticism shared by the other critics mentioned above, but his discussion focuses on the centrality of the literary coterie (*bundan*) in modern Japanese letters. Most modern Japanese prose narratives are confessional, Itō argues, and his assessment of *Hakai* is conditioned by his ideas about the relationship between the *shishōsetsu* and the *bundan* (literary coterie or salon that has come to dominate and determine the literary mainstream). He states that novelists of the Meiji period were cut off from mainstream society, which, to begin with, offered no space for individualized exploration. But the development of a group of "naturalist" writers around a literary coterie provided the opportunity and a ready-made audience for writers of this in-group. As Itō sees it, the social pressures of everyday Japanese life led them to produce involuted prose narratives focused on the private struggles born of their disjunction from society. Without an audience of like-minded estranged figures (members of this *bundan*), confessional novels would not have become the defining form of serious modern prose narratives.[9] It should be noted that Tōson was an anomalous *bundan* figure, always on its periphery. In Itō's words, "people like Ōgai, Shiga, and Tōson could not completely abandon the real world;

8. Nakamura Mitsuo, *Fūzoku shōsetsu ron* (Kawade shobō, 1954).

9. Itō Sei, *Nihon bundan shi* (Kōdansha, 1979), 24 vols. For a rigorous extension of this thesis, see H. D. Harootunian, "Between Politics and Culture."

they tried to blend in with society, the family."[10] Tōson's novels such as *Ie* (The Family, 1910–11), says Itō, are chronicles of his attempt at finding a place in the family to mediate between individual and society. If the literary characters required the family as mediation, in real life, Itō may well argue, the writers themselves required the mediation of a *bundan*.

Whether critics read *Hakai* as a novel of individual expression, social tensions, naturalistic depiction of life, or a provincial work, their discussions typically rest on the shared perception that the text represents a modern novel that deviates from the lineage of Edo literature and the contemporary "popular fiction" that was seen as derivative of *gesaku*. The shift from Edo-period literature of frivolity to modern fiction has been captured a number of ways: as a transition from feudal to modern, communal to individual, traditional literary styles (*gabuntai*) to colloquial (*genbun'itchi*), and frivolous to serious. With *Hakai*, Tōson is placed in a post-Edo literary trajectory that begins with Kitamura Tōkoku and Futabatei Shimei, the font of modern romantic individualism and the writer credited with the first successful *genbun'itchi* novel, respectively. *Hakai*'s position in this genealogy of modern narrative rests on its participation in the discourse of Western individualism, around which the new Japanese prose narrative was to write itself. Accordingly, realist critics have insistently equated the protagonist Ushimatsu with Tōson, if not in the form of autobiographical identity then as a projection of the author's own personal struggles over his identity as an individual. The current essay attempts to question the sovereignty of the unified subject, a view that insistently underwrites critical discussions of *Hakai*.

To the critical reappraisal of essentialized subjects stated earlier, another is suggested by Paul Jay's identification of the central contradiction in any autobiographical text: "the ever-present ontological gap between the self who is writing and the self-reflexive protagonist of the work. . . . We shall see that it is the implicit, or at times explicit, recognition of such a gap—and the author's consequent response to it—that in large measure

10. Itō Sei, "Tōson no hassō to sutairu," in *Shimazaki Tōson zenshū, bekkan* (Chikuma shobō, 1983), 37–39.

determines both the method and the form of a work."[11] In language that shares Kamei's notion of the separation of perceiving and perceived subjects, Jay's thoughts aptly critique the problem of the unproblematized acceptance of the "individual." In the late Meiji and early Taishō periods, the desire to produce literary subjects took the form of *shishōsetsu* out of uncertainty over how to express in narrative form such relativized subjects. In a discussion of *Ukigumo*, it will be recalled, Kamei Hideo states that Futabatei's third-person narrator (whose perceptions and sensibilities he characterizes as being *shomin-teki*) helped to clarify the distinction and tension between the creating self and the created self.[12] In Kamei's view, a clear separation of these subject positions is necessary before one can create a subject capable of direct expression, around which events can unfold. Kamei's critical approach takes two important hints provided by recent Western textualist criticism: perspective as a material expression of subject positions and the notion of texts as productive. The following discussion of *Hakai* takes these same issues and recasts them in a historicist framework, leading to the convergence of these concerns in Tōson's figuration of the narrators in *Kyūshujin* and *Hakai*.

NARRATING BEYOND *GESAKU*

Like many other writers of his time who chose to distance themselves from the apparent frivolity of the *gesaku* tradition and follow many of the standards of Western realist literature, Tōson experienced difficulty in creating a new narrative style that would seem natural and also would be appropriate to these new conventions. The opening sentences of *Hakai* provide an expansive view of the story's setting and of the problems encountered by Tōson as he attempted to mimic the Western realist narrator.

> Rengeji dewa geshuku o kaneta. Segawa Ushimatsu ga kyū ni yadogae o omoitatte, kariru koto ni shita heya to iu no wa, sono ku-

11. Paul Jay, *Being in the Text: Self-Representation from Wordsworth to Roland Barthes* (Ithaca: Cornell University Press, 1984), 29.
12. Kamei, *Kansei no henkaku*, 52.

> ritsuzuki ni aru nikai no kado no tokoro. Tera wa Shinshū Shimominochigōri-iiyama-machi nijūnangaji no hitotsu, Shinshū ni fuzoku suru kosetsu de, chōdo sono nikai no mado ni yorikakatte nagameru to, ichō no taiboku o hedatete Iiyama no machi no ichibubun mo mieru. Sasuga Shinshū dai ichi no bukkyō no chi, kōdai o me no mae ni miru yō na shōtokai.
>
> (40)
>
> Rengeji doubled as a boarding house. The room that Segawa Ushimatsu rented after one day suddenly choosing to move was upstairs in the priest's house adjoining the temple. Gazing out from the window of this old temple of the Pure Land sect, one of over twenty temples in the town of Iiyama in Shimominochigōri, Shinshū, [one] could even see part of the town of Iiyama beyond the massive gingko trees. Befitting the place in Shinshū where Buddhism has flourished most, the town of Iiyama presented itself to the eye like antiquity itself.[13]

The text continues its condensed panoramic scene-setting, somewhat reminiscent of the opening to Futabatei's *Ukigumo*, by sweeping over the landscape even to show the reader the school where Ushimatsu teaches. The traces of traditional literary forms are evident in the use of an extended place name that I have romanized as a single hyphenated word to suggest its use in the original text as a marker used for the rhythmic effect of syllables strung together without break. (Frequently seen in premodern texts, they are used repeatedly in Ōgai's historical tales to impart the feel of earlier works.) Such strings of noun-ending phrases set off by commas and serving as noun stops also occur frequently in Japanese premodern literary forms. Both practices are rooted in oral literature, where rhythm and sound contribute prominently to the pleasure of the text. The use of noun stops (*meishidome*), as in the "sentence" ending with *tokoro*, is suggestive of rapid-fire, emotive cadences of oral recitation. Direct self-referential markers such as *sasuga* and other more overt signs that point to an individuated perspective appear throughout the text. According to the annotation of the text by Yamada Akira, Tōson's use of *ateji*, which designate Japanese *kun* readings for Chinese compounds (such as *yadogae* for *tenshuku*, *me*

13. The translations are my own.

no mae for *ganzen*, and *arisama* for *kōkei*), shows language caught between an orality affirming a populist orientation toward colloquially based literature and the precision of meaning afforded by *kanji* serving as ideographs.[14] In all these ways, *Hakai* shares with the work touted as Japan's first modern novel, Futabatei's *Ukigumo* (serialized from 1886 to 1889), the vestiges of pre-*genbun'itchi* texts, nearly two decades after the latter text was begun.[15]

Hakai's narrator resembles its *gesaku* progenitors in another way: It lets the reader know how to judge each character as he or she is introduced. The reader's first encounter with Ginnosuke occurs as Ushimatsu runs into him after leaving the bookstore: "The honest and solicitous Ginnosuke immediately noticed his clouded visage. The eyes which had once been deep and clear had lost their lustre, imparting instead an unnameable anxiety. 'There must be something wrong with his health,' he thought to himself as he listened to Ushimatsu tell him about his search for new lodgings" (44). The narrator does not always tell the reader outright how to receive a given character. Nonetheless, characters are *given* to us in no uncertain terms: "According to this principal, education was in essence a set of regulations. Hence, the inspector's words were analogous to the commands of a superior officer. The principal had always believed in the value of military-style discipline for the children, and both his private life and his school activities were imbued with such an ethos. . . . Fidelity to these principles had brought success—well, at least in his own eyes—for he had been awarded a gold medal with the inscription 'in recognition of meritorious service'" (52). The ironic tone, revealed by the use of military imagery in concert with the parenthetic qualification of success, strongly inveighs against the character of the principal of the school where Ushimatsu teaches. The "well, at least in his own eyes" signals an abrupt shift from "detached" description to individual judgment. The combination of *gesaku*-like self-

14. Yamada, *STS*, 40 n. 6.

15. In Mitani Kuniaki's view, noun endings and "present-tense" inflections in Futabatei's *Ukigumo* represent a continuation of *togaki*, stage direction-like scene-setting, with occasional commentary thrown in. See Mitani, "Kindai shōsetsu no gensetsu joshō," 49.

reference, emotive narration, and irony produces an individuated subject perspective (belonging to the narrator) that governs the depiction of characters and events. As we might expect from narration that tells us definitively how the reader is to receive a character, Ushimatsu's conversations with school officials, or with his nemesis Bunpei, are wooden and predictable, unable to escape the overdetermination that comes from almost parodically vilified characters.

The most important vestige of a *gesaku* legacy is the text's orality. A problematic that looms large not only in premodern but modern Japanese literature as well, in *Hakai* it is vigorously reworked in the narrator function. Here, the narrator is the site that reproduces most clearly the contradictions of the text's signs: Does it wish to present the text as a document of truth; is the authenticity of the mental anguish leading to confession the object of privilege; how is the notion of individuated identity to be pursued; what discursive functions are available to express the private subject? In an era when a break from existing discursive forms of prose narration informs the narrative enterprise, writers like Tōson were attempting to install in their writing subjects that were not written in the discourses of "pre-enlightenment" (pre-Meiji) Japan. But as Tōson's repeated incorporation of imperial signs suggests, the difficulty facing the creation of narrative subjects came from another direction—the Meiji state as the arbiter of subject creation.

The contradictions of an imperial nation bent on shaping a new citizenry through a more egalitarian educational system are compressed in a series of signs trumpeting imperial nationhood: Ushimatsu's school, like every other school in the nation, celebrates the emperor's birthday with the singing of "Kimigayo," a reading of the Imperial Rescript on Education, a round of banzais, and a principal's speech on filial piety. Juxtaposed to this is another series: the humiliation of Senta, the *burakumin* boy who is ostracized from the games and the celebration, the forced retirement of the loyal and hard-working Keinoshin, and the report of the *burakumin* activist Inoko's failing health. Just as the closing scene of *Kyūshujin* links glorification of the emperor to the scene of adultery, the two series of events and images in *Hakai* implicitly criticize the imperial state. The promise held forth by education is undercut by the absence of places in the new society for decent people such as Inoko, Senta, Keinoshin, and Ushimatsu.

Let us return to the narrator, the "site" that most clearly reveals the problems surrounding the task of narrating subjects in texts of this era. Upset at a scene he has just witnessed wherein an earlier boarder has been forced to vacate his room because his *buraku* origins have been discovered, Ushimatsu has decided to leave his lodgings for a room in the temple, Rengeji.

> Tochi no narawashi kara "okusama" to agamerarete iru kono uhatsu no ama wa, mukashimono to shite wa tashō shokyōiku mo ari, miyako no seikatsu mo manzara shiranai demo nai rashii kuchi no kikiburi de atta.
>
> (42)

> This nun who never actually received the tonsure, and in accordance with local custom was addressed as the priest's wife, was not without old-fashioned education, and her manner of speech suggested that she might have lived in Tokyo at one time.

The degree of uncertainty suggests an angle of observation closer to Ushimatsu rather than to the perspective of the narrator, who, on other occasions, can state with unwavering certitude that Bunpei was a conniving opportunist. The day after the eviction incident, Ushimatsu passes in front of a bookstore advertising the book of Inoko Rentarō, the activist *burakumin* who has been campaigning for human rights on behalf of his fellow outcasts. "Mireba ni sannin no seinen ga misesaki ni tatte, nanika atarashii zasshi demo asatte iru rashii (43; [Ushimatsu] noticed three youths standing in front of the bookstore apparently foraging for new magazines). Here the conjectural suffix *rashii* assigns the source of perception (and the statement) to Ushimatsu again. The narration vacillates between firm statements suggestive of omniscience and a more qualified and equivocating perspective indicative of Ushimatsu. In the next passage, which begins chapter 3, narrative "uncertainty" is employed differently:

> Takajōmachi no geshuku chikaku kita koro ni wa, kane no koe ga achikochi no sora ni hibikiwatatta. Tera-dera no yoi no otsutome wa hajimatta no de arō.
>
> (45)
>
> By the time Ushimatsu reached his lodgings in Takajō, the skies reverberated with the ringing of the temple bells. Evening services must have begun at these temples.

In this occurrence, the conjectural marker *rashii* does not signify a shift to Ushimatsu's vantage point; the uncertainty belongs to the narrator, who makes a statement that simulates a situation of spoken communication. In direct conversation, there is a marked tendency in Japanese to "soften" statements by injecting a degree of uncertainty. This use of *rashii* marks the statement as uttered in conversation rather than in scripted style, directing the statement directly at the reader.

But *Hakai* is also replete with shifting focalization, defined by Rimmon-Kenan as "the angle of vision through which the story is filtered in the text."[16] Ushimatsu is on his way to his father's funeral when he encounters the politician Takayanagi:

> Nisan chō hanarete, kuruma no ue no hito wa kyū ni nanika omoitsuita yōni, *kochira* o furikaette mita ga, betsu ni Ushimatsu no hō dewa ki ni mo tomenakatta. [Emphasis added]
>
> (124)
>
> When he had gone two or three blocks the man in the carriage abruptly turned and looked this way, but Ushimatsu took no particular notice of it.

This kind of shift in perspective—here it has shifted from a narrator position removed from the characters to the spatial coordinates inhabited by Ushimatsu himself—occurs repeatedly. Another instance of narratorial "indecision" and shifting can be seen in the narrator's use of indirect narration; in the scene that follows, Keinoshin confides his problems to his close friend, Ushimatsu, at a local watering hole.

16. Shlomith Rimmon-Kenan, *Narrative Fiction: Contemporary Poetics* (New York: Methuen, 1983), 43.

> Kikeba kikuhodo, Ushimatsu wa kinodoku ni natte kita. Naru hodo, sō iwarete mireba, rakuhaku no esugata sono mama no yōsu no uchi ni mo, dōyara bushi rashii igen o sonaete iru yō ni omowaruru.
> (96)

> The more Ushimatsu heard, the more pity he felt. Somewhere in this picture of poverty itself, he could somehow sense the traces of samurai dignity.

The thoughts depicted belong to Ushimatsu, but the narrator has lapsed into a rather stiff written style (*bungo-tai*) with the expressions *rakuhaku no esugata* and *omowaruru* (classical inflection)—clearly not Ushimatsu's own words. The boundaries separating the narrator from Ushimatsu are continuously dissolved in this manner, revealing perhaps shifting identification by the writer and a language without conventions arguing for clear-cut separation of represented and representing subjects. There is a long-standing practice in Japanese literature of rendering internal thought as quasi-direct discourse. The following somewhat extended passage, in which Ushimatsu thinks about a just-concluded visit by friends, illustrates a prose in which the stylistic conventions are not firmly in place.

> Tomodachi ga kaetta ato, Ushimatsu wa kokoro no gekkō o osaekirenai to iu fū de, jibun no heya no naka o aruite mita. Sono hi no monogatari, ano futari no itta kotoba, ano futari no kao ni arawareta hizai na kanjō made omoidashite miru to, nantonaku munajiji no rurueru yōna kokochi ga suru. Senpai no bujoku sareta to iu koto wa, dai ichi kuyashikatta. Senmin dakara toru ni taran. Aa, shuzoku no sōi to iu wadakamari no mae niwa, ikanaru atsui namida mo, ikanaru shijō no kotoba mo, ikanaru tettsui no yō na mōretsu na shisō mo, sore o ugokasu chikara wa nai no de arō. Oku no zenryō na shinheimin wa kō shite yo ni shararezu ni hōmuri sararaururu no de aru.
> (80)

> After his friends had gone home, Ushimatsu paced back and forth in his room, as if unable to contain his agitation. Recalling all that was said, even the subtle expressions of feelings that he had seen on their faces, he shivers. That Inoko had been insulted embittered him most. To be dismissed out of hand just because he was an eta—just thinking about such irrational words angers him/me. Ah, but

> no matter how many tears are shed, no matter how passionate, powerful, and sincere the arguments, how could such prejudice be overcome? So it was that a large number of fine upstanding "new commoners" would go to their graves, their plight unrecognized by the world at large.

Here the third-person referent "Ushimatsu" and the *to iu fū de* mark a vantage point belonging to the narrator removed from Ushimatsu. The concluding verb form of the second sentence (present tense) shortens the distance between Ushimatsu and both the narrator and reader. *Senmin dakara toru ni taran* (Because he is a lowly being, he doesn't matter) is closed by a period, but this diacritic is more a breath mark than a period as conventionally used in Western writing. In the context of its appearance in this passage, it takes on the appearance of direct discourse, but at the same time this brief "sentence" is linked to the following sentence by the *kō iu* . . . as one in a series of thoughts rendered as (narrator-mediated) indirect discourse. Appropriated by the sentence that follows it, this short sentence (*Senmin.* . . .) ends up being what might best be called quasi-direct discourse. The feelings belong to Ushimatsu, but the words conveying those feelings cannot be attributed clearly to either Ushimatsu or the narrator. As if to further underscore this ambivalence, the concluding narrative form (*de aru*) belongs to the narrator, but the exclamation (*aa*) is either a representation of Ushimatsu's direct utterance (*aa*) or the emotive display of an over-identifying narrator; or, like one of the uses of *rashii* above, it shifts the words from writing to conversation (again with the reader).

In *Hakai* there is a pronounced tendency for Tōson to render other characters' words through direct quotation and to reserve quasi-direct discourse for depicting Ushimatsu's thoughts and words.[17]

17. For a cogent discussion of quasi-direct discourse, see Volosinov, "Quasi-Direct Discourse in French, German, and Russian," in *Marxism and the Philosophy of Language*, 141–59. For an interesting discussion of quasi-direct discourse as "the new embodiment of the reflective function of the author," see Bakhtin, "Discourse in the Novel," in *The Dialogic Imagination*, 259–422. The quotation is from the introduction to Hirschkop and Shepherd, eds., *Bakhtin and Cultural Theory*, 10.

> Naka niwa tachitodomatte Ushimatsu no tōru tokoro o nagameru mo ari, nanika hisohiso tachibanashi o shite iru no mo aru. "Asoko e iku no wa, a'rya nanda—un, kyōin ka" to itta yō na kaotsuki o shite, hanahadashii keibetsu no iro o arawashite iru no mo atta. Kore ga jibunra no azukatte iru seito no fukei de aru ka to kangaeru to, asamashiku mo ari, haradatashiku mo ari, niwaka ni fuyukai ni natte sukusuku arukihajimeta.
>
> (43)

> There were some who stood still and stared at Ushimatsu as he passed; others glanced at him contemptuously, as if to say, "and who is *that*—oh, a teacher, isn't it?" When he thought that among them, perhaps, were parents of children in his own class, he felt rage and humiliation. Seized by such despondency, Ushimatsu quickened his pace.

There are three subject positions present in this passage: the thoughts of passersby rendered in direct quotations, Ushimatsu's own thoughts given in quasi-direct discourse, and the narrator positioning itself in Ushimatsu's perspective. But it is often difficult, if not impossible (as in the present passage), to distinguish the narrator's position from that of Ushimatsu. We can "explain" these narrative acts in terms of literary linguistics, as Edward Fowler has done in his discussion of language in *shishōsetsu*. Departing from the linguist S.-Y. Kuroda's reportive–nonreportive paradigm ("A narrative is reportive if related by a single-consciousness narrator who addresses a specific audience as if engaged in an act of communication; it is nonreportive if related by a multi-consciousness narrator whose utterances are not a part of actual linguistic performance") and Ann Banfield's discussion of the "unspeakable sentence" (a sentence peculiar to narrative "which reconstructs or 'represents' in a fictional 'here and now' the speech and thought of characters in a prose fiction"), Fowler characterizes Japanese narrative writing as predominantly "written reportive style."[18] In his words, "the written reportive style, with its restricted point of view, is the overwhelming preference of authors writing in a language that favors the transcription (in as literal a way as possible in

18. Fowler, *The Rhetoric of Confession*, 30, 32.

writing), over the representation, of speech and thought."[19] The examples I have cited from Tōson's text and the apparent ambiguities of perspective may be profitably explained as the result of such "transcriptive" narration in a language that allows it. But to Fowler's extension of Kuroda and Banfield, let us note that the singleness of perspective or consciousness that is attributed to the "reportive" side of the reportive–nonreportive dichotomy can be "single" only in an abstract opposition to the nonreportive. That is, I think it helpful to invoke Bakhtin's conceptions of language, giving agency to unorthodox units such as words, phrases, even placement, thereby replacing a transcendental subject—which happens to underwrite the notion of "written reportive style."

Fowler's contribution to the discussion of Japanese language, grammar, and point of view in literature is considerable, and while this is not the place for representing or even distilling the major points of his argument, it is important for our purposes to acknowledge his own recognition of competing perspectives that divide opinion on the nature of narrative language. "Like Kuroda, Banfield argues against the hypothesis put forth by Todorov and others that every text has a narrator and hence conforms to the communication model." In fact, Fowler's designation of written reportive style rests upon what he calls a "recorder-witness" paradigm, which "rejects the wholly representative author-reader paradigm of the nonreportive style while approximating the communicative speaker-hearer paradigm of discourse."[20] While he rightfully recognizes the significance of dialogics (here between speaker and hearer), it remains relegated to a secondary role that serves to perpetuate fixed and transcendent categories of subject expression (such as author, speaker, character). Meaning is often produced precisely in these relationships, in reading the gaps, analogous to what John Miller Chernoff indicates is required for comprehending West African music: "Sensing the whole in a system of multiple rhythms depends on comprehending, or 'hearing,' as

19. Fowler, *The Rhetoric of Confession*, 38.
20. Fowler, *The Rhetoric of Confession*, 33, 39.

[West] Africans say, the beat that is never sounded."[21] Dialogics offers another advantage—it takes language not for its abstract, iterable qualities but for the particularities that arise in enunciation, especially in its intertextual engagement with other texts. Fowler's conclusion that "context, not grammar" distinguishes represented speech from direct utterance in Japanese also applies beyond the boundaries of this linguistic distinction. Japanese linguistic criticism explains "perspectival inconsistencies" as a characteristic feature of Japanese, but as it manifests in *Hakai* I feel it can be more fruitfully viewed in terms of Bakhtin's studies of quasi-direct discourse—an approach that foregrounds language in its enunciative moment. Since such half-mimetic, half-representational discourse involves reworking a character's words or thoughts by another (here the narrator), some disjunction in value, intention, and perspective invariably occurs. Significance lies not in merely identifying such differences but in meaning that is produced in these slippages. Insofar as different subject positions emerge, the represented words (subject) are (re)accented differently; in other words, there is no such thing as an unmotivated or disinterested perspective or subject position. But do the narrator's words, which (re)present Ushimatsu to the reader, serve as a metalanguage with higher authority than those directly attributable to Ushimatsu? Or, to use Bakhtin's terminology, does this text succumb to monologic perspective? We might best pursue this question by reconsidering the significance of authority and authenticity to post-Restoration narratives. Let us make our way to such a consideration by way of Tōson's text.

Japanese critics whose works have been informed by Conti-

21. John Miller Chernoff, *African Rhythm and African Sensibility: Aesthetics and Social Action in African Musical Idioms* (Chicago: University of Chicago Press, 1979), 155. Quoted in Ward, "What They Told Buchi Emecheta," 88.

In another important sense, Hirosue Tamotsu shows the value of reading the gaps of a text in his analysis of Saikaku's work. Through improvisation, linking by association, leaps in logic, and abrupt shifts in the cadence and rhythm of language, Saikaku, he argues, opens up to text. In place of a conjunctive logic (teleology), Saikaku's prose requires "reading the logic of gaps." See Hirosue Tamotsu, *Saikaku no shōsetsu: jikū ishiki no tenkan o megutte* (Heibonsha sensho, 1982), 78.

nental textualist theories in recent years have opened avenues away from merely reconfirming content-centered readings. Sugiyama Yasuhiko observes that in *Hakai* everything is viewed through Ushimatsu's perspective.[22] But his assertion stands only by ignoring the narrator as a separate locus of perspective. Ushimatsu does not exhibit any ironic distance from himself, but he is not entirely devoid of the capacity to be self-reflective, for he lives with an unrelieved tension that stems from his fear of becoming the object of the "others'" knowing vision.[23] As has been indicated by Noguchi Takehiko, the distinction between *miru* and *mirareru* metaphorically expresses Ushimatsu's position in society while showing the reader how this very disparity between seeing and being seen determines the boundaries of subjectivity.[24] Limited to the privacy of his own anguish and living in fear of the gaze of others, Ushimatsu effectively remains a subject with no possibility of affirming his agency. Like *Kyūshujin*'s narrator, whose place in society permits no socially engaged praxis, Ushimatsu must turn to confession as the only way to affirm his subjectivity. But he must wait for an act of nature—the bull who spears his father—to enable him to take even this act.

Hakai presents in story form the conditions of its own existence as a text in Meiji Japan: It must resort to oblique gestures in the direction of its reader—gestures that draw attention to the fictiveness of *Hakai*, its identity as a material product—to articulate subjectivity, something it cannot do in the confines of the text. There is no "communication" among characters, if by that is meant an exchange between parties that is characterized by the possibility of change in one or both. Ushimatsu is presented as a generalized image capable of being influenced to

22. Sugiyama Yasuhiko, *Sanbun hyōgen no kikō* (San'ichi shobō, 1974), 140.

23. There are many parallel scenes between *Hakai* and *Chikumagawa no suketchi*, a work consciously modeled on a program of linguistic sketching (*shasei*). *Shasei* valued the relationship between the observer and the observed, and, in line with this, *Chikumagawa* is more concerned with how the world appears to the observer/character. *Hakai*, in contrast, employs the mediating intervention of a narrator.

24. The separation of seeing and being seen arises in Noguchi's comparison of Tōson to Shūsei. See "'Eibin naru byōsha' no bunpō: Tokuda Shūsei no shōsetsu buntai o megutte," *Umi* 13 (August 1981): 192–95.

some extent by others (Inoko) but without the capacity to influence others. The apologeticness of his public confession that he is a *burakumin* can be seen in his decision to leave his job and home and flee to Texas rather than to carry on the path charted by the activist Inoko, for example. *Hakai* attempts to limn a subject position through indistinct but repeated gestures of the narrator, who (perhaps unwittingly) discloses him/herself as the site of contest, if not of narrated subjecthood.

Tōson was able to capture what Bakhtin-Volosinov calls the "generative process of language" in the school principal, who can extemporize in a flowery ceremonial idiom and then switch to a private language of complicity with his sycophantic lackey, Bunpei. To the extent that this principal is removed from the narrator, he is afforded a measure of independence so that his words are allowed to engage in dialogue with others. But depiction of the principal is strongly conditioned by the voice of the narrator. In the overwhelming task of criticizing a backward and hypocritical educational system to which the principal's words belong and in turn help create, the narrator's voice threatens to impose its own perspective on all.[25] The discourse of a centrally controlled national educational system is articulated through the principal in his interactions with other local officials and politicians, with Ushimatsu and the other teachers, and with the students.

If the state plays an overt other, the absent cause that leads Ushimatsu to attempt claiming a place for himself in this new society is his father (tradition). Framed as a confession, *Hakai* is apparently a tale concerned with Ushimatsu's agony, which leads him to an act (confession) carried out apologetically. The scene in which Ushimatsu speaks to the school inspector on behalf of the timid Keinoshin, who will lose his retirement pension because of the principal's manipulation of a technicality, is the only place where the reader sees a bold and forceful Ushimatsu. He can affirm the values of reason, social justice, and private expression only on behalf of another and do so without disturbing a deep-rooted injunction against self-advocacy. The

25. John Frow states "that all discourse is informed by power, is constituted *as discourse* in relation to unequal patterns of power" (*Marxism and Literary History*, 61).

words he utters on behalf of Keinoshin are clear and forceful precisely because they express criticism of systemic injustice to which Ushimatsu himself is victim. Yet challenging this injustice on his own behalf would have undermined the effectiveness of the advocacy. Even as "individualism" is being touted as a sign of the new modern era, its manner of expression remains subject to contradictory rules. Put differently, within the economy of various discourses, the status of "individualism," *once placed within a specific enunciative environment,* is less powerful than the discourse of subjecthood that has been in place for a good many years.

A closer look at the narrative of Ushimatsu's confession testifies to the problems of subject affirmation. His name contains a homophone for the word "cow," a somewhat glaring paradox in light of his father's determination to keep their *buraku* origins secret. It may be more appropriate to affix the "responsibility" for such naming not to Ushimatsu's father but to the author of the text; this is a gesture that shows the trace of *Hakai*'s textuality, a departure from the strategies of mimeticist writing. That the naming seems more the hand of an agent other than his father is further indicated by the narrative line, which makes a cow responsible for the killing of Ushimatsu's father. Ushimatsu must kill his father—the sign of familial obligation that has prior claims on his subjecthood—in order to affirm his selfhood in the form of confession. The sense of disappointment in post-Restoration Japan can be seen in the manifold expressions of disenfranchisement, be they of the popular rights movement (*jiyū minken undō*) or the tendency of intellectuals and writers to turn sharply inward. The early years of Meiji provided the promise of bringing honor to one's family or community through *risshin shusse*, but by the turn of the century the term had come to reflect a more personalized and self-serving pursuit of material success.[26] In *Hakai,* Ushimatsu must reject the stifling obligations of filial piety to write himself in an idiom

26. For a cogent discussion of *risshin* and literature, see Maeda Ai, "Meiji risshin shusse shugi no keifu," *Bungaku* 33, no. 4 (April 1965): 10–21. An informative account of its development in Meiji Japan is provided by Kinmonth in *The Self-Made Man in Meiji Japanese Thought.*

that received sanction neither in the limited avenues of entrepreneurial *risshin* nor in government service.

Among those who became educated but could not abide by these two avenues of careerism, a third possibility presented itself: retreat to the recesses of the self. This narrative of the inward turn that begins with Kitamura Tōkoku, extending to such "naturalists" as Tōson, Katai, and Shūsei and culminating in the *shishōsetsu* of the Taishō era, has been frequently and convincingly argued by historians and literary critics alike, and indeed it was a significant phenomenon in modern Japanese letters. But, rooted in the subject-centric tendencies of Western humanist realism, historians and critics have tended to ignore the mediating social forms that have engendered such writerly retreat. In a study that challenges such ahistorical considerations of the phenomenon, H. D. Harootunian argued that avenues of self-expression were effectively limited by state policy that systematically eliminated realms that mediate the private and the subject—that is, the space of political participation.[27] Just as the direct curtailment of private space must be seen as part of a larger statist discourse to forge a strong centralized nation and consolidated subjects (*kokumin*), it is important to see government support for encouraging the development of a clear, spare, and colloquially based writing style in a similar light: state interests in promoting a standardized and uniform language that would assist in effectively renarrativizing Japan as a modern (pragmatic, scientific, commercially and militarily updated) *kokka*.

For Sugiyama Yasuhiko, the development of *genbun'itchi* is fundamentally a question of positioning and expressing newly reordered social relationships in a society that embraced the notion of civilization as arising from the fusion of culture and daily life. Futabatei's *Ukigumo* figures in the discussion of these points. "[He] was the first to consider perspective or point of view of an individual in relation to his surroundings. The issue of a character and his relationship to his environment was the true objective of *genbun'itchi*. . . . The difficulties of represen-

27. H. D. Harootunian's examination of the problem remains an exception. See "Between Politics and Culture," 110–55.

tation come from the problem of positioning the expressed subject; where to place him, how he relates to his environment—such questions are contained in *genbun'itchi*."[28] Although Sugiyama recognizes that the reordering of interpersonal relationships lies at the heart of *genbun'itchi*, he fails to develop the ideological implications of his observations. Karatani Kōjin, on the other hand, sees *genbun'itchi* as a manifestation of the modern Japanese state. He inverts the standard causal interpretation of the relationship between interiority and *genbun'itchi*, arguing that the establishment of a system called *genbun'itchi*, that is, a tool enabling the expression of abstract thought, led to the discovery of an interior.[29] Implicit in this view is the recognition that Japan has become a centralized state that directly impinges on the material life and consciousness of the individual. But, not merely something neutral and instrumental as the word "tool" may sound, *genbun'itchi* was socially created within the discourse of "Western" utilitarianism eagerly promoted by the state to the ends of strengthening and consolidating the newly reordered nation. The well-established tendency to view *genbun'itchi* as an attempt to create a written style approximating spoken Japanese ignores the politics of standardization that was perhaps the most important impetus behind the government's appropriation of the movement. Colloquial Japanese, like the spoken language in any other country, is marked by tremendous range and variation. The very formula that defines *genbun'itchi* as a written representation of spoken language (as if there were such a monolithic entity) reveals an ideology at work.

It is precisely this characteristic of the spoken, its uncontainability and its refraction into thoroughly dispersed and individuated forms, that explains the centrality of Tōson's oral-based narrative strategies, and the ambivalence that surrounds them, in *Kyūshujin* and *Hakai*. In the context of Tōson's historical moment, orally based narration is not simply a relic from earlier literary forms. We would have to await the work of various folkloricist developments in the succeeding decades, for example, to see a more explicit valorization of orality, though more recently, particularly in jingoistic invocations of speech as a mark

28. Sugiyama, *Sanbun hyōgen no kikō*, 102, 114.
29. Karatani, *Nihon kindai bungaku no kigen*, 42, 67.

of authentic nativeness, orality would be accorded a privileged status. *Hakai* was written under the sign of a modern literary text, responsive to the demands of realism and a transparent, colloquially based writing that hides its own presence. At the same time, it resists, however ambivalently, simply affirming as natural and given the discourse of *genbun'itchi* that remains complicit with the narrative of a unified modern nation. In the name of egalitarian opportunity, the new imperial education system imposed a mantle of standardization to help create a skilled and educated citizenry for nation building.

The "break" that reveals itself in the relationship between the narrator and Ushimatsu is part of a "double voice" narration, and it signifies a profound discomfort with a totalizing discourse (monologism) of a seamless, effaced narration that has already been appropriated by the center (state). The authorities viewed the suppression of orality and the dispersed subjectivities that it implied as a necessary condition for the success of its mission of national consolidation. Ushimatsu was faced with a personal dilemma involving his father, but the very conditions that necessitated this vow of silence are inscribed in Ushimatsu's own work. Ostensibly set up to level social distinctions and to disperse opportunity among its citizenry, the Meiji educational system demanded the suppression of difference.

THE SPATIAL METAPHOR OF CITY/CENTER-COUNTRYSIDE/PERIPHERY

A metaphor of the center (defined by its other, the periphery) links the issues of *genbun'itchi* and orality to the figuration of subjects in Meiji Japan. *Hakai* expresses the contradictions of a text that remains vigilant not simply to substitute the object of its criticism (that is, a unified nation-state, particularly its educational system) with another authority, a seamless, authoritative narration. *Genbun'itchi*, which began as a signifier of Western rationalism (*genbun'itchi*'s signified) had already become naturalized as a new sign of the state (authority). The very form of the *genbun'itchi* narrative—texts modeled on nineteenth-century Western realistic novels—signals texts underwritten by the authority of a rationalist-utilitarian statist discourse. Broadly speaking, the avenues open to prose narrative writing seeking expression of subject positions not defined or aligned with the state would be forced to the outer perimeters of Japanese society, where they would diverge, one way leading to the involuted "romantic" self-articulation exercises whose ends would be authenticity, the other to the affirmation of local, nonstandardized voices (e.g., Izumi Kyōka, Nagai Kafū). Both courses represent deflections away from narrowly defined and sanctioned subject positions, resulting in the loss of agency for subjects.

By the 1910s and 1920s, the *shishōsetsu* would come to rely on the pretense of unmediated reality despite "fictiveness" or figurative and rhetorical strategies that differed little from other prose narrative forms.[30] Authenticity would be enough for these texts, but in turn-of-the-century Japan, literary texts sought authenticity and authority separately. Then, it was not enough to provide a slice of reality and presume that the question of authority was irrelevant, either because the life depicted was self-authorizing or because over the years a right to assert individual desires and perspectives had been abdicated by writers inhabiting the marginalized ghettos of Japanese literary society. Another way to put this is that a work inhabiting *Hakai*'s enunciative moment, still relatively free of the sublation of authenticity and authority (determined largely by state policies that swiftly eroded possibilities for private expression), could still take a contestatory stance toward authority.

Confronted with a choice between embracing a narrative strategy that implicitly ratified the centrist discourse of the state or claiming subject positions devoid of agency, *Hakai* manages, almost in spite of itself, to bring into question the state practice of appropriating the countryside and nature. *Hakai* breaks from other "naturalist" texts, including Tōson's own *Kyūshujin* and *Warazōri*, by seeing nature and the countryside as socially constructed.[31] In Kamei's view, nature can function as a means for

30. In *The Rhetoric of Confession*, especially 6–16, Fowler convincingly demonstrates just how fictive and fabulated the *shishōsetsu* is.

31. The standard view of "naturalist" literature locates explanation of human behavior in nature; thus, Doppo's work and Tōson's early texts are said to depict man as being powerless against urges and drives that belong to nature, out of his direct control.

developing *kansei*, a sensitivity that is opened up in dynamic relation to some other.[32] For Ushimatsu, nature serves as that other, playing partner to his ruminations and even prompting them. "Nani mo kamo chichi no shi o meisō saseru tane to naru" (138; Everything [in nature] became the source of reflection about his father's death). In this work, locale is not used as *meisho* (scenic landmark) but rather as a lived place—the *fūkei* that Karatani Kōjin attributes to Kunikida Doppo as having discovered. *Fūkei* (landscape), he argues, gave birth to subject–object distinctions.[33] Doppo's *Wasureenu hitobito* (Unforgettable People, 1898) placed humans in nature in a way that led to the "discovery" against the backdrop of nature, a figure with an urban sensibility. Doppo's discovery of *fūkei* marks a realignment of the relationship between an individual and her/his environment.

In *Hakai*, "urbanity" can be seen as the center (Tokyo), against which and in terms of which all else is constructed or invested with meaning. The provinces have already been partially reconstructed by the center, seen in the education system and its bureaucratic forms. As Togawa Shunsuke has noted, Ushimatsu always lives in lodgings outside the protective space of the Japanese family; *Hakai* chronicles the difficulties of a life lacking the mediation of such a structure.[34] Official recognition of equality had come to the so-called *shinheimin* in 1871, but *burakumin* continued to suffer from severely circumscribed opportunities, relegated to do work considered unclean. In Tōson's text, such contradiction has been displaced in the folds of urban–rural tensions. With a story set in the countryside where family and lineage maintain their authority, the secret of a hidden pariah identity gains urgency. Neither city nor country offers refuge from injustice, and nature itself (in the form of the cow that spears Ushimatsu's father to death) can only provide a dispassionate and incidental comfort.

The narrativization of nature was to find sophisticated expression in the following decades of early twentieth-century Japan. The agrarianism of such figures as Gondō Seikei and Tachibana Kosaburō, who "dramatized the ideal of an Asian

32. Kamei, *Kansei no henkaku*, 259.
33. Karatani, *Nihon kindai bungaku no kigen*, 36.
34. Togawa Shunsuke, *Shimzaki Tōson* (Chikuma shobō, 1979), 63.

agrarian community independent of the state,"[35] and Yanagita Kunio, who wrote to enhance the status of country and village folk, is prefigured in the scene where Ushimatsu reminisces about his childhood while watching Keinoshin's family toil in the fields.

> Patches of evening mist hid the opposite bank of the Chikuma River, and the peaks of the Kosha mountain range were blanketed in darkness. Just as the western sky appeared to turn a deep russet brown, the setting autumn sun hurled its last rays against the surface of the rice fields. Then, darkness settled over the forests and the farmhouses. Ahh, if only one could fully enjoy the pastoral beauty of such a scene, without worries and suffering, how blissful one's youth would be.
>
> (90–91)

Unlike the later agrarianist texts, which tend to invoke the emperor as a central part of their discourse, Tōson's *Hakai* couches its agrarian yearnings in terms that are critical of the imperial institution. The locale Shinshū contains mountains and nature undomesticated by humans, nature reworked by humans (agriculture), and traces of a new centralized nation (educational system). No longer is the countryside immune to the incursions of modern ways, its state of flux mirroring the effects of the new nation-state on the new parameters given to subjecthood. Reaction against the city, particularly Tokyo as the symbol of national consolidation and rapid appropriation of the trappings of Western industrial societies, is found widely in the literature of this period.

The countryside in *Hakai* subverts the standard use of *inaka* or *kokyō* as a "culturally domesticated homeland"[36] that stands as a comfortingly whole and unified Japan. His father in self-imposed exile in the mountains to protect the secret of his *buraku*

35. See Thomas R. H. Havens, *Farm and Nation in Modern Japan: Agrarian Nationalism, 1870–1940* (Princeton: Princeton University Press, 1974), and Tetsuo Najita and H. D. Harootunian, "Japanese Revolt against the West: Political and Cultural Criticism in the Twentieth Century," in *The Twentieth Century*, ed. Peter Duus, vol. 6 of *The Cambridge History of Japan* (Cambridge: Cambridge University Press, 1988), 711–74.

36. The expression is from Paul Anderer, *Other Worlds: Arishima Takeo and the Bounds of Modern Japanese Fiction* (New York: Columbia University Press, 1984), 9.

origins, Ushimatsu not only lacks a family but also does not have the ultimate refuge, a *kokyō*, which represents the union of family to place. The value of *kokyō* rests on its apparent naturalness; Tōson's *Hakai* offers instead a narrative that points to the constructedness of *kokyō* and, by doing so, reveals how it has been subjected and appropriated by the Meiji state. Hardly the repository of enduring traditional values and the soul of Japan, the countryside is already touched with the winds of social change.

Earlier I suggested a major change in the metaphor that aptly describes the social arrangements of Japanese society, a change from the metaphor of a vertically structured filial hierarchy to that of a spatial construct of a center (Tokyo) and its periphery. (It might be argued that this new schema allows a place for the West as an other, but far removed from the center.) *Hakai* enacts the new metaphor on several levels. Most obviously, it is a text that narrates a subject with no filial (family) connections. Ushimatsu has no family and is redrawn instead as a figure who is removed from the center and who feels compelled to move far away from the center, to the United States. The difference spelled by elements of the rural periphery and the city center graphically presents Ushimatsu's status as a marginal figure. The older fellow teacher Keinoshin and his wife cannot seem to make the adjustments to a modern life, which takes the form of increased depersonalization and the proliferation of bureaucratic layers in all aspects of life. Ushimatsu's father, who works as a cowherd in the mountains, has additional reasons to seek security in the fold of nature, far removed from human society. The *eta*, Kamei has written, has been given the sign of a liminal figure halfway between animal and man. He works at the fringes of mainstream society in work associated with animals—tanning, butchery, shoemaking. Even in Meiji Japan, a nation dedicated to refashioning itself through a new meritocratic system based upon education, there is no place for *burakumin*.

The metaphor of center and periphery that replaced the vertically conceived formulation of the social order prevailing in Tokugawa Japan mirrors the very worldly conditions that gave shape to events that culminated in the Restoration. Western imperialist pressures forced Japan in the Meiji era to reconceive nationhood in international terms, particularly according to military and economic imperatives. Such responses to threats from an external other required rather different modes of legitimation that, in the seventeenth century, Nobunaga had faced in his task to forge unity on a field of internal conflict. As Timothy Brennan notes, "European nationalism was a project of *unity* on the basis of conquest and economic expediency."[37] While legitimation was sought in temporal-filial terms in the figure of the emperor, geopolitics of the late nineteenth century compelled Japan to seek identity and legitimation in spatial, other- (Western-)directed terms. On the domestic front this configuration of center and periphery provided a way for the state to represent Meiji society as repudiating hierarchically defined social relations when in fact such inequality persisted. The requirement for Japan to position itself in (spatial) relation to a dominant other (the West, over there) was reproduced within national boundaries in such differentiations as urban–rural, public–private, and native–foreign.[38]

If Japanese mythology narrates the relationship of emperor to nature, *Hakai* registers its ambivalence toward this conceit (used to legitimate the state) by juxtaposing signs of the emperor system and the playing out and construction of social inequity in the heartland of rural Japan. In the semiotic conventions of *Hakai*, the countryside plays on the increasing valorization of the urban, only to show that rural Japan is marked by the problems that are engendered by the system. If there is nostalgic appropriation of the rural, this countryside can finally only serve as a figure that clearly articulates social inequities expressed in spatialized differentiation. Tōson's *Hakai* marks a moment (whose shorthand designation is "modernity") in which the relationships between self and social institutions could no longer be adequately explained or apprehended by the self-enclosed "trope" of tradition (history).

37. "The National Longing for Form," 58.

38. The determination of "Japan" by this discourse of differential relations, especially as marked by economic yardsticks, persists in undiminished form.

4

BETWEEN STYLE AND LANGUAGE

The Meiji Subject and Natsume Sōseki's *Neko*

History has been curiously removed from studies of Natsume Sōseki (1867–1916) and his work despite the fact that, more than any other writer of the modern era, he has invited depiction as an emblematic figure of his time.[1] On the one hand the presumed congruence of his texts with their "historical contexts" has served to establish his stature as a writer and intellectual, while on the other hand the supposed absence of connections to history in his early prose continues to underwrite the diminution of such works as *Wagahai wa neko de aru* (I Am a Cat, 1905–6), *Botchan* (The Young Master, 1906), and *Kusamakura* (Pillow of Grass, 1906), which have been routinely dismissed as humorous, experimental, and nonnovelistic.[2] Even the few avowedly historical examinations of Sōseki,[3] like the more recent new historicist approaches to literary criticism, tend to

1. The representation of Sōseki as a symbol of transitional Japan emerges insistently from the vast corpus of essays discussing Sōseki in terms of notions such as individualism, egotism, and *sokuten kyoshi* ("pursue heaven and forsake the self"). For example, see Etō Jun, *Natsume Sōseki* (Keisō shobō, 1965), Ozaki Yoshio, *Sōseki to sokuten kyoshi* (Hobunkan, 1968), Senuma Shigeki, *Natsume Sōseki* (Tōkyō Daigaku shuppankai, 1970), and Miyoshi Yukio, *Sōseki no jidai to shakai*, vol. 4 of *Kōza Natsume Sōseki*, ed. Miyoshi Yukio, Hiraoka Toshio, Hirakawa Sukehiro, Etō Jun (Yūhikaku, 1982).

2. Fukae Hiroshi, for example, omits *Neko* from his book *Sōseki chōhen shōsetsu no sekai* (Ōfusha, 1982). See also Yoshida Seiichi, "Sōseki bungaku no shutten," in *Shizenshugi no kenkyū* (Tōkyōdō, 1955), 1: 354.

3. In *Sōseki to sono jidai*, 2 vols. (Shinchō sensho, 1970), Etō weaves together biography and Meiji history to underscore the persistent motifs found in Sōseki's work. Following a widely held practice, Yoshimura Yoshio uses conceptual categories such as naturalism, egotism, romanticism, and rationalism to stand for particular moments of history. See *Natsume Sōseki* (Shunjūsha, 1980).

reduce the complex, interanimating relationship of a text and its historical moment to a static, self-validating binarism.[4] In other words, such valuation of a literary work by its association with a history conceived either as context (background) or determinant of the literary text inadvertently trivializes both text and history by writing out the vital contestatory interaction between text and social process and the creative possibilities of that encounter. As suggested earlier, a similar dualism, mirrored in the familiar opposition of Japan to the West, pervades the study of modern Japanese literature, and unfortunately it has continued to prevent us from seeing a text as a field in which the past is reprocessed in a complex intertextual collision of words, voices, and conventions.

The historian Dominick LaCapra articulates a corrective to the problem this way: The text "must be . . . seen with reference to both the problem of relating a text to its times and to the way texts may *place in radical question their own seemingly dominant desires and themes*" (emphasis added).[5] The present essay attempts to restore what the application of "naive historicism" (by no means restricted to the new historicists) has effectively suppressed in Sōseki's *Wagahai wa neko de aru*: its active engagement with the discursive currents of modernization in the beginning of the twentieth century. An examination of the formal properties of *Wagahai wa neko de aru* (hereafter abbreviated *Neko*) allows us to position the work squarely within one of the key problematics of modernity in Meiji Japan—the creation of a new private subject. *Neko* inhabits that moment when the notion of the self was reshaped by the imperative for every individual to become an obedient imperial subject.[6] Attention to its form allows us to resituate *Neko* in its historical place, revealing how

4. For a critical discussion of new historicism, see Edward Pechter, "The New Historicism and Its Discontents: Politicizing Renaissance Drama," *PMLA* 102 (May 1987): 292–303.

5. LaCapra, *Rethinking Intellectual History*, 43.

6. Selfhood can be seen with more "dispersed loyalties" in pre-Meiji Japan, embedded in the fabric of local units such as villages and domains, for example. For discussion of government pressures to forge a more uniform citizenry, see Carol Gluck, *Japan's Modern Myths*. Miriam Silverberg shows how in subsequent years the populace was transformed into "consumer-citizens" ("Living on the Urban Edge: Culture and Subculture in Taishō Japan," paper presented at the Annual Meeting of the Association for Asian Studies, Chicago, March 23, 1986).

it not only challenged the wholesale appropriation of Western literary conventions but offered a powerful critique of the ways in which this private subject was being reconstituted through these conventions.

Consistent with this study's larger aims to interrogate the essentialized subject, this reading departs from earlier discussions of Sōseki by its characterization of the "self" as an issue of narrativization.[7] Critiques of the humanist subject, as David Carroll persuasively argues, inevitably find grounding in their own subjects.[8] As the present study has suggested all along, the point is not the rejection or acceptance of the subject but the necessity of its reconception. Recent theoretical critiques suggest that (1) the subject is *created* rather than given; (2) it is often not singular but plural; (3) it can be protean, defined by its absence as well as by an explicit textual manifestation; and (4) its status as the guarantor of meaning for a text represents a particular ideological perspective within the discourse of Western humanism and as such is open to challenge. By no means a gratuitous substitution of a term with fashionable jargon, *subject* signifies the restoration of historical specificity lost in the notion of a transcendent and a priori *individual.*

A similar empiricism accounts for the insistent practice of focusing upon *Neko*'s literal content; in such cases the work has been represented as entertaining satire with a protagonist modeled on the author. Released from such a belletristic assessment, which authorizes its dismissal, this work positions itself in a vitally transformative period of Japanese history through what Hayden White would call the content of form. He notes: "Narrative, far from being merely a form of discourse that can be filled with different contents, real or imaginary as the case may be, already possesses a content prior to any given actualization of it in speech or writing."[9] It is this blindness to the signifying aspect of form and structure that has prevented critics from seeing how *Neko* definitively breaks with Tokugawa literature. If *gesaku* can be read as a "carnivalized" expression of the oth-

7. In "Neko no kotoba, neko no ronri," in *Kindai Nihon no bungaku kūkan* (Shinyōsha, 1983), Maeda Ai gives a provocative analysis of *Neko*'s language and the way it is inscribed with conflict.

8. Carroll, *The Subject in Question.*

9. White, *The Content of Form,* xi.

erwise powerless private subject in Tokugawa Japan, Sōseki centers a new subject who no longer asserts him/herself through sexual play and the body. In the Meiji period, private expression instead takes the form of language. *Neko* dramatizes this shift both through its content and by what I call its "dialogic structure." My reassessment of this misunderstood work begins with a brief examination of some key assumptions implicit in existing textual commentary on *Neko* and, indeed, in critical approaches to Japanese literature in general. The interrogation of these practices is followed by some theoretical considerations regarding the subject, both as a matter of literary interpretation and as an important political issue in an era of national consolidation. The reading of *Neko* in the last half of this chapter shows how its dialogic structure constitutes a form of protest against *genbun'itchi,* which had been appropriated as an ideological expression to claim the subject in Meiji Japan by the time of *Neko*'s appearance in 1905.

A FRAMEWORK FOR READING

In the sober utilitarian spirit of the late Meiji period, Sōseki's early texts appeared rooted in the legacy of *gesaku,* a literature of amusement. Jay Rubin provides an evaluation of Sōseki by thirteen prominent writers (the evaluation appeared in the March 1908 edition of the journal *Chūō kōron*): "They saw him as an original stylist, a pioneer in humor, a writer attempting to transcend the real world, and a man 'incapable of writing tragedy' whose works 'are finally not modern fiction.'"[10] Rubin's summary is written from a perspective that anticipates the reversal of these points by Sōseki's subsequent texts—novels that critics have characterized as serious pieces, probing the troubled psyche of contemporary man, works that in style and substance exemplify Japan in transition.[11] Like Sōseki's contemporaries, critics today continue to approach his early prose narratives by

10. *Chūō kōron* (March 1908): 53–54. Quoted by Jay Rubin in "The Evil and the Ordinary in Sōseki's Fiction," *Harvard Journal of Asiatic Studies* 46 (December 1986): 335.

11. Reduced to purely textual terms, the modernity of these later texts consists of writing that attempts to conceal or to reduce the markers of the narrator (*genbun'itchi* attempts this) and the representation of an enclosed subject through a controlled and localized point of view.

stressing their humor and their biographical links to Sōseki. Through the eyes of a housecat, *Neko* takes a satiric look at the foibles of humankind as displayed in the conversations that take place in Kushami's study. Its association with a literary legacy of frivolity accords it the status of a work straddling the old and the new. The Japanese critic Okitsu Kaname, for example, showcases its debt to the vaudeville comic form *rakugo* in trying to reclaim the author as a native son.[12] His studies admirably challenge the overwhelming tendency to represent Sōseki as the quintessential Westernized writer by rooting his early writing in a native comic tradition. But his revisionism can also unwittingly reify the familiar opposition of Japan against the West, recast here as the early playful (even unstable) writer and the later serious intellectual, questioning the costs of Western influence.

The representation of Sōseki as a man of his times is by no means confined to discussions of his later texts. As it arises in connection with the early Sōseki, it frequently takes the form of questions about his mental health. Sōseki's own ironic reference to his neurasthenia in *Bungaku ron* (Essays on Literature, 1907) has perhaps unintentionally fostered this approach: "Since my return home it has been said that I have been suffering from nervous strain and insanity. I have no basis to plead my innocence, as even my own relations confirm this verdict. However, when I consider that I owe the production of *I Am a Cat* to this instability . . . I feel I must acknowledge my debt to this condition."[13] Etō Jun, perhaps the most influential Sōseki scholar-critic (and, more recently, unflagging polemicist for the right) is among those who have stressed *Neko*'s cathartic function for Sōseki's struggle with doubts, angst, and depression dogging the writer just returned (in 1903) from a punishing sojourn in England. This, he argues, was a work of "self-dismantling" (*jiko kaitai*).[14] In a similar vein, Kamiyama Mutsumi notes that the silent frustrations Sōseki kept locked away had to be released

12. Okitsu Kaname, *Meiji kaikaki bungaku no kenkyū* (Ōfusha, 1969) and *Nihon bungaku to rakugo* (Ōfusha, 1971).

13. Natsume Sōseki, *Bungakuron*, vol. 9 of *Sōseki zenshū* (Iwanami shoten, 1967), 16.

14. Etō Jun, *Natsume Sōseki* (Shinchō bunko, 1979), 70. For other examples see Mizutani Akio, "Neko no sekai," in *Natsume Sōseki zenshū bekkan* (Kadokawa shoten, 1975), and Kamiyama Mutsumi, *Natsume Sōseki ron josetsu* (Kokubunsha, 1980).

in the form of critical satire.[15] Such views of *Neko* as amusing satire or a vehicle for psychic release stop at and rest upon the framework of an all too familiar hagiographic construction of the writer. The equation of Sōseki with the cat's master Kushami, seen in virtually every discussion of *Neko*, echoes the varying but finally unified description of modern Japanese literature as "the revelation and discovery of the individual."[16] This characterization is derived from conventions governing the realist novel, which is defined by the union of a view of language as primarily transparent and referential and the assumption of a transcendent private self.

The explicit expression of this ideology of the private subject takes the form of mimeticism in literature, its dominance and ubiquity over the years attested to by its presence in such apparently divergent critical practices as Anglo-American criticism, reflection theory, and homological constructs of Marxist theory. The particular point of contention informing the current chapter is the tendency of mimeticism to obscure rather than clarify how a literary work occupies a moment vitally connected to the past and the present. The relationship between text and extrinsic world involves a complex interweaving of social relations, ideological meanings, and material practices.[17]

A much needed reformulation of the subject in narrative terms, a reformulation that can steer us away from facilely linking Kushami to Sōseki, is suggested in Benveniste's separation of *discours* and *histoire*: "Discourse . . . [is] every utterance assuming a speaker and a hearer, and in the speaker [resides] the

15. Kamiyama, *Natsume Sōseki ron josetsu*, 159.

16. Walker, *The Japanese Novel of the Meiji Period*, 28.

17. Where the "old" New Critics treat the text as an enclosed, sealed-off entity, the "new" new critics see textuality itself as a kind of boundary, mediating an externality that is never really separate. In discussing the relation of the literary text to a cultural text, John Frow writes: "Intertextuality is always in the first place a relation of a text to the literary canon . . . and only through this a relation to the general discursive field. . . . Reference to the authority of nonliterary modes of discourse then is always structured by the force of reference to the literary norm" (*Marxism and Literary History*, 128). Frow reminds us that a literary text participates in a field of discourse and particularly in canonized forms or genres that mediate between a given text and its textual environment—what he calls a "general discursive field" (which displaces the notion of the "real world").

intention of influencing the other in some way. It is primarily every variety of oral discourse of every nature." Because *discours*, "which is dependent on a speech act," serves to recenter the subject, its absence spells the loss of highly individuated and differing subject expressions. *Histoire*, he claims, "is today reserved for written language characterizing events of the past in a form without any intervention of the speaker in the narration."[18] Paradoxically, the very absence of a speaking subject reinforces the authoritativeness of a statement. In recent years textualist critics like Barthes, Benveniste, and White have shown us how nineteenth- and twentieth-century Western literature, particularly the novel form, has produced a narrative that suppresses the speaking subject.[19] In other words, the text seeks validation through the resulting sense of heightened objectivity and truthfulness conveyed by a statement without a specified speaker.

Not merely a matter of stylistics as has often been thought, *genbun'itchi*, it was suggested above, was at the center of this issue of subject expression. Attempts to produce and establish a new style of writing corresponding more directly to contemporary spoken Japanese had received their share of vigorous criticism in the early Meiji period.[20] Yet by the 1890s a widely felt sense of urgency to modernize in all ways had led to the establishment of stylistic conventions that could loosely be called *genbun'itchi*. In the world of letters, such writing was viewed as the essential handmaiden of Western realism, necessary for incisive and nuanced psychological portrayal. As early as 1885, Tsubouchi

18. Émile Benveniste, *Problems in General Linguistics*, trans. Mary Elizabeth Meek (Coral Gables: University of Miami Press, 1971), 209, 206.

19. Recent studies in linguistics and literature suggest the difficulty of suppressing the markers identifying the speaker of a Japanese sentence. Chiyuki Kumakura, for example, claims that Japanese is an "essentially 'speaker-oriented' language; that is, everything is 'viewed' from the speaker's standpoint" ("Interpersonal Speaker: The Point of View in Japanese Narrative," paper presented at a colloquium, Center for Japanese Studies, University of California, Berkeley, May 5, 1986).

20. As Nanette Twine notes: "[It] was vital to the success of the new order, but many intellectuals and statesmen regarded it as a threat to the security of their long-cherished, rigid views on the nature of scholarship and literature" ("The Genbunitchi Movement: Its Origins, Development, and Conclusion," *Monumenta Nipponica* 33 [Autumn 1979]: 333).

Shōyō in his well-known disquisition on the novel ("Shōsetsu shinzui") had affirmed the union of spare, colloquial writing and realistic depiction of an individuated subject. But as the critic-scholar Sugiyama Yasuhiko has observed, *genbun'itchi* was not merely a matter of writing style; it represented an attempt to link, for the first time, quotidian life to culture (*bunka*).[21]

Like nineteenth-century Western texts that inspired it, the *genbun'itchi* movement was empowered by the impulse to elevate the authority of the written word by concealing its subject.[22] Yamada Bimyō experimented with the copula *de arimasu*, and Ozaki Kōyō tried out abrupt, noninflected forms, not only to level social distinctions implicit in Japanese language but also in an attempt to eliminate the speaking subject. The adoption of such subject-suppressed narration reflected the desires of Meiji writers to enhance the status of literature, which had never been highly regarded as an art form in Japan. If the Western novel could be useful in elevating the Japanese *shōsetsu*, it was through the former's claims to "truthfulness." And to the extent that *genbun'itchi* could make the speaking subject less obtrusive, if not completely effaced (as could be done in Western prose), it was seen as effective in investing the novel employing it with claims of truth and reality.

Japan has long had what one might call a native tradition of subjective literature, the *nikki*, *zuihitsu*, and poetry being obvious examples. But clearly the status of the subject in such writing differed from that held by their counterparts in the West. As shaped in the nineteenth century, the Western novel claimed self-validation through the subject, which served simultaneously as the locus of perspective, the organizational center, and the guarantor of truth and meaning. And, as stated earlier, the practice of concealing the narrator by employing a third-person preterite narrative lacking markers for any speaking subject further enhanced the authority of a text. In contrast to the cen-

21. Yasuhiko, *Sanbun hyōgen no kikō*, 103.

22. Sentences lacking an apparent speaker are often associated with the most "authoritative" of narrative form—that presented through an omniscient narrator. For an extended discussion of sentences and the speaking subject, see Ann Banfield, *Unspeakable Sentences: Narration and Representation in the Language of Fiction* (Boston: Routledge & Kegan Paul, 1982).

trality accorded the subject in the Western novel, however, such "premodern subjective Japanese genres" as *zuihitsu* and *nikki* proclaimed their own identities in relation to a specific speaking subject, who made no further claims of authority beyond his or her role as speaking subject.

The monologic[23] (single-voiced) tendencies characterizing the new expression of subjectivity (through *genbun'itchi*) clearly troubled Sōseki, and it is no accident that his earliest major prose narratives *Kusamakura* and *Neko* implicitly challenged the standardization of such narratives. Years later when *genbun'itchi* had become common practice, Sōseki's tale served to defamiliarize it by employing an orational style—a hybrid language inscribed with conventions of orality and scripted form—intoned by a household cat. In *Neko* the very "neutrality" and effacement of the speaking subject sought in *genbun'itchi* was tacitly questioned by the use of yet another (nonstandard looking) "colloquially based" style, a narrator who proclaimed the strangeness of his own status as narrator, and the employment of a detached, third-person narrator. Sōseki's odd fusion of narrating subject with language reminded his reader that what was fast becoming the standard form of narration was merely a convention recently naturalized and one among many possible forms of literary expression. The question we must raise regarding this cat is not, then, as Japanese critics have frequently asked, whether Sōseki borrowed his cat from Hoffman[24] but what it signifies within the constellation of narrative arrangements found in late Meiji writing.

23. In a series of essays, Mikhail Bakhtin provides a rich theoretical discussion of language, arguing that, contrary to its common conception as monologic (i.e., defined by a single perspective), language is essentially dialogic—composed of utterances constituted by and oriented to other utterances and expressed through fragments of statements, books, institutions, or any other definable subject positions. Critical of the blindness to diversity inscribed within any text, he notes that "ultimately, monologism denies that there exists outside of it another consciousness, with the same rights, and capable of responding on an equal footing, another and equal *I* (*thou*). . . . The monologue is accomplished and deaf to the other's response" (*Problems in Dostoevsky's Poetics*, 318).

24. See, for example, Yoshida Rokurō, *Wagahai wa neko de aru ron* (Keisō shobō, 1968).

CITY SPACE AND TEXTUALITY[25]

Sōseki's inclination to resist adopting a single, standardized language in his early prose explains his foregrounding of spoken language, which, in *Neko*, appears not only as the cat's direct discourse but as *rakugo*, popular songs, epigrams, and a host of other forms with strong traces of orality.[26] In the mid-Meiji period, the literary terrain still offered Sōseki a plurality of narrative schemas as alternatives to monologism in representing the subject in modern Japanese prose. Higuchi Ichiyō's narrative in *Takekurabe* (1895–96), for example, had departed from a focused, third-person perspective neatly organizing the text into a whole. Instead, her narration was interlaced with choral voices of townspeople, epigrammatic observations, and popular songs. The anonymous orality of Ichiyo's townsfolk finds itself transformed into the oxymoron of a cat with a distinctive voice in Sōseki's work. The apparent contradiction indicated in this split between subject and voice epitomizes the dialogic structure of *Neko*—a work in which meaning is generated from the collision of "differences" between languages, voices, perspectives, and anecdotes. Sōseki's discomfort with central authority was illustrated by his decision to leave Tokyo Imperial University for the newspaper *Asahi* in 1907 and his refusal to accept a degree of Doctor of Letters offered by the Ministry of Education in 1911. Such distaste for bureaucratic regulation takes the form in *Neko* of narration that directly challenged the standardization of a prose style promoting a closed-off, monologic perspective. *Neko* displays a spirited juxtaposition of voices that, in daily life, find little opportunity to engage one another. The playful pedantry of Meitei, the lively Edokko bluster of Kuro the cat, Mikeko the female cat's refined *yamanote* elocutions interlaced with

25. The text of *Wagahai wa neko de aru* used for this essay comes from Matsumura Tatsuo, ed., *Nihon kindai bungaku taikei*, vol. 24 of *Natsume Sōseki shū* (Kadokawa shoten, 1971).

26. The contrastive opposition of literacy and orality is highly problematic for reasons beyond the one suggested by Walter Ong's observation that "language is so overwhelmingly oral" (*Orality and Literacy* [New York: Methuen, 1982], 7). The connection between spoken language and song, carefully examined by Albert B. Lord in *The Singer of Tales* (Cambridge, Mass.: Harvard University Press, 1960), is illustrated in the diverse representation of "sung" genres in *Neko*.

affectations of young girls' speech, Kaneda's duplicitous language of the coarse *nouveau riche*, snatches of popular songs and rhymes, and many other distinctive voices populate the pages of *Neko*.[27]

The accommodation of such diversity is encouraged by *Neko*'s use of the narrative present. This temporal perspective is asserted from the well-known opening of *Neko*, the words of its loquacious cat ringing with the self-proclaiming bombast of orational-style Japanese: "Wagahai wa neko de aru. Namae wa mada nai" (I am a cat. As yet I have no name). With a tentativeness that marks its own moment of enunciation, the cat then tells us "shokugyō wa kyōshi da sōda" (his profession is teaching, I hear). There are instances in which chronological sequence matters, as in the events surrounding the Kaneda affair (an opportunistic businessman and his wife want to see their daughter married to Kangetsu, though only if the latter actually completes his doctorate), but for the most part the work expunges time as an active force.

A persona with no history and nameless to the end, this narrator deviates from both the effaced narration characteristic of *genbun'itchi* prose and the traditional Japanese storyteller, who even while commenting did not insert himself in the narrative. The narrating cat signifies the absence of temporality in a work from which genealogical links to the past have been erased—from the cat and from all the other characters who parade through Kushami's study. The self-referential first-person delivery effectively foregrounds the role of narration, but the use of a cat that lacks filial connections and social position disrupts expectations of "reliability" the reader seeks in a participating narrator-character.[28] It is not particularly important that we

27. Itahana Junji identifies many other voices, including pedantic *kanbun* style, *shaseibun* (sketching), Chinese poetry, parody of English poetry, the language of students, and the speech of shopkeepers. See "Wagahai wa neko de aru ron," *Nihon bungaku* 31 (November 1982): 1–12.

28. A term of linkage and exclusion, filiation refers to vertical connections, found for example in the family or *iemoto* systems in which transmission of privileged knowledge in an exclusive institution serves a self-authorizing function. Chapter 5, which discusses *Kokoro*, illustrates the endurance of filial relations, this time asuming the form of patriarchy. For a discussion of filiation see Edward Said, "Secular Criticism," in *The World, the Text, and the Critic*, 1–30. Said also discusses it in *Beginnings: Intention and Method* (New York: Basic Books, 1975), 81–88.

know Kushami's ancestry, as the events take on meaning only in the context of these spaces. Sōseki's use of a first-person participating narrator cat placed in and bound to the timeless present with the other characters whom he observes effectively disallows any editing, selecting, and arranging of scenes and events; that is, this scheme militates against the imposition of a single, monologic order to the depicted events. The conjunction of spoken language and present aspect engenders a kind of equality that permits different voices to interact freely with one another while denying the cat an omniscience that freedom from temporal coordinates binding the characters would confer.

The term "chronotope," coined by Bakhtin, designates the two primary categories of textual presentation—time and space.[29] *Neko* shares with *gesaku* a chronotope weighted in favor of space; episodes are organized by the cat's movement through a textual terrain carved up by a fixed set of spaces—Kushami's study, the Kaneda residence, Mikeko's house, and boundary areas like the street outside of Kushami's house. In *Neko*, place has been transformed into privatized space. Unlike "place"—rooted in socially and historically shared association with well-known persons and events—ahistorical and anonymous "space," which derives its value from functionality, provides the context for common people in daily life. *Neko* is filled with the "non-events" of quotidian life taking place in privatized spaces that shape the very events they contain. Sōseki thereby shows us the private space of the individual in Meiji society—space rather different from the space found either in Edo popular culture (where it typically displays the drama of human emotions as it collides with codes of social obligation) or in the public space of official conduct in turn-of-the-century Japan.

Far from being merely background, these new sites have the power to shape events and human behavior. The thin walls enclosing Kushami's study encourage indulgence in private behavior; thus, we see him extracting his nose hairs with impunity or invariably dozing off after reading a page of any written material. More significant, such privacy promotes the variety of discussions, both personal (Kangetsu's misadventures with women, for example) and not so personal, that fill out the pages

29. Bakhtin employs the concept to distinguish one genre from another in historical perspective.

of this work. But at other times, it is the permeability of the walls ostensibly providing privacy that engenders activity, as when the Kanedas hire their neighbors to eavesdrop on Kushami and his guests. The private space depicted here is hardly airtight, but, however imperfect, what effectively encourages the storytelling, gossiping, and other personal verbal acts to occur is the *sense of privacy* afforded by this enclosed space.

Bakhtin's notion of "chronotope" suggests the inextricability of the notions of space and time, and the present discussion necessarily echoes this realization in seeing how *Neko*'s use of space influences, and is conditioned by, its use of the present moment. The intersection of (present) time and (private) space is critical to this rereading of *Neko*. By virtue of its distinctive representation of time and space (its chronotopic characteristic), Sōseki's work becomes a truly transitional text. *Neko* shares with nineteenth-century Western novels a rootedness in the present—a condition with more than serendipitous connections with the enhanced function of verbal expression and communication associated with modern urban life—and focuses on the increasing availability of enclosed spaces designed for such encounters (i.e., salons, cafés, houses with rooms affording privacy).[30] The human body no longer expresses itself through sexual encounter or display as one sees in Tokugawa *gesaku*.[31] Instead, *Neko* illustrates perhaps one of the most significant characteristics of the "modern bourgeois novel"—the displacement of physical action by *words as action*. Rumination, talking to oneself, and conversation take center stage. If in *gesaku* the boxy interiors of the brothels afford hilarity and sexual encounter, the framed events of *Neko* consist of dialogic encounter. It is precisely such dialogic exchange giving shape to *Neko*'s distinctive chronotope that accounts for the creation of meaning in this work.

This dynamic of interacting voices complements Okitsu Ka-

30. I am *not* arguing against well-established contentions that city life promotes alienation and diminished communication. I simply wish to point out that material conditions of urban life (e.g., the presence of a critical mass to engender and support private and public meeting places) have led to the emergence of verbal expression as an activity in its own right (meeting in cafés, visiting in salons) rather than remaining an incidental function in daily life.

31. A seminal study of the economy of space in early modern Japanese urban culture is H. D. Harootunian, "Late Tokugawa Culture and Thought," in *The Nineteenth Century*, ed. Marius B. Jansen, vol. 5 of *Cambridge History of Japan* (Cambridge: Cambridge University Press, 1989), 168–258.

name's discussion of Sōseki and his debt to *rakugo*. For Okitsu, Sōseki's strong interest in raconteurs like Yanagiya Kosan and San'yūtei En'yū signifies a deep-rooted populism. In my view, Sōseki's piece does not have a transgressive spirit (such as Bakhtin sees in the carnivalesque humor of Rabelais's cultural criticism),[32] but *Neko*'s use of *rakugo* does permit dialogue across socioeconomic boundaries. *Rakugo* is characterized by the formulaic relationship of set-up and punchline: words, phrases, and other units of language relate to one another in dialogic patterns instead of unfolding in a linear fashion over time (as straight narrative does). Words employed in such a framework primarily attend to the immediate environment they inhabit. Like the set-up and punchline organization of *rakugo* dialogue, *Neko* organizes words, phrases, and longer units of language in response to one another. A text composed of a series of such units clearly differs from one consisting of linear narratives: Where meaning is created in the moment of enunciation in dialogic exchange, in linear narration meaning is created by the temporal consequentiality of its segments.

The dialogic organization of *Neko* is illustrated in an extended vignette in chapter 2 when Meitei, Kangetsu, and Kushami in turn entertain each other with accounts of their experiences with the supernatural. Ostensibly, the characters talk to each other, but in fact meaning resides at the level of narration, as the *anecdotes*, not the characters, "interact." Meitei begins with an event taking place on a blustery January night when, walking along the embankment of the palace moat in order to relieve his depression, he suddenly finds himself in front of a pine tree. According to legend, the tree inspires its beholders to hang themselves. Just as he decides to try out one of its branches Meitei remembers an appointment he has made and decides to return after his promised rendezvous. Informed that his friend has canceled the meeting, he rushes back to the tree, only to discover that someone else has beaten him to it.

Kangetsu then relates an event following a year-end party where he is informed that a young lady-friend had been taken

32. The subversive potential of carnivalesque laughter is developed in Bakhtin's *Rabelais and His World*.

ill and in her delirium has been calling out his name. Walking home from the party on a dark moonless night, he hears a faint voice calling to him as he is about to cross a bridge. He finally determines that the voice is beckoning him to join it in the depths of the river, and the anecdote ends with Kangetsu jumping off the bridge railing, only to discover that he has leaped not into the water but onto the middle of the bridge.

Both tales, while comic, occur on a cold wintry night and are cloaked with a sense of mystery and the supernatural. Not to be outdone, Kushami chimes in that he too has a strange experience to relate. As the story goes, after repeatedly giving excuses, Kushami reluctantly agrees to his wife's persistent plea to see a *gidayū* (narrative chanting) performer. But on the day of their planned excursion he suddenly becomes ill. In a rush to get well before the arbitrarily appointed departure time of four o'clock, he calls a doctor, who arrives at ten minutes before the hour, diagnoses the illness as nothing serious, and leaves him with medication. Fighting the queasiness in his stomach, Kushami manages to down the medication at exactly four, and at ten minutes past the appointed hour he recovers completely.

> "Then did you go to the theater?" Meitei asks, looking like he has somehow missed the point of the story.
>
> "We wanted to go, but since my wife had previously indicated that there was little hope of getting a seat if we left after four o'clock, what could we do? We didn't go. If my doctor had arrived just fifteen minutes earlier I could have kept my promise and my wife would have been satisfied. Just fifteen minutes would have made all the difference. What a shame. Whenever I think about it, I can't help feeling what a close call it was."
>
> My master, who has come to the end of his tale, looks as if he has just completed his duty. He appears to feel that he has matched the tales told by the other two. The sound of his wife clearing her throat can be heard from the adjoining room.
>
> (108)

Kushami's tale shares none of the key elements contained in the other two, and only he fails to see this. Where Kangetsu and Meitei's accounts are shrouded in mystery and sustained by narrative interest (we don't quite know how they will end), Kushami's experience is firmly rooted in the mundane and is devoid of suspense. The case of the abruptly vanishing ailment is a mystery only to Kushami himself. Sōseki has given us a series of tales that, aside from their intrinsic interest, create meaning through their interaction: Kushami's tale is "meaningful" because of the gap that separates it from the other two, to which it stands in contrast. This section is built upon a "failed dialogue" between Kushami's tale and the other two; the genre requirements characterizing the first two tales are not echoed in the third. These tales are invested with meaning by addressing (or misaddressing) each other in this way.

It is not just the placement of its parts, an arrangement whose organizational principle I have called dialogic, that distinguishes *Neko*. As a work that defamiliarizes the standardization of a colloquially based language, it positions itself in the currents of changing conventions governing language use. *Neko*'s structure is quite different from the linear development characterizing *genbun'itchi* prose, and it underscores its own contestatory stance further by topicalizing language itself. The following scene thematizes the material properties and the productive possibilities of language. As usual, Kushami is in his study, brush poised for action:

> After a prolonged pause he writes in broad stroke, "Burn incense." The opening lines of a poem or haiku, I wonder, thinking that it is almost too clever for my master, but no sooner have these thoughts registered than he has abandoned his opening words and has started a fresh line, which reads "I have been thinking about the natural saint." But now the brush refuses to budge. Holding the brush he cocks his head to the side, but inspiration apparently remains elusive and he begins to lick the tip of the brush. His lips have become black with ink as he begins to draw a small circle at the end of his sentence. To this he adds two dots for eyes, a small nose with gaping nostrils, and a straight line for a mouth—hardly the makings of good prose or haiku. Even my master's patience seems at its end as he smudges over the face. He begins a new line. Merely beginning a new line, he seems to think, can somehow lead to poetic expression. . . . After a while he writes swiftly in colloquial style, "The natural saint was a man who was to undertake a study of space, to read the *Analects*, to eat baked yams, and to suffer from a runny nose." His writing style is not smooth. Without hesitation he reads the line aloud and laughs. "Haa haa, that's good . . . but

> the part about the runny nose is a bit much," and he draws a line through that phrase. Where one line will do, he draws two and then three lines. The neat parallel lines multiply, and he continues to draw more, even as they spill over into the neighboring columns for writing. After eight lines have been drawn he still seems unable to resume writing, and this time he abandons his brush and begins twisting his mustache.
>
> (113–14)

Here, where language production is event, we witness Kushami's writing degenerate into doodling. Kushami begins with an affected poetic conceit, but the resistance encountered in the act of writing redirects his efforts to an epitaph for the natural saint; mid-sentence his writing takes a comic turn. The lines striking out the comic description of the runny nose exceed their simple copy-editing function to become graphic artifacts in their own right—the eight parallel lines that stretch beyond the boundaries of the writing lines. Words here are not merely referential; they are themselves productive, participating in and altering events.

In many places, *Neko* playfully subverts the illusion of the separateness of text from real life as if to further mock the premise of "straightforward subjectless narration" that language simply functions as a transparent medium for depicting real life. In the following scene, Kushami's parlor is peopled with virtually the full cast of characters, and Kangetsu is asked about the acquisition of his first violin. The young Kangetsu lives in a boarding house in the country where the locals do not look too kindly on young men interested in cultivating their skills in music. In response, he feigns illness and stays home from school to wait for the cover of dusk.

> "Well then I burrowed back under the covers and shut my eyes, breathing a silent prayer asking the gods and Buddhas for nightfall to come quickly. I waited for what seemed like three or four hours and stuck my head out, but the rays of the bright autumn sun are still beating on the six-foot shoji, and near the top I could see the shadows of strung persimmon swaying."
>
> "We've already heard about those."
>
> "But this happened over and over. I crawled out of the bedding, opened the shoji, ate one of the sweet-dried persimmons, went back

to bed, and prayed to the gods and Buddha for the quick arrival of nightfall."

"We've heard all that before."

"Please, don't be so impatient. So then I endured another three or four hours in bed, thinking surely it must be evening by now, but when I stick my head out the bright autumn sunlight is still beating down on the shoji, the long shadows of drying persimmon swaying in the breeze."

"We're getting nowhere."[33]

[In response to a chorus of complaints from his audience, Kangetsu replies:]

"Since all of you find this a bit trying, I will cut it short. I completed this alternation of eating persimmons and ducking under the covers until all the fruit was gone."

"By then surely the sun must have set."

"You would think so but in fact it hadn't. After I ate the last persimmon I crawled back into bed and then stuck my head out again, only to find the fierce autumn sun beating down. . . ."

"I've had enough of this story. It keeps going on and on."

"It is boring for me as the storyteller too."

"With the perseverance you've shown, you ought to be able to endure almost anything. If we don't interfere, that fierce autumn sun will be casting its rays until tomorrow morning. Tell me, just exactly when do you intend to purchase that violin?" Even the indefatigable Meitei seems worn out. . . .

"You ask when I will buy the violin. Well I intend to buy it as soon as nightfall arrives, but it is not my fault that no matter how many times I peer out from under the covers the sun is still blazing away. . . . My dear Tōfu, I felt so wretched that I wept."

"That doesn't surprise me. Artists tend to be very emotional, and I sympathize, but I do rather wish that you could speed up the story a bit."

"I want that sun to set as much as you do, but it just wouldn't set. . . ."

My master is nearing the end of his patience as he interjects, "It's very hard on the listeners to put up with that sun. . . . We'll listen, but hurry up and make it set."

33. The editor of this edition notes that this repetitiveness is like a child's bedtime story (*mukashi banashi*), in which monotonous repetition is used to induce sleepiness. This information is attributed to Yanagita Kunio's *Mukashi banashi to bungaku*, "Hatenashi hanashi" (see 433 n. 5).

> "You ask the impossible, but in deference to your wishes let us just say that the sun has set."
>
> (433–35)

The elision of text and real life in this passage effectively underscores the constructed nature of both. The assumption that a tale is a representation of a preexistent reality is questioned by the excessive zeal with which narrative account mimics what it purports to represent. The passage also illustrates what Bakhtin calls double voice: "It [speech] serves two speakers at the same time and expresses simultaneously two different intentions: the direct intention of the character who is speaking, and the refracted intention of the author."[34] Here the collision of narrative intent (the presentation of events in temporal order) with comic intent (the slippage between actual event in Kangetsu's life and his account) causes Kangetsu to lose his audience.

The materiality of language is further suggested in the *rakugo*-like vignettes centered on conversations that illustrate the unimportance of communicative or referential functions, where miscommunication and failed connections govern the exchange of words. In the following scene, a policeman comes to investigate in the wake of a burglary at the Kushami residence.

> "And about what time was it when you were burglarized?" The policeman asks a stupid question. If they had been aware of the time of burglary they most likely would not have been victimized. My master seems unaware of this as he debates the issue in earnest with his wife.
>
> "What time was it?" he asks.
>
> "Let's see . . ." she says thoughtfully. She thinks that thinking deeply will give her the information she lacks. . . .
>
> "What time did you go to bed last night?"
>
> "It was after you did."
>
> "Yes, that's right, I went to bed before you did."
>
> "I wonder what time it was when I woke up."
>
> "It must have been seven-thirty."
>
> "So what time would that make the burglar's break-in?"

34. Bakhtin, *The Dialogic Imagination*, 324.

> "It must have been the dead of night."
>
> "Of course, we know that. I'm asking about the specific time."
>
> "I can't say for sure unless I give it some more thought." His wife still seems intent on producing the information through careful thought. The officer seems impatient listening to this pointless conversation since he had asked the question as a matter of routine and is not the least bit concerned about the exact time or the accuracy of the response.
>
> (198–99)

The policeman's responsibilities have been reduced to asking questions with little regard for the content of the responses. Dialogue, conversations snatched through eavesdropping, gossip, storytelling, writing, delivering speeches—these anchor *Neko* in place of narrative development, plot, and revelation of concealed thought. The foregrounding of the speakers' words as performance rather than as information infuses an irony distancing the cat from the scene, thereby undercutting monologic appropriation of the events by this narrator. The scene just quoted also effectively employs a double voice: The speakers address each other, but the scene itself is mediated by the cat addressing the reader.

The rhetorical strategy employed in *Neko*—the dialogic structure, its use of language underscoring its material properties, the prominence of spatialization, the substitution of "narrative interaction" for communication between people, the primacy of spoken languages, and its use of a narrating cat with no filial connections—reveals a dogged resistance to rescripting Japanese literature in accordance with a monologic form that increasingly characterized modern Japanese prose narratives in the Meiji era. The issue at the center of these endeavors—how to express or represent the private subject—echoed the problem of fixing the private citizen (balancing the demands of a consumer-citizen within a modern nation-state) in the revamped social structure of Meiji Japan. Sōseki's uneasiness with the emerging form of the subject can be seen in *Neko*'s narrative strategy, which disperses the subject.

In recent years, the subject and language have been linked by theorists in a radically different sense. In the words of Émile Benveniste, "it is through language that man constitutes himself as a *subject*, because language alone established the concept of 'ego' in reality, in its reality, which is that of being."[35] Meiji writers did not, of course, articulate the relationship of language to the subject in these terms. Yet astute Meiji intellectuals sensed the direct relationship between narrativity and the subject beyond the mere association of a spare colloquial style with realistic character presentation. The implications of standardizing narrative form prompted vigorous response from thoughtful critics in the late-Meiji and Taishō periods. As Harootunian has stated, "The ensuing struggle over identity and the terms of difference prompted writers like Yanagita Kunio . . . and Origuchi Shinobu to enlist the earlier nativist narrative (*kokugakuron*) announcing subject positions for the folk and their 'household duties' to combat a storyline which was upholding the march of modernization led by bureaucratic rationality serving the imperial state."[36] *Genbun'itchi* as the sign of a new age enjoined the conjuncture of the private subject with an evolutionist narrative. A few years earlier than Yanagita Kunio or Origuchi Shinobu, Sōseki had expressed discomfort with the appropriation of the subject in the Meiji state. Like the two, Sōseki questioned the status of the subject in Westernizing Japan. His incorporation of various native and popular cultural forms, be they *rakugo*, popular songs and ditties, or *kōdan* (a strategy distinctively different from the nostalgic evocation of the past or the affirmation of native traditions seen in Origuchi or Yanagita), revealed a method of organization best characterized as one of dialogic exchange firmly rooted in both the narrative present and its own historical moment.

Seeing form as a matter of narrowly conceived stylistics, critics have failed to notice the decisive mediating function that language reform in Meiji Japan had in shaping *Neko*'s critique of the private subject. *Neko*'s *rakugo*-like vignettes showcased language in its moment of enunciation—that place in a text

35. Benveniste, *Problems in General Linguistics*, 224.

36. H. D. Harootunian, "Disciplinizing Native Knowledge and Producing Place: Yanagita Kunio, Origuchi Shinobu, Takata Yasuma," in *Culture and Identity: Japanese Intellectuals during the Interwar Years*, ed. J. Thomas Rimer (Princeton: Princeton University Press, 1990), 101. See also the epilogue to Harootunian, *Things Seen and Unseen*.

wherein "subject, situation and intention are all integrated into a single speech act."[37] Shunning reported speech and similar alterations of language that write out diversity, the work displayed the cacophony of variegated voices in a richly striated society. *Neko* distinguishes itself as an actively interventionist work, enmeshed in the fray of discursive strains competing to claim and consolidate an orthodox representation of the subject in the middle and closing years of Meiji Japan. In a period in which the mantle of national interest was required to justify every thought and activity, and the articulation of a private voice was increasingly banished to the margins in highly privatized cultural forms (witness the Japanese *shizenshugi* writers a few years later), Sōseki recuperated the performative nature of literary form. Aware that the subject is continually created and re-created within history, he sought through form to reclaim the subject from its authorized expressions as either imperial subject or the seeker of *risshin shusse*. A text that self-consciously underscored the idiosyncraticness of its own structure, *Neko* dared to question the private subject in modern society by situating itself in the spirited contests over the standardization of writing in Meiji Japan.

In this, Sōseki's first commercially successful prose narrative, question and contest over the subject are manifest as an exploration of the paradox of *écriture*, the "ensemble of features of a literary work such as tone, ethos, rhythm of delivery, naturalness of expression, atmosphere of happiness or malaise," or what might be dubbed "personal utterance."[38] *Écriture* arises from Barthes's recognition of the impossibility of separating language (the systemic) from style (the individual). I say "paradox" because *Neko* is finally a text that rejects claims to any sense of individuated agency at the same time that it seeks to challenge the discourse of *genbun'itchi* so often invoked precisely to avow such "individuality." Sōseki's text affirms the productivity of the *relationship* between language and its intended referent—the in-

37. This definition of enunciation is from Sakai, "Voices of the Past: The Discourse on Language in Eighteenth-Century Japan," 130–33.

38. Quotations are from Susan Sontag's preface to the English language edition of Roland Barthes, *Writing Degree Zero*, trans. Annette Lavers and Colin Smith (New York: Hill and Wang, 1968), xiii.

dividuated subject—the gap that is the intersection of the social and the individual. Several years hence, as if to keep pace with the centripetal forces of industrializing Japan, Tokuda Shūsei's prose was to figurate changing social relations through the grid of a new urban geography. Where Sōseki's texts would continue to confront the very notion of the subject and its vulgar appropriation, Shūsei would track the dispersion of subjects, not as things ominously seeking transcendental glory but as unwitting products of the textures of city life.

5

DEATH, EMPIRE, AND THE SEARCH FOR HISTORY IN NATSUME SŌSEKI'S *KOKORO*

Natsume Sōseki's *Kokoro* (1914) has been widely read as a work that depicts the forced privatization of the subject in post-Restoration Japan, but most studies of this, his most celebrated prose narrative, fail to address the imprint of the larger world which the text suppresses as a requirement for its canonization. That is, Sōseki's text obscures the very conditions of modernity and nationness that give rise to this text. While *Kokoro* continues to be read as one of the most sensitive portrayals of a modern Japanese intellectual failing in his attempts to negotiate the complications of Japan's modernization, the very notion of the modern is generally left unexamined, treated as if it were self-evident and fixed. This chapter will address aspects of Japan's experience of modernity—the vital links between the discourse of nation building, Japan's colonialist behavior on the Asian continent, and the sense of lost history that deeply colors Japan's experience of the modern—aspects that remain conspicuously absent in the secondary literature on *Kokoro*. Concentrating on the issues of modernity and nationness that the text itself yields, I shall establish these links by focusing on the role that suicide plays in the text, arguing that such death not only marks the end of the Meiji era but also serves as the precondition for the narrative creation of *Kokoro*.

Sensei's death and his injunction aimed at Watakushi (hereafter the student) to remain silent spells not only an unbridgeable gap between generations but the breakdown of filial transmission from teacher to student in the modern period. This radical breach marked by death is crucial; we shall see how a chain of deaths exhorts the reader not merely to look back on an era just past but also points to the need to narrate a new "modern" history (i.e., of post-Restoration Japan) at a time when Japan's earlier history appears to have been rendered irrelevant. Visual and textual evidence of activity on the continent circulated in the print media, and Sōseki's text shared space in the *Asahi shinbun* with splashy coverage of increased Japanese military presence on the Asian continent and developments in Europe that culminated in the First World War. While *Kokoro* "recognizes" the "loss of history" as an important part of Japan's experience of modernity, it fails to connect the modern to Japanese nationhood, particularly as the former becomes manifest as expansionism on the Asian continent. The subsequent canonization of *Kokoro* in part rests upon the text's very inability to articulate this connection. Instead, as a work that comes at the end of an era, *Kokoro* earns its place in modern Japanese literary history by inaugurating the problematization of modernity as a question of lost history—an acute sense of loss that would contribute to the turn toward overt military adventurism in the 1920s and 1930s.

MODERNITY AND THE CANONICAL TEXT

Whether we take note of the sheer volume of studies on Sōseki's works, his standing in the "most admired" polls taken of school children, or his portrait gracing the thousand-yen note, his stature is indisputable. Anyone who chooses to study *Kokoro*, let alone Sōseki's many other writings, must confront the daunting task of engaging an overwhelming corpus of secondary works. By one count, *Kokoro* is the main subject of well over 300 Japanese studies of varying length, including many books, and there is no hint of a slowdown in the process of its institutionalization.[1] Another clear sign confirming this work's canonical status is the secure place it occupies on the list of required reading and study in the Japanese general education curriculum, though it should be noted that only the third, or last, part of

1. Ishihara Chiaki, "Kokoro," in vol. 1 of *Kindai shōsetsu kenkyū hikkei*, ed. Yūseidō henshū bu (Yūseidō, 1988), 158.

Kokoro is excerpted for reading.[2] To understand a work's canonicity is to address the disparate strands of institutionalization such as the conditions of a text's production, its reception over the years, and the extended process that is inherent in the term "canon." The focus of this chapter prevents a proper examination of these areas, compelling me to address canonicity only rather narrowly as an inescapable condition that shapes our reading and interpretation of a text whether we openly acknowledge it or not. I touch upon the question both because the enormity of the investment made in *Kokoro* over the years cannot be ignored by any contemporary study of this text and, most importantly, because discussion of *Kokoro* as a canonical text reveals connections between narration and the modern nation-state, linkages that have been overlooked in previous studies. Such ties between textual expression and nation are captured by Fredric Jameson's linking of national allegory to literature this way: "The telling of the individual story and the individual experience cannot but ultimately involve the whole laborious telling of the collectivity itself."[3] In the context of the twentieth century, the collectivity that canons narrate is the nation. We shall be particularly concerned with the way in which this work, like virtually every other text from the modern Japanese literary canon, refuses or is unable to address the imperialist dimensions of Japanese modernity.

The aspect of canonicity that concerns me here is not the production and maintenance of a literature as belles lettres but the social function or significance of canonization. Frank Kermode notes that "canons are essentially strategic constructs by which societies maintain their own interests, since the canon allows control over the texts a culture takes seriously and the methods of interpretation that establish the meaning of 'serious.'"[4] This view of the literary canon resists the common practice of banishing it to the realm of aesthetics set apart from the

2. See Komori Yōichi, "*Kokoro* ni okeru hantensuru 'shuki': kūhaku to imi no seisei," *Kōzō to shite no katari*, 415–37.

3. Fredric Jameson, "Third World Literature in the Era of Multinational Capitalism," *Social Text* (Fall 1986), quoted in Homi Bhabha, "DissemiNation," in *Nation and Narration*, ed. Homi Bhabha (New York: Routledge, 1990), 292.

4. Frank Kermode, "Institutional Control of Interpretation," *Salmagundi* 43 (Winter 1979): 72–86.

vital contestatoriness that marks any modern society. While canons are erected from texts of the past, they speak far more to the prevailing values that reign over the selection of this literary corpus. Lost under the assumption of widely assumed consensus is the contest that Charles Altieri puts this way: Canons are "simply ideological banners for social groups: social groups propose them as forms of self-definition, and they engage other proponents to test limitations while exposing the contradictions and incapacities of competing groups."[5] At the smallest level of differentiation, the canonization of Sōseki's work competes against the similar installation of a literature that today might best be designated *shizenshugi-shishōsetsu* (henceforth designated "naturalist") narrative, an approach to literature that flourished in variant forms particularly from the turn of the century to well into the 1920s; at a higher level, the text is defined by a canon drawn against other canons divided by national borders. *Kokoro* can be designated as a site in which issues of canon and nation meet in the particular shape we can discern as Japanese modernity. Put differently, as the canon that is today designated *kindai bungaku* began to take shape early in the twentieth century, it was closely associated with the forces of modernity that helped construct a modern Japanese society that could accommodate Western ideas, material, and practices. What was sought was the fusion of existing cultural and social identities to a modern European form of the nation-state. The notion of a literary canon is important from the vantage point of reading *Kokoro* in the late twentieth century because it permits us to discern the text's exclusion of the Japanese state as it increasingly defines its own contours in international terms or, more explicitly, as an imperialist power.

The very idea that a body of literature becomes a canon rests

5. Charles Altieri, "An Idea and Ideal of a Literary Canon," *Critical Inquiry* 10 (December 1983): 39. It must be noted that Altieri's description describes a scenario that he sets up to explicitly challenge. Positioning himself critically against what he calls a "critical historicism" and a "hermeneutics of suspicion," he argues that "the past that canons preserve is best understood as a permanent theater helping us shape and judge personal and social values, that our self-interest in the present consists primarily in establishing ways of employing that theater to gain distance from our ideological commitments." See p. 40.

upon a unity constructed from a shared culture and a sense of a social whole inscribed within national boundaries. Thus, viewed paradigmatically in relation to other (national) canons, a particular literary canon will appear unified and even stable. But just as those constituent conditions of canonicity change over time, so does a category like the canon. In a passage reminiscent of Bakhtin's description of heteroglossia, Richard Ohmann draws our attention to the mutability of categories (be it the English novel or American literature) and the struggle that often attends their change: "At any given moment categories embody complex social relations and a continuing historical process. The process deeply invests all terms with value: since not everyone's values are the same, the negotiating of such concepts is, among other things, a struggle for dominance—whether between adults and the young, professors and their students, one class and another, or men and women."[6] The notion of literary canon, like many of the other terms we use to discuss Japanese literature in the West, is fraught with difficulty. If canon is to designate a privileged mainstream literature in modern Japan, it must arise from such considerations as the literary coterie, the Monbushō and its educational policies, reader reception, publishing firms and their relation to writers, the production of collected works so popular in Japan,[7] and even popular media attention to literature. The text called *Kokoro* as we see it today has been "produced" by the combined effect of these forces; it should be readily apparent that what we assume to be a completed and stable product (this text) is hardly immutable and fixed and will continue to bear the effects of changing times. No one can deny that *Kokoro* has negotiated the various sectors mentioned above in such a way that *today* it continues to command a privileged place in modern Japanese literature.

The process of canonization unfolds over time across a variety of social sectors (publishing, the accumulation of scholarly ratification, etc.), making its representation as a set of stable criteria

6. Richard Ohmann, "The Shaping of a Canon: U.S. Fiction, 1960–1975," *Critical Inquiry* 10 (September 1983): 199.

7. See Silverberg, *Changing Song*, 163–68, for a discussion of canonicity and *zenshū*.

hazardous at best. The purpose of the present study is not to enumerate these changing criteria but to identify an oft-neglected requirement that denominates the modern Japanese canon—to avoid marking the text with its own worldly conditions, specifically the aspect of modernity that manifests itself as international aggression.[8] *Kokoro* shares with other early twentieth-century works an unstated imperative that, if it is to win mainstream acceptance, it must ignore the aspect of Japanese modernity that shapes the nation's relations with other non-Western (i.e., Asian) lands. Stated in more "positive" fashion, this work owes its place in the canon to its contribution to the installation of what would become the central figure in modern Japanese fiction—the isolated, bourgeois figure who will quickly come to outgrow the confines of "class" to stand for the whole of Japanese society. Such disregard of contention-ridden difference (class) is not fortuitous, and it does not simply reflect the appropriation of values implicit in Western literary practices (romantic and realist literature). Modern Japanese narratives that come to occupy what we can only metaphorically call the heart of the canon observe a kind of social contract to occlude such differences as class and competing political interests in Japanese society—that is, the serious consideration of alterity, whether it be conceived in domestic or international (but only non-Western) terms. A text like *Kokoro* does not simply or neatly eliminate traces of social and political differentiation; but the very internal contradictions and differences of that text must be suppressed so that it can be made to belong to, and to construct, a modern Japanese literary canon. Restated in terms that exceed the structures of textuality, we might argue that *Kokoro* has been accorded a privileged place in the modern Japanese literary canon because the text confronts important issues that grow out of Japan's experience of the modern. But the text's refusal to address some of the more troubling contradictions of Japan's modernity—most pointedly the refiguration of the nation's relations to its Asian neighbors in colonialist terms—also tacitly

8. To use the words of Marx, literature participates in the sometimes conscious and often unconscious requirement to "share the illusion of that epoch." Quoted from "The German Ideology," *The Marx-Engels Reader*, ed. Robert C. Tucker (New York: Norton, 1978), 165.

underwrites the venerated status of this particular text. Before we pursue the question of *Kokoro*'s complicity in this silence, let us consider briefly the notion of the modern, a vast topic that defies adequate treatment within the space of this study.

The modern designates a collective diversity of events, developments, shifts in perception, and altered relations among things and people; the centrality of change makes modernity an extended moment whose nature and limits are difficult to specify. Its defining paradox—foregrounding the juxtaposition of the present moment and the past—is captured in David Harvey's identification of Baudelaire as a key European modernist figure: "[Modernity] is the transient, the fleeting, the contingent; it is the one half of art, the other being the eternal and the immutable."[9] The subjective experience of such disjunction is captured by Marshall Berman, who endows the modern with a "paradoxical unity, a unity of disunity: it pours us all into a maelstrom of perpetual disintegration and renewal, of struggle and contradiction, of ambiguity and anguish. To be modern is to be part of a universe in which, as Marx said, 'all that is solid melts into air.'"[10] In a spirit of passionately committed humanism, Berman sees modernity as universal, cutting "across all boundaries of geography and ethnicity, of class and nationality, of religion and ideology."[11] While undoubtedly modernism as it has migrated from its European context maintains these characteristics, as many historians have pointed out, it is essential to see the specific inscription of a hegemonic West in the very notion of the modern in discussing Japan's modernity.[12]

Berman's attribution of contradiction to the modern may very well characterize all "modernities," but one of its central expres-

9. Harvey, *The Condition of Postmodernity*, 10.

10. Marshall Berman, *All That Is Solid Melts into Air: The Experience of Modernity* (New York: Simon and Schuster, 1982), 15.

11. Berman, *All That Is Solid*, 15. For a thoughtful critique of Berman's book, see Perry Anderson, "Modernity and Revolution," in *Marxism and the Interpretation of Culture*, ed. Cary Nelson and Lawrence Grossberg (Urbana: University of Illinois Press, 1988), 317–33.

12. For example, see Naoki Sakai, "Modernity and Its Critique: The Problem of Universalism and Particularism," *South Atlantic Quarterly* 87 (Summer 1988): 475–504, particularly his discussion of Koyama Iwao and Kosaka Masaaki's views on world historical representation.

sions in Japan can be located in the conjuncture of the sense of history made inconsequential and the desire to narrate an immediate history that would move beyond the boundaries of Japan's own borders. Demographic upheavals that accompanied rapid urbanization, the quickening rhythms of daily life, the insinuation of new urban culture into the everyday life of virtually everyone—those conspicuous signs of modernity—are all familiar signs in the discussion of Japan's emergence as a modern nation-state. But what has continued to be relegated to later in the century—Japan's encroachment onto the Asian continent in the 1930s—is one of the most striking features of Japan's modernity that already forms the fabric of the nation-state at the time of *Kokoro*'s appearance in 1914.

Used to apprehend early twentieth-century Japan, the term "modern" almost always erases Japan's own reproduction of imperialist behavior and instead signifies the introduction of Western thought and material goods. While forced subjugation of a foreign people is not a practice specific to modernity, the modern nation-state has typically engaged in such behavior. Japan begins to actively position itself as an agent of such behavior around the turn of the century, a time in which the Japanese are forced to conceptualize their own unity in the context of global imperialist contest. The coincidence of Japan's experience of modernity and the consolidation of a "modern" nation-state is hardly accidental. Like the preceding forms of modernity in Europe, the experience of the Japanese modern must be closely linked to the establishment of a mass urban population. Rural life promotes a sense of community by differentiating one's own small locale from other localities (which can take the form of villages, valleys, towns). A sense of connection will have to come differently in the city, which forces a large number of strangers to share a rather large, variegated living space, where the conduct of daily life typically requires frequent movement within its confines. Sandwiched between the emergence of a vigorous popular culture in the Edo period and the rise of a new mass culture in the 1920s and 1930s, Sōseki's Tokyo is not so much a cluster of disconnected villages, as this city has often been characterized, as it is a population transformed into new dimensions. Benedict Anderson suggests how an even larger space, the nation, achieves wholeness: "I propose the following definition of the nation: it is an imagined political community—and imagined as both inherently limited and sovereign. . . . It is imagined because the members of even the smallest nation will never know most of their fellow-members, meet them, or even hear of them, yet in the minds of each lives the image of their communion."[13] In his study of nationalism, Anderson goes on to show the importance of "print communities formed around newspapers and novels" in constructing such imagined community. It is worth noting that during the Meiji period, the "print community" facilitated the emergence of cultural heroes that were discursively created, and such figures were often employed in ways that (sometimes intentionally, at other times unintentionally) served the cause of national consolidation. Thus, the image of the Meiji emperor was given different spins according to the needs of the moment, and the representation of General Nogi Maresuke (1849–1912) quickly shifted from that of an inept strategist, responsible for heavy casualties among the Japanese army on the Asian continent, to war hero cum educator and guardian of such virtues as selflessness, military valor, and dedication to the nation.[14]

For our discussion, the salient characteristics of Japanese modernity are these: the rise of nationhood, given shape by the growth of cities and such manifestations of urban culture as the "development of print-as-commodity, . . . key to the generation of wholly new ideas of simultaneity,"[15] and the exploitation of the means of creating and circulating ideas or images (e.g., General Nogi) in a short time to a mass populace. Such are the

13. Benedict Anderson, *Imagined Communities: Reflections on the Origin and Spread of Nationalism* (London: Verso, 1983), 15.

14. Carol Gluck addresses the changing figuration of the Meiji emperor in *Japan's Modern Myths*, 221–26. Telling confirmation of the prominence of worldly events in late Meiji society is found in the memoirs of Nakano Shigeharu. In her discussion of his *Nashi no hana* (Pear Flowers, 1957–58), Miriam Silverberg observes that the "expansion of empire, the execution of Kōtoku Shūsui, and the passing of the Emperor are embedded in the narrative, as Meiji history enters the village through the eyes of a child giving meaning to his immediate surroundings" (*Changing Song*, 18). For an extended discussion of print culture and political consciousness in Meiji-Taishō Japan, see Silverberg, *Changing Song*, 16–30.

15. The quotation is from Anderson, *Imagined Communities*, 41.

conditions that give shape to Sōseki's *Kokoro,* which appeared initially as a newspaper novel serialized in 110 installments from April 20 to August 11, 1914. While the tale itself is fictive, it is tied to its moment by the incorporation of the two figures mentioned above, the Meiji emperor and General Nogi; not simply important historical personages, they are figures whose much-larger-than-life dimensions had been created by a commodified print culture. Despite the ambivalence that Sōseki seems to have shared with his countrymen at the time regarding Nogi's anachronistic suicide, *Kokoro* appropriates an image of General Nogi associated with military valor, moral rectitude, and unflinching loyalty.[16] Sōseki surely knew that these images were at odds with the history of a soldier who had been suspended from the military on three different occasions, a man who had been dismissed from his post as governor of occupied Taiwan for administrative ineptitude, a general whose outdated strategies and intransigence caused the senseless slaughter of nearly 58,000 of his own men at the battle of Port Arthur, won only after he was replaced by another commanding officer.[17] Despite these facts, the eventual "victory" over the Russians helped elevate Nogi to mythic proportions, and in 1907 he was appointed director of the Peers School "because the government maintained popular respect for Nogi's image as hero of Port Arthur while excluding the failed general from the inner circles of power."[18] In *Kokoro* such reversals that link Nogi to the inaugural events of Japanese expansionism are replaced by a general, created by media, whose final image has been imprinted by his suicide. Characteristic of modern fiction, *Kokoro* treats the everyday life that is also the moment occupied by the text. More important, in *Kokoro*'s eschewing of a complicated historical figure at odds with its ideologically motivated image, we confront the text's complicit silence concerning Japanese adventurism on the continent.

16. Gluck surveys the ambivalent reaction to Nogi's *junshi* in *Japan's Modern Myths*, 219–56.

17. Robert J. Lifton, Shuichi Katō, and Michael R. Reich note that during the Russo-Japanese War, "Nogi was denounced as an inept, 'no-policy' general who was senselessly murdering the nation's youth" (*Six Lives, Six Deaths: Portraits from Modern Japan* [New Haven: Yale University Press, 1979], 51).

18. Lifton, Katō, and Reich, *Six Lives, Six Deaths*, 54.

The process of canonizing a modern Japanese literature occurred at a time that directly overlaps the period of Japan's confrontation with Western culture, which at once provided a model for the Japanese to emulate and an object to resist; but very quickly it became clear that successful resistance to Western material and cultural phenomena—that is to say, the maintenance of national sovereignty—would require appropriation of the very things being resisted. *Kokoro* narrates the experience of modernity transplanted to Japanese soil, as at once something radically foreign that was forced upon Japan and as a new moment signaling the sudden irrelevance of Japan's own history, which might have helped the Japanese negotiate the present. Perhaps like the European modernity that was experienced on its native ground thousands of miles removed, Japan's modernity can only be perceived as confirming one of the irreducible facts of modern life—that it is radically contradictory. And, not unlike the upheavals of nineteenth-century Europe characterized by Nietzsche's declaration of the death of God, the events following the Imperial Restoration of 1868 spelled alternating, sometimes simultaneous, movements of repudiating the past, questioning it, and resurrecting it as the enduring repository of what is essentially Japanese.

Kokoro textualizes the irony of its protagonist's inability to speak by placing it within a modernity that ostensibly redefines time and space to permit increased occasion for city-dwellers to meet and to interact with others. In the remaining pages, I will examine the function of the cameo appearance by a Westerner early in the text, connecting it to the text's refusal to admit any meaningful consideration of events outside of Japan's borders. Then I trace the path of the protagonist Sensei's entombment in silence, to his suicide, and finally to the narrator-student's subsequent textualizing in response to the blankness of Sensei's death. Here, in the very transformation of a serialized one-part newspaper narrative into a book in three parts, *Kokoro* reproduces the attempt to narrativize something called a "modern" Japanese history. Within the next decade, such narrative activity would be depicting an imperialist mapping of Asia rivaling that of the Western powers.

SYNOPSIS

Kokoro is narrated in the first person by a student who befriends an older man at a beach where they are both vacationing. The student is drawn to Sensei by the mystery of the latter's unexplained loneliness, and the gradual revelation of Sensei's life provides a way for the student to shed his innocence and confront the dangers that lie in following the stirrings of his own heart. The first part, titled "Sensei and I," tells the circumstances that lead to the friendship between Sensei and the narrating student. It serves mainly to raise questions that remain unanswered until Sensei's revelations in his letter (part 3): Whose grave does Sensei dutifully visit alone every month? In spite of the love between Sensei and his wife, why is there no joy in his life? And despite his education, why does Sensei live with no job, almost completely cut off from society?

Part 2, "My Parents and I," recounts the student's return to his home in the country to be with his dying father, a man whose unreflective security in his own conventionality contrasts sharply with the anguished intellectual figure of Sensei. As the student's vigil lengthens into summer, a long letter arrives from Sensei. The student's father's impending death prevents him from reading the letter from beginning to end, but in quickly skimming it he is stung by the line that reads "by the time this letter reaches you, I shall probably have left this world—I shall in all likelihood be dead." In an act that leaves the door open for the student to relive the same sense of guilt and despair that consumes Sensei, he immediately leaves his dying father and rushes back to Tokyo. Part 3, "Sensei and His Testament," consists entirely of Sensei's letter written to the student, a letter that presumably clarifies the mysteries of a man who lives each day tormented by his past. It reveals how, left in the care of his uncle after the death of his parents, the school-age Sensei is subsequently tricked out of his inheritance. With what is left from his inheritance, he comes to study presumably at what was then Tokyo Imperial University. Sensei falls in love with the daughter of a widow in whose house he takes room and board. In the meantime, Sensei is worried about a classmate whom he identifies solely by the initial "K." Concerned about his friend, whose religious concern with an ascetic spirituality makes daily living somewhat hazardous, Sensei persuades K to move in with him. Despite K's puritanical insistence on living a spiritual life, he too falls in love with the widow's daughter, Ojōsan. Upon hearing K confess his feelings for her, Sensei is seized with panic for having missed the opportunity to declare his own feelings (and presumably to make prior, more legitimate claims on Ojōsan). Fueled by the jealousy he feels during those occasional moments when he perceives Ojōsan to be favoring K, Sensei plays on K's sincerity and ridicules him for straying from his path of the mind and spirit. Whether moved by his own heart, goaded by jealousy toward K, or influenced from some other direction (the text is ambiguous), Sensei quickly asks for Ojōsan's hand in marriage but is unable to tell K about it. When K discovers what has happened, he takes his own life. There is no accusation in his short suicide note, which simply ends with "why did I wait so long to die?" Sensei later marries Ojōsan, but he never confesses his part in the drama of K's death, out of fear, he writes in his last letter, that telling her would "taint her whole life with the memory of something that was ugly." As a result, Ojōsan must suffer through living with a man who has renounced any intention of living, never certain how she herself might be the cause of his unexplained misery.

DEATH, TEXT, AND THE PROBLEM OF LOST HISTORY

Kokoro's use of a mythic General Nogi, together with the cameo appearance of a Westerner in the second chapter, an appearance that has baffled critics over the years, alerts us to the text's refusal to admit any meaningful consideration of events outside of Japan's borders. Only because he is noticed by the student does the Westerner become visible in the text, but the abruptly truncated appearance serves only to signal an absence from the work. What strikes the narrator-student about this white man is the attire that distinguishes him from other foreigners—he is wearing a genuine Japanese *yukata* (*junsui no Nihon no yukata*), which he discards to reveal "his white body, covered only by a loincloth that we Japanese wear" (kare wa ware ware no haku sarumata hitotsu no hoka nanimono mo hada ni tsukete inakatta).[19] A succession of incongruities confronts the student's gaze, from a white man in a crowd of Japanese to a foreigner unlike other foreigners (the student notes the contrast between this Westerner, or *seiyōjin*, and the others he had seen two days earlier at another beach where they had worn Western-style swimming outfits that covered much more of their bodies). In this passage the Westerner enacts a series of subverted connections between outward appearance and expectations. The suggestive focus on such details that frame the student's initial encounter with Sensei recalls the detective-mystery story frame that is employed in many of Sōseki's works and throughout this one. The association of this Westerner with Sensei plays upon the fact that *Kokoro* at least appears to maintain narrative interest by revealing more and more of Sensei. But just as the expectations are overturned, this detail, the curious Westerner, turns out to be a false lead that tells us nothing about Sensei.

If thematically this apparently dead-end appearance of the Westerner inadvertently reveals an aspect of the historical context that the text is not prepared to pursue, viewed formalistically the false clue serves to reveal the text's status as fiction. Despite the intrusion of actual historical figures like the Meiji emperor and General Nogi, *Kokoro* aspires to a kind of "mimesis for mimesis's sake." We can apply Simon During's characterization of Jane Austen's unmotivated novel to Sōseki's work: "With this lack of motivation comes a new principle of organization and delimitation—organic unity. . . . It operates a formal requirement of autonomous texts intent on providing a scene adjacent to the nation-state. The text's unity is the unity of culture—a set of overlapping, unprogrammable connections and analogies within the strictly delimited frame of the work itself."[20] What is described here is the realization of textual convention that is affirmed in the modern era, where narrative practice is "accorded" its own status by being relegated to the realm of

19. *Sōseki bungaku zenshū* 6 (Shūeisha, 1983), 366. All quotations from *Kokoro* are from this edition.

20. Simon During, "Literature—Nationalism's Other? The Case for Revision," in *Nation and Narration*, 147.

cultural creation. If realism values literature's apparent likeness to "the real world," it also rests on the presumption that the two are finally separate. It is the ambivalence of Sōseki's text, the way in which it gestures to historical events and people while affirming mimeticist views of art as autonomous, that makes *Kokoro* a profoundly engaged work.

The relationship of Sensei to the Westerner, particularly as it remains a mystery, raises the suspicion that Sensei is not as isolated and asocial as the student presents him to be. But insofar as the text rests on the promise of gradual disclosure, it must do what it can to thicken the mystery. For that sense of mystery is the textual strategy that *Kokoro* uses to realize its primary task: to interrogate the relationship between Sensei and the student.[21] Earlier interpretations attribute inconclusiveness or irresolution to this text largely because Sensei's death is not adequately explained by his testament. In my reading, the problem of indeterminacy is most vividly inscribed in this relationship between "teacher" and "student." It is "vacancy" that marks their relationship—the absence of firm grounds for knowledge and knowing (that a teacher ought to impart to students), of a modern history, or of awareness that one's own country seeks nationness through colonial expansion. As the narrator, the student presents a monologue of a dead father (Sensei), whose words must steadfastly focus on the private (the urban, nuclear family with little contact with the outside world) and whose only links to the social are orchestrated images of the emperor and his former general. The state, its modern history, and knowledge are disavowed or pointedly absent in Sensei's private account, and it is through the student's relationship to him that we can recognize these "absences." It is in that sense that the brief appearance of the Westerner in the beach scene makes more sense when viewed as signaling an absence.

The problematization of the student–Sensei relation is in fact

21. While removed from the concerns of the present study, the relationships between Sensei and K, the Westerner, and the student suggest personal affinities that are not entirely asexual. Doi Takeo pursues this matter in *The Psychological World of Natsume Sōseki* (Cambridge, Mass.: Harvard University Press, 1976).

an attempt to come to grips with modernity, and *Kokoro*'s opening lines inaugurate this process.

> I always called him Sensei. I shall therefore refer to him simply as "Sensei," and not by his real name. It is not because I consider it more discreet, but it is because I find it more natural that I do so. Whenever the memory of him comes back to me now, I find that I think of him as "Sensei" still. And with pen in hand, I cannot bring myself to write of him in any other way.
>
> (1)

Literally denoting priority by birth (born before), *sensei* is most commonly a word used by students to refer to their teachers or a term of direct address that signals the respect one has toward a person who is knowledgeable and wise by virtue of his or her age and experience. *Kokoro*'s opening lines make sense only if the person designated by this referent does not properly fit the conditions of the appellation and thus requires a disclaimer. The narrator is a college student, and while we are told that Sensei is a graduate of the university and has conducted research, he does not teach or work at all. Sensei's attitude toward scholarship and learning is expressed in his answer as to why he is no longer interested in books: "Perhaps it is because I have decided that no matter how many books I may read, I shall never be a very much better man than I am now" (54).[22] The thematics of *Kokoro* indicate that matters of the heart are favored over learning and knowledge, but it is a text whose narrative quest for deeper understanding ultimately signals the valuation of the latter. If the disjunction between content and form bespeaks the ambiguities of modernity, the split also enacts Sōseki's singular ability to straddle what has been a rigid divide in Japanese letters between serious and popular fiction.

Sōseki represents the erasure of what in later years would become a widely accepted opposition between serious literature (*jun bungaku*) and popular narratives. It is not surprising that

22. Over the years, many critics have focused on the relationship between the student and K, some arguing that K signifies a pre-Meiji spirit, others that he is a symbol of a modern orientation to learning and knowledge. For a discussion of the relationship as governed by an "objectifying gaze," see Ishihara Chiaki, "Manazashi to shite no tasha: *Kokoro* ron," *Tōyoko kokubungaku* (March 1985).

such a writer's work looks critically upon the separation of knowledge and learning set in motion by focusing on the status of the *sensei*. Among the unspoken requirements for inclusion in the canon of serious literature is a text's ability to contribute to the cultivation of a literate and intelligent reading population that is bound together by common discourses of knowledge (and its transmission). In *Kokoro*, Sensei is constructed to overlap the domains of scholarly knowledge and wisdom gained through personal experience. But the very grounds upon which both of these are rooted—Japan's past—have been shaken by the incursion of a more recent historical phenomenon called modernity. In large part, the value accrued to knowledge comes from its claims to represent time-tested practices of the distant past. History as the guarantor of knowledge has been undercut by the experience of modernity, leaving in *Kokoro* a *sensei* without the traditional roles given to a person with his title. *Kokoro*'s strategic response to this dilemma consists of the narrating student's act of framing Sensei's death note with his own narrative act.

There is special meaning, then, in the way the questioning of knowledge and its transmission is linked to muteness and death as responses to the overwhelming contradictions of an era that Sōseki's text unsuccessfully attempts to comprehend. *Kokoro* invokes a narrative of patriarchy for this task, letting family ideology mediate *Kokoro*'s engagement with the modern. Let us defamiliarize its use in *Kokoro* by looking briefly at Doris Sommer's discussion of Latin American novels. After acknowledging Anderson's connection between nation-building and print communities, Sommer argues that in order to explain why these novels are so "relentlessly attractive" we must not overlook in them the romance that "legitimates the nation-family through love." She continues: "I suggest that this natural and familial grounding, along with its rhetoric of productive sexuality, provides a model for apparently non-violent national consolidation during periods of internecine conflict. To paraphrase another foundational text, after the creation of the new nations, the domestic romance is an exhortation to be fruitful and multiply."[23]

23. Doris Sommer, "Irresistible Romance: The Foundational Fictions of Latin America," in *Nation and Narration*, 76.

Kokoro contrasts sharply with this construction of "nation-family" and a "rhetoric of productive sexuality." Instead, it reduces Ojōsan, the sole female who might have played a larger part in the text, to a figure who cannot contribute to the ostensible central objective of this work: to explain Sensei.[24] While Sōseki's text suggests the deterioration of the "traditional" Japanese family (e.g., the student's family living in the countryside), it cannot write out the narrative of patriarchy that the Meiji state institutionalized through the promotion of "family" modeled on the samurai family. *Kokoro* displays the effects of relentless state policy of governing its citizenry by reappropriating filial discourse, the law of the father, in post-Restoration Japan.

The narrator-student interrupts his study to return to the countryside to be with his ailing father, who closely follows the daily newspaper accounts of the dying Meiji emperor. The death of the monarch causes his father to fade rapidly, as if their fates were somehow linked. It is his father who first sees the news of General Nogi's death in the paper. A few days after the emperor's death, Nogi takes his own life in atonement for having lost the last banner, resurrecting a practice called *junshi* (following one's lord to the grave), which had been outlawed since the 1600s. Like the student's father, Sensei himself will link his own impending death by suicide to these two public figures representing the tumultuous years of the Meiji period. Here are Sensei's thoughts on the emperor's death: "I felt as though the spirit of the Meiji era had begun with the emperor and had ended with him. I was overcome with the feeling that I and the others, who had been brought up in that era, were now left behind to live as anachronisms. . . . I had almost forgotten that there was such a word as *junshi*. . . . I did feel that the antiquated word had come to hold a new meaning for me" (245). While Sensei mourns the passing of an age, his suicide is not cast as the re-creation of a traditional, public act. Within the line of male figures linked by death—Emperor Meiji, General Nogi, the student's father, and Sensei—are we to insert the narrator-student, who appears to

24. Several writers rightfully point to a more significant function given to Ojōsan. For example, Komori Yōichi suggests that the student returns to Tokyo as he reads Sensei's testament in order to enter into a relationship with Ojōsan that is more than that between mentor's wife to student.

ensure himself a future fraught with guilt and torment by leaving his father on the brink of death?

Let us remember that the break between Sensei and the student is anticipated by the questioning of the very notion of *sensei*, a word that signals its own relationality (mentor–student). We must shift registers in the way we view Sensei's death in order to see how its signification escapes a "traditional" meaning of death and also shapes the text as a whole. My students have often been baffled by Sensei's inability to "simply communicate," whether with Ojōsan, his close friend K, or with the student, to whom he finally writes his long epistle. Differences in time, place, and sensibility clearly separate textualized Sensei from today's inquisitive Western readers of *Kokoro*, but the question can guide us to matters that bear on the canonization of this work.

It is worth noting that the inability to express feeling recurs frequently. In part 2, the student returns to his parents in the countryside, sitting in vigil with his older brother, who has rushed home from western Japan to be with their dying father; the two sit and wait, unable to admit that both of them await their father's death. When K confesses to being in love with Ojōsan, Sensei can say nothing in response to the revelation. Instead, he seeks out Ojōsan's mother and asks for her daughter's hand without mentioning it to K. Several days after hearing of Sensei's action, K quietly kills himself. To the very end, Sensei shields his wife from the truth about K's suicide, revealing his tale of betrayal solely to the student as his last testament.

The penultimate instance of broken communication is, of course, the death of Sensei. *Kokoro* explores the relationship between speaking and death, the latter as the precondition for the former. Sensei's death is almost always attributed to such markers of Japanese modernity as the disintegration of the family unit, the ascendance of self-oriented conceptions of society, and the pernicious effects of an industrialized, increasingly materialistic nation. However, Sensei's death must also be seen together with the frustration of speechlessness, the loss of voice, and the erosion of familiar avenues by which the sense of subject could be affirmed, all of which must have assailed many of Sensei's generation. More functionally viewed, death engenders the production of Sensei's letter and in turn the student's acts of textualization. Put differently, it is the very possibility of textualizing life, of organizing it in accordance with the laws of writing and narrativizing, that paradoxically gives rise to the impossibility of speech.

Sensei's life, which is governed by the inability to speak and communicate with others, is revealed in the form of a last will and testament—a document that reinforces the new signifying relations governing narrativizing and death. For a man who remains trapped in his own silence to the end, only the immediate emptiness of death can engender the production of a long letter to break that silence. As if "he were listening to his own death," Sensei produces a written account tracing the events that lead him to live life as if he were dead, a life punctuated by his own suicide. Foucault's discussion of the function of language in the *Odyssey* can help us illuminate the status of language in *Kokoro*.

> The limit of death opens before language, or rather within language, an infinite space. Before the imminence of death, language rushes forth, but it also starts again, tells of itself, discovers the story of the story and the possibility that this interpretation might never end. Headed toward death, language turns back upon itself; it encounters something like a mirror, and to stop, this death which would stop it, it possesses but a single power: that of giving birth to its own image in a play of mirrors that has no limits.[25]

The student to whom the testament is written inserts himself at that very point at which a stop might be made of endless interpretation. But he is not positioned as the authoritative interpreting agent or "next" in the chain of filial transmitters of knowledge. *Kokoro* speaks to the limits of such institutionalized intellectual labors. And, acting much like what Barthes calls a writerly text, *Kokoro* invites the reader to assume the very position given to the student, to narrativize and hence to interpret the story of Sensei.

In a sense, Sōseki himself "reinterpreted" the text when he took the serialized newspaper version, which was one continu-

25. Michel Foucault, "Language to Infinity," in *Language, Counter-Memory, Practice: Selected Essays and Interviews by Michel Foucault*, ed. Donald F. Bouchard (Ithaca: Cornell University Press, 1977), 54.

ous narrative subtitled "Sensei and His Testament," and reissued it in book form after dividing it into three parts (as we know it today).[26] The first two parts provide background information on the student, the circumstances of his encounter with Sensei, and his truncated visit to his dying father in the country. Parts 1 and 2 are also replete with hints about Sensei's past and his impending suicide—in short, those matters that await revelation in part 3, "Sensei and His Testament." Death provides that point from which the past (whether that of Sensei, the student, or Japan's immediate history) must be narrated or created anew.

In *Kokoro,* death generates such narrative activity in a form that evinces its own status as writing. Note that the exfoliation of the student's narrative is a response not to the death of Sensei but to the narration of his dying (the testament/letter). And it is not the veracity of Sensei's disclosures that matters, for overwhelmingly the text speaks to the nature of representation and its uses in modern civil society. Thus, the revelation of Sensei's past occupies the thematic center of this text, but the real interest moves outside of Sensei's life to the student who responds to him, first by befriending him and then by narrating his story. The text "owes" its existence to the student's "narrative response" to Sensei's death, and the thematic weight of the text falls on the student—what will be his fate?

Kokoro was written during the years in which, in spite of a wide range of approaches, literature legitimated by claims that it offered unmediated recording of real life continued to reign as orthodoxy. We must recognize that Sōseki's work eschews the designation *shizenshugi* literature, contributing instead to a body of writing whose "truth" or "falsity" is secondary to the task of representation itself. I have borrowed During's words used to describe English literature of the "civil Imaginary," works that reenact everyday life, typically assuming the form of letters, memoirs, and other written forms. Such literature, During states, "reproduces representations of manners, taste, behavior,

26. While there are minor stylistic revisions, the original newspaper version and the Iwanami book edition remain virtually the same.

utterances for imitation by individual lives."[27] As are the narrators in such works, *Kokoro*'s narrator "is explicitly socially located in the writing, the text's occasion being made apparent."[28] Reinforcing the effect produced by introducing a Westerner (which I identified earlier), the narrator-student serves to highlight fabulation by gesturing to the very conditions that engender the text—by a character whose function is limited to that of witness and writer. The central contradiction in Sōseki's text, which is narrativized by a character whose participation in the production of text clearly differentiates him from the protagonists of *shizenshugi* literature, is expressed as a break between Sensei, for whom "truth" is primary, and the student, whose concern is representation (here, storytelling).

By framing Sensei's confessional testament within the conditions that occasioned the creation of a larger text, the student has shifted *Kokoro* from the register of *shizenshugi* to a text about representation. (The anticipatory signs in the first two sections, hints that are more fully revealed in the testament section, might well be read as awkward and at times uncertain duplications of a self-adequate text.) In what formalists would designate as a motivated text, both the prominence of private confession and the insertion of a perceiving writer to whom the confession is directed affirm the troubled status of the individual in Meiji society and the highly privatized way in which the text must write itself—that is, around suicide. But, just as "death" is ambivalently associated with both the private (Sensei and his quiet suffering) and the public spheres (the Meiji emperor and General Nogi) in *Kokoro*, the status of the individual subject remains in question.

When Ojōsan is left behind by an overprotective husband who leaves his wife with no explanation for his own death, in what position does that leave the student? Passing references in the first two parts indicate that he has kept his promise to Sensei and not conveyed to her even the existence of the testament, let alone its contents. In effect, Sensei has left the student with the

27. Simon During locates the origins of such literature in eighteenth-century England. In "Literature—Nationalism's Other?", 142.

28. During, "Literature—Nationalism's Other?", 143.

imperative to remain mute, to reproduce the path of betrayal, self-loathing, and despair. The student's response to this imperative is the fabulation, the narration of *Kokoro* beyond the borders of Sensei's own testament. Such transgression, it appears, is the only way by which the student can avoid becoming yet another figure in the chain of institutionalized patriarchy and death that threatens to persist in modern Japanese society. At the same time, the student's act comes marked as a "creative destruction" that is a central figure of modernity.[29] Accompanying the destruction that clears away tradition, that reduces human relations to a depersonalized calculus of money and profit, that engenders war as a means of subjecting people to colonial rule, there is a ratification of "creation" that is tightly implicated in moments of "destruction"—the "other" to creation in the dialectic of modernity.

Kokoro is written in relation to other texts that constitute the field of literature, but that realm does not exist apart from larger "situations." Japanese naturalist literature—confessional writings that signaled their own veracity by the luridness of the author's revelations—peaked in 1908. Such prose would largely determine the shape of the Japanese canon, resurrected as the I-novel of the 1920s and 1930s. Sōseki's *Kokoro* overtly challenges the naturalist–I-novel trend by centering death, which can have no role in narratives that impart the sense of unmediated depiction of the writer's own ongoing life. Death establishes *Kokoro* as derisively gesturing in the direction of naturalist literature and its practitioners who continued to occupy key positions within the Japanese literary establishment. Death also plays a role in situating the work in the world. *Kokoro* raises questions about a Japanese experience of modernity, the juxtaposition of silence, textuality, and death relating this work not only to the literary currents of its time but to the sense of nationness defined in global terms. In the coming decades, Japanese intellectuals would articulate more explicitly their concerns with a "world history" that excluded Japan.[30] Sōseki's work can only forecast in oblique gestures (the fleeting appearance

29. See Harvey, *The Condition of Postmodernity*, 18–19.

30. Such culturalists of the 1920s and 1930s as Watsuji Tetsurō, Kuki Shūzō, and Nishida Kitarō immediately come to mind.

of a Westerner), through a text marked by absence (the dead father, Sensei), the complicity of intellectual and military responses to this exclusion that would lead to heightened expansionist activity on the Asian continent.[31] As surely as a helpless silence and death would fuel and encourage narrative activity in *Kokoro*, confrontation with Japan's own mordant history would lead Japan to emulate the imperialist trajectories of the Western powers and to narrate its own history of coercion onto the map. Here again, *Kokoro* contests Japanese *shizenshugi* literature, which displaced historical awareness with the "present," or contemporaneity, as a signifier of modernity. By linking Sensei's suicide with the Meiji emperor's death, Sōseki's work attempts to create what is absent from *shizenshugi-shishōsetsu* literature and from the Meiji era itself—a history of modern Japan. In *Kokoro*, death urges us to look back at the events leading to that null point and to seek meaning in individual lives from such a frame, thereby memorializing the first epoch of post-Restoration Japan.

The question of Sōseki's complicity in Japan's expansionist sentiment is beyond the scope of this paper, but in passing we should note that in 1909, four years after the Russo-Japanese War and five years before *Kokoro* began serialization, Sōseki traveled through Manchuria and Korea on assignment for the *Asahi shinbun* to write about the social conditions he observed.[32] The signs of continuing Japanese activity on the continent are clearly visible on the pages of the large-circulation newspapers of his time, including the *Asahi*. Sharing space with the later installments of *Kokoro* are articles and photographs of European mobilization for war. Photographs of impressive German and British officers and implements of war alternate with images of

31. While the Sino-Japanese War of 1895 is a convenient milestone to date the beginnings of Japanese adventurism on the Asian continent, we must remember that increasing government presence in Korea can be discerned from the 1880s. See Ramon H. Myers and Mark R. Peattie, *The Japanese Colonial Empire, 1895–1945* (Princeton: Princeton University Press, 1984). By all accounts it is the Russo-Japanese War of 1904–5 that clearly marks the early moments of "social acceptance" for colonialist behavior by Japan.

32. In addition to diary entries, some of Sōseki's impressions of his travels are found in his work "Man-kan tokoro dokoro," in vol. 8 of *Sōseki zenshū* (Iwanami shoten, 1975), 153–270.

Japanese men of war in the July and August 1914 editions of the *Asahi shinbun*. Sōseki's text shared space not only with such visible records of military behavior abroad but with prominent ads for Lion toothpaste for boys and girls, *miruku-meido* milk, and Dunlop tires.[33] Along with the "content" of such coverage of international events and these new products, the *Asahi* was unmistakably projecting itself as the purveyor of modernity.

What Sōseki's prose fiction (including *Kokoro*) demonstrates is a blindness to the connection between Japan's experience of modernity, about which he felt tremendous ambivalence, and Japan's extraterritorial activities. Thus, what we might observe as one condition of the canonization of works such as *Kokoro* is a narrowly constricted focus on minute nuances of private perceptions, thoughts, and feelings. At a time when Japan's own search for subjecthood—for proclaiming a place in world history—was so acutely felt, Sōseki's canonized works would pointedly ignore the grammar of nationness within which Japan sought recognition. Yet, as I have argued here, the text's engagement with issues of modernity that arise in the narration of silence and death unwittingly reproduce the concurrent narratives of nation and empire and the construction of a "modern" Japanese history—those conditions that governed the simultaneous creation of a new literary canon. Japan might be included in Timothy Brennan's assertion that "the rise of the modern nation-state in Europe in the late eighteenth and early nineteenth centuries is inseparable from the forms and subjects of imaginative literature."[34] Just how writing and nationness express their relationship deserves close attention, case by case.

33. See, for example, *Asahi shinbun*, August 11, 1914.
34. Brennan, "The National Longing for Form," 48.

6

CLAIMING THE URBAN LANDSCAPE

Tokuda Shūsei as Discursive Creation

His writing never appears in the literary curricula of Japanese schools, but Tokuda Shūsei (1871–1943) has enjoyed muted respect as a writer's writer in his own country.[1] A remarkably strong consensus among critics has conferred upon this figure the title of the most "naturalistic of naturalist writers." Despite his distaste for so-called *shizenshugi* literature, Natsume Sōseki had praise for much of Shūsei's writing, but in an observation more critical than laudatory, Sōseki also expressed what has since become the canonical view of Shūsei as a representative of *shizenshugi* literature when he stated that his prose "captures reality as it is, although there is no 'philosophy' behind it."[2] Here, absence of "philosophy" indicates an uneasiness regarding subject position, or agency (which occupied Sōseki's thoughts throughout his career), while the "reality as it is" (*aru ga mama*) has become the hallmark of a "literature of sincerity" (the *shizenshugi-shishōsetsu* movement) and the signature of a writer whom, separated from us by geographical, cultural, and temporal distance, we can only apprehend as a discursive creation called Tokuda Shūsei. Shūsei comes overdetermined as a

1. Kawabata Yasunari and Akutagawa Ryūnosuke, for example, have raised their voices in praise of Shūsei's writing. In 1912, *Waseda bungaku* noted that Shūsei had contributed more to modern Japanese literature than anyone else. See Hiroe Yōko, "Kabi no ichi to sono shitsuyō sei," in *Rōnko Tokuda Shūsei*, ed. Kōno Toshirō (Sakufūsha, 1982), 47–66. More recently, the novelist Nakagami Kenji has expressed admiration for Shūsei's prose.

2. From Yoshida Seiichi, *Shizenshugi no kenkyū* (Tokyodō, 1955), 2: 680. Sōseki is quoted as saying that life is indeed like this, but that's all he leaves the reader. Shūsei doesn't move or touch the reader, he just depicts life as it is, leaving values removed.

"naturalist" writer par excellence, and the ambivalence signaled by Sōseki's assessment provides a way to read his texts and contest the narrative practice of *shizenshugi*, a key constituent of a larger discourse called *kindai bungaku*.[3]

Like the writers associated with this literary movement, Japanese naturalism is marked by diversity and difference: Candid disclosure of the self through confession, the depiction of "mental states," narrative without editorial comment, the proclivity to highlight the sordid aspects of life, critical exploration of the clash between individual interests and the traditional family, a renewed portrayal of women, animal drive as explanation for human behavior, and isolated depiction of the individual in the provinces all have a high profile in what has been grouped under the practice called *shizenshugi*, or Japanese naturalism.[4] Shūsei occupies a central position in the *shizenshugi-shishōsetsu* movement, not so much because he prominently featured distinctive female protagonists (which we will take up below), nor for his frequent though not exclusive use of autobiographical material, but because both detractors and supporters alike consistently have attributed to his texts the quality of depicting life "just as it is" (*aru ga mama*). Shūsei's texts provide the occasion to consider the larger socially determined meaning that underlies this connection between *aru ga mama* and *shizenshugi*—that is, Japanese "naturalism" as a discourse, freighted with political contest and competing interests and desires. By examining the historical meaning inscribed in what can aptly be viewed as the ideology of *aru ga mama*, we can begin to free Shūsei's texts from the fixed category called *shizenshugi bungaku*, where they have remained canonized since the early decades of this century.

A central feature of *shizenshugi-shishōsetsu* literature, *aru ga mama* (sometimes *ari no mama*) shares with *shasei* (sketching from

3. In "Tokuda Shūsei and the Representation of Shomin Life" (Ph. D. diss., Yale University, 1989), Richard Torrance persuasively argues that Shūsei is miscast as a *shizenshugi* writer. His deviation is captured, in part, this way: "As the new literary language became more standardized, Shūsei rebelled by incorporating greater literary diversity into his narratives—onomatopoeia, slang, urban and rural dialects, and even items from the nonstandard pseudo-classical lexicon and grammar" (141).

4. See William F. Sibley, "Naturalism in Japanese Literature," *Harvard Journal of Asiatic Studies* 28 (1968): 166–68.

life, practiced by the poet Masaoka Shiki and members of his salon) the objective of "disinterested" depiction of life as it is with no accompanying commentary or value judgment. But we must dispute the implied promise in the contract between writer and reader of faithful and unadulterated transcription (never possible) in *aru ga mama* narration.[5] While it is beyond the scope of this study to pursue the question of why this movement has dominated the field called modern Japanese literature, we cannot avoid this fact as we examine the texts of one of its most celebrated practitioners. Consistent with a caution sounded at the beginning of this study, we shall not only avoid but actively discredit the recurring tendency among both Japanese and American critics either to consider *shizenshugi-shishōsetsu* as an imitation of European naturalist literature or to see it as a modern expression of enduringly Japanese literary sensibilities.

Our task is to see how Shūsei's texts have been made meaningful through their placement in the narrative practices that effect *aru ga mama*, which, in turn, empowers the discourse of *shizenshugi-shishōsetsu*. By examining how his narratives impart or eschew *aru ga mama*, we will see their relationship to (the sign of) everyday life (*shomin seikatsu*) as it is shaped and redefined by the city. In Shūsei's texts, *aru ga mama* comes together in a metaphor linking the city and the country, not merely as a way of domesticating[6] but of transforming the very terms by which the West and the modern would inform everyday Japanese life. In this extended interrogation of *aru ga mama*, the particular

5. Edward Fowler's study of the *shishōsetsu* is a sustained argument for the materiality of narrative practices, even in a form consistently viewed as transparently referential (the referent being the author's lived life). He notes that "originality never became the touchstone that it has been in western literature since the rise of the novel in the eighteenth century, because the writer saw his task as the faithful transcription of a reality there for all to see rather than the creation of one in need of illumination" (*Rhetoric of Confession*, xxvi). Fowler's discussion of the *shishōsetsu* in materialist terms goes far in opening up this category to question.

6. Paul Anderer argues that modern Japanese writers tended to avoid overt engagement with the upheavals wrought by the introduction of Western ideas, material goods, and ways of thinking. While it is true that texts, such as Kawabata's *Asakusa kurenaidan*, that obviously challenge this view are rare, Anderer misrecognizes the mediating strategies of texts (e.g., urban–rural tension, narrative experimentation, etc.) as retreats to safe, native practices. See his *Other Worlds*.

form that the attribution of "naturalism" to Shūsei's texts most insistently takes, we shall see the limitations of *shizenshugi* readings and then look briefly at Karatani Kōjin's study that sought to question the very status of naturalism by problematizing the *kindai shōsetsu* (which the discourse of naturalism has played a significant role in shaping).[7] In these readings of *Arajotai* (The New Household, 1908), *Kabi* (Mold, 1911), and *Arakure* (Reckless, 1915), I shall show how urban life signals a renewed emphasis on exteriority and how Shūsei's prose narrates Japan's transformation from a largely rural nation to an urban society through a vocabulary of facial expression (*warai, me, miru*). We shall also explore the way in which the city helps figurate Shūsei's works, noting particularly how he incorporates the signs of war with other countries in texts that seem narrowly focused on worldly events in distinctly local rather than global terms. Finally, *Arakure* will be shown to display the constraints of narrowly sanctioned *risshin shusse* and a female protagonist's production of difference to claim subjecthood amidst the regimentation and uniformity of war-driven, urbanizing Japan. Read together, these texts point to their own place in the larger narratives of production and consumption that shape "modern" Japanese society.

The imported term "naturalism" (*shizenshugi*) gained currency in Japan toward the end of the first decade of Meiji, when it emerged as the dominant topic of literary discussion among a fast-growing circle of literary critics. While the period of intense production of so-called naturalistic texts was between 1906 and 1911, the issues subsumed under the rubric remained central to literary debate for years to come. *Shizenshugi* is directly implicated in the construction of a discourse called *kindai bungaku*, not only as it exemplifies the relationship of the literary guild or *bundan* to literary expression but as itself the site of contest over the signs (many enumerated above) of modernity (*kindai*).

Shūsei participated in placing himself and his own texts in a

7. I have truncated my discussion of Karatani's text in view of the incisive and perceptive commentary on it by Brett de Bary, "Karatani Kōjin's *Origins of Modern Japanese Literature*," *The South Atlantic Quarterly* 87 (Summer 1988): 591–613.

narrative of modernity (expressed through such terms as *kindai bungaku, kindai-teki buntai,* and *kindai shōsetsu*) that authorizes literary naturalism. In a prefatory essay to *Arajotai,* about to be serialized in the newspaper *Kokumin shinbun,* Shūsei situated his own text between those written by "naturalist" writers and those following the dictates of *shasei* (sketching from life), admitting that *Arajotai* was closer to the latter.[8] His statement does not signify differences between naturalism and *shasei* (*shizenshugi* writers' affinity for *shasei* is illustrated in Tōson's eager adoption of "sketching from life" in *Chikumagawa no suketchi* and in *Hakai*) so much as an intention to proclaim a break from his close ties with the antiquarian work of Ozaki Kōyō (1867–1903), a key figure in the professionalization of writers in turn-of-the-century Japan and leader of the *Ken'yūsha* (Friends of the Inkstone). The critic Yoshida Seiichi, for example, has observed that Shūsei's idealism, which translated into an interest in politics and social problems, distinguished him from his fellow *Ken'yūsha* members whose concerns extended only to clothing, taste, and conduct in the pleasure quarters.[9]

That critics point to social conscience and awareness of class interest as a way of contrasting Shūsei with *Ken'yūsha* fiction suggests an aspect of Japanese naturalism that needs to be reemphasized: the interrogation of the subject and its place in society. According to Yoshida Seiichi, Shūsei was frustrated by existing social conditions that promised little hope for changing existing, essentially feudalistic, social arrangements or for promoting individuals' rights.[10] In a slightly more ambiguous ratification of Shūsei's interest in such issues, another critic, Wada Kingo, questions Shūsei's sympathies for the working class, arguing that his oeuvre has been misrepresented by the practice of critics focusing on his I-novelistic works, thereby preventing them from seeing that many of his longer nonautobiographical texts (Wada uses the words *kyakkan-teki buntai*—"objective texts") de-

8. From Noguchi Fujio, *Tokuda Shūsei no bungaku* (Chikuma shobō, 1980), 76.

9. Shūsei had joined the Kenyūsha in 1891, and while his prose was considered to be naturalistic, hence markedly different from the *gesaku*-like standard Kenyūsha fare, he remained faithful to his mentor Ozaki Kōyō until the latter's death in 1903. An account of Kōyō's death appears in *Kabi.*

10. Yoshida Seiichi, *Shizenshugi no kenkyū* (Tōkyōdō, 1955), 1: 430.

pict ex-samurai and middle-class characters instead of those from the lower classes. Wada admits that Shūsei's attitude toward bourgeois figures is generally critical; Shūsei, he says, remarked that "the niceties of bourgeois life cover up a person, obscuring his essence."[11] The view that Shūsei was a champion of the working class extends to critics who have interpreted his "detached, realistic" depiction of the underclass as an indicator of the author's sympathy. Interestingly, his son, Tokuda Kazuho, has questioned this perspective, stating that his father's feelings toward the daily life of the masses was marked by a strong ambivalence.[12]

It is not surprising that the protracted debate over Shūsei's disposition toward the working class frequently turns on the assessment of his writing as spare, detached, objective, and lacking in judgment or world view. They are linked in discussion, of course, because the laconic, apparently uneditorialized depiction of people leaves the critic/reader wondering just how to interpret his texts. The extent to which critics have been disconcerted by the apparent absence of subjective view attests to the strength of textual conventions revolving around agency. We might say that Shūsei's texts mark a moment in literary history wherein *narrative style has become the subject of the text.* Echoing Sōseki's lament over the absence of philosophy, Yoshida Seiichi presents the established view that Shūsei does not probe the complexity and depth of the pain accompanying self-awareness—an avoidance that the times demanded.[13] Similar assessments abound: The writer Morita Sōhei observed that *Kabi* (like many of Shūsei's texts) has no development or climax.[14] These and virtually every critic who has written on Shūsei's work have pointed to the absence of an organizational framework, narratorial comment, or some other material evidence of the writer's philosophical perspective. They are asking for what Hayden White has identified as being at the heart of

11. Wada Kingo, *Shizenshugi bungaku* (Shibundō, 1966), 289, 290, 292.

12. Tokuda Kazuo, *Tokuda Shūsei shū*, vol. 21 of *Nihon kindai bungaku taikei* (Kadokawa shoten, 1973), 28.

13. Yoshida Seiichi, *Shizenshugi no kenkyū*, 2: 227, 681.

14. Shinozaki Hideki, "Kabi no kōzu," in *Ronkō Tokuda Shūsei*, ed. Kōno Toshiro (Sakufūsha, 1982), 227. Yoshida Seiichi also claims that there is no climax or plot in Shūsei's prose. *Shizenshugi no kenkyū*, 2: 682.

historical narratives: "Demand for closure in the historical story is a demand . . . for moral meaning, a demand that sequences of real events be assessed as to their significance as elements of a moral drama. . . . We need to invest things with moral authority, and we narrativize to do this."[15] Recast in terms of White's depiction of the Western historical narrative (which takes its cue from Western literary textuality), Shūsei's texts would be closer to annal than to narrativized story.[16] According to White's typology of historical representation, "annalistic . . . accounts deal in *qualities* rather than agents, figuring forth a world in which things *happen* to people rather than one in which people do things."[17] The implicit message of Shūsei's annalistic style (and of other rhetorical strategies discussed below) is that what is being depicted is unadorned truth, which, as such, requires no commentary. In the context of post-Restoration letters, annalistic prose signaled "realism" as convincingly as narrativized story came to impart historical veracity in the context of European writing culture.

This juncture, where Western conventions of realism intersect Shūsei's "nonnarrative" prose, provides us with an opportunity to rethink the issue of the subject so central to Western realism and ostensibly "absent" or "new" to Japanese textual practices (according to deeply ingrained views that differentiate Japanese and Western society and narratives). Thorough transparency of language and of narrative technique underwrite the claims of *aru ga mama* narration, thereby giving center stage to the object of representation, the private subject. By examining how the *aru ga mama* effect is realized, we shall see that subjects do not simply mean individuated characters. Thus, the subject of Shūsei's prose is, at different points in the text, the reader, the new urban geography as it works in tandem with the country to narrate acting agents, or even the wars that seem almost ab-

15. White, "The Value of Narrativity in the Representation of Reality," 23.

16. From a similar perspective comes Masao Miyoshi's views, which cast considerable doubt on the practice of equating the *shōsetsu* with the Western realist novel. See Masao Miyoshi, "Against the Native Grain."

17. White, "The Value of Narrativity in the Representation of Reality," 10. See also his introduction in *Metahistory: The Historical Imagination in Nineteenth-Century Europe* (Baltimore: The Johns Hopkins University Press, 1973), 1–42.

sent in the way they have been domesticated into the fabric of daily life.

The narrativization of subjects is closely linked to the tension between urban growth and the countryside, rediscovered and invested with cultural fecundity in contrast to the culture of modernity associated with the city. It is a tension that Shūsei himself wore, not merely as a figure who came from the outlying regions to Tokyo (virtually every writer followed this path) but in his role as a writer both of so-called belles lettres (*jun bungaku*) and of popular narratives (*tsūzoku shōsetsu*), which had a mass audience not restricted to the educated classes in the cities. Even after *Arajotai* and *Kabi* secured his position as a writer of serious fiction, Shūsei continued to write in women's magazines, children's periodicals, tabloids, and newspapers for audiences that did not exist just a decade or two earlier. Shūsei, then, seems precariously caught between the role of the Edo style (*gesaku*) writer methodically churning out popular works for the consumption of a growing literate population and the Meiji writer cum intellectual, whose pedigree and education helped impart seriousness and honor to the avocation of fiction writing. Shūsei's oeuvre (his serious texts, which fall under the rubric of *shizenshugi* literature) is empowered by the ambiguous signs of seriousness and *shomin seikatsu* (everyday life of the common people). His texts signify contemporaneity by projecting a sense of homology between *what* it depicts (the here and now) and *how* it depicts (as if unmediated). Appropriating the landscape of urbanization that belongs to the common man and woman, and narrating texts that signify an absence of agency directed from above, Shūsei creates subjects that are given meaning in a social network and that owe their existence to the city.

FŪKEI AND THE CRITIQUE OF *SHIZENSHUGI*

Our examination of the relationship between the subject and urban life requires the mediation of Karatani's discussion of *fūkei* (landscape).[18] Aimed at destabilizing the accepted views of

18. Here I have truncated my dissertation's ("The Subject in Meiji Prose Narratives," University of Chicago, 1986) more extended look at Karatani's *Nihon kindai bungaku no kigen*. For an incisive and perceptive discussion of *Kigen*, see Brett de Bary, "Karatani Kōjin's *Origins of Modern Japanese Literature*."

modern Japanese literature, Karatani's study enlists the insights of recent Western (mostly French) critical theories to reveal the familiar shibboleths of Western mimeticism—the conception of prose narrative as individual-centered, a view of language and literature as representational, and the position that modern Japanese narrative is derivative (of the West)—that authorize and create the discourse of modern Japanese literature. To his credit, Karatani makes explicit the politics involved in his choice of *fūkei* (landscape) as both method of critique and as a term denoting an epistemological shift in the relationship between subject and environment. As de Bary astutely notes in her essay on Karatani's *Kigen*, his use of *fūkei* "acts to foil those who would read the book as another application of Western methodologies to the Japanese case, or to see in it the subjugation of 'Japan' to the hegemony of a new, postmodern Western discourse."[19] Karatani treads on sensitive ground, however, when he invokes the notion of *fūkei*, for it cannot help but recall associations with the discourse of Japanese cultural essentialism.[20] Due credit must be given, however, for Karatani's use of *fūkei* serves as a provisional move to contest the realist conventions of Western textuality that have served to install Japanese naturalism at the center of the *kindai shōsetsu*. (As a means of subverting the Western realist conventions that underwrite views of the *kindai shōsetsu*, Karatani turns to the material properties of language itself, particularly in his discussion of *genbun'itchi*.) What I am questioning in this admittedly rich conception is a too rigid association of *fūkei* with nature and, by implication, with the "premodern." A more open and historicist sense of *fūkei*, for example, would have prompted Karatani to consider socially created phenomena, particularly the city, as *fūkei*. *Fūkei* is not simply landscape that through its ability to defamiliarize passively permits a similar discovery of human beings. As we shall see later in this section, the city in Shūsei's texts (especially in its relationship to the countryside) is an enabling condition serving to narrativize subjects.

Karatani's discussion is also important for what it implies but

19. de Bary, "Karatani Kōjin's *Origins of Modern Japanese Literature*," 602.
20. Watsuji's essay on climate ("Fudō," 1935, wherein climate produces a distinctively Japanese landscape and society) stands out in this regard, though the literature on *fūkei* over the years has been vast.

does not articulate: To use de Bary's words, Karatani uses *fūkei* "to challenge and invalidate the epistemological foundations of modern positivist history."[21] It may be "curiously, abstractly pastoral," a strategy of which Karatani undoubtedly is aware, employing it for its egalitarian, horizontal sensibility. But, when we apply it to texts such as Shūsei's, we can see the sense of difference that marks not only his work but his moment in history. There is present in his texts a newly emerging sense of utility and contemporaneity that depends upon a sense of radical difference from the past.[22] Much of this is due to the specific rhetorical devices employed in his texts, but it must be remembered that such presentness depends upon a sense of profound difference from the past. In Shūsei's texts this sense of radical difference takes the form of contentiousness that divides city from country. This difference is captured in terms of shifting figures: from a society in which cultural continuity and sameness come from a sense of temporal connection (distance too is marked by this linearity of relationship) to a culture that increasingly rewrites itself in the space of the moment, in which changes seem frequent and unremitting, and in which the changes themselves seem to stand for developments that defy explanation according to linear or developmental causality. In short, the very landscape of everyday life in urban areas results in change that leaves little or no trace either of the geography or the history that once was.

Shūsei's texts represent sites wherein *fūkei* is transformed into the confluence of everyday life. If place, as symbolized in the role given to *meisho* (famous place), always tied history to itself, in Shūsei's texts the narrative of everyday life no longer insists on such a connection. Eschewing links to a past that confers culturally shared meanings on place, the city finds validation in the functional anonymity and replaceability of its parts. Put differently, city life is meaningful in its spatiality, where everyday life is constructed by movement and location; the urban geography of twentieth-century Japan begins to valorize daily life

21. de Bary, "Karatani Kōjin's *Origins of Modern Japanese Literature*," 598.
22. Noguchi Takehiko ("'Eibin naru byōsha' no bunpō," 198) states summarily that modern Japanese literature is distinguished from earlier literature by its location in the present.

empowered not by a sense of continuity with earlier times but by a newly constructed emphasis on the present. In Shūsei's prose, place (the city, either alone or in relation to the countryside, as there was no "countryside" until the development of urban areas) functions not as some location celebrated by its association with a person or event from the distant past but as the faceless reality of now. Place becomes one of many elements in the constellation of signs (the city) that, in relation to other signs brought together by the phenomenon of urbanization, engender the construction of new meanings. Much as Bakhtin's conception of the novel as dialogic represents the production of a new space in which hitherto unrelated genres, narrative practices, and voices could interact, the sense of place given shape in Shūsei's work reveals the dialogics of modern Japanese society.

It was common practice for government ideologues in post-Restoration Japan to invoke a sense of cultural continuity and identity located in a common past in order to promote national consolidation. Whether it was an energy subsumed under the rubric of Western, by the Taishō period *modān* (modern), or literary movements such as *shizenshugi*, what was deeply disquieting to the authorities was the creation of culture as lived and created in the present moment. In short, such a way of conceptualizing a sense of existence represented a shift in agency from one that could be claimed by the state (linear narratives of legitimation that invoked, for example, the imperial line) to one that dispersed agency to uncontainable and ongoing enunciative moments.[23]

In line with the readings of other texts in this study, I am interested in examining how narratives construct subjects. With Shūsei's texts, we must account for the repeated representation of his prose as "naturalist"; the way out of the endlessly repeated affirmation of *shizenshugi* comes from reading his narratives as intertexts of an urbanizing Japan. In *Arajotai*, *Kabi*, and *Arakure*, the city participates in the figuration of subjects. As they inform Shūsei's prose, subjects are not confined to the borders of the

23. Tokugawa period fiction, *gesaku*, can be identified as a literature representing a similar shift from "temporal to spatial" textuality.

text. My readings must also attend to a critical condition of textual production: the environment of reading in early twentieth-century Japanese society. Whether one examines Shūsei's popular texts written for quick, mass consumption by women and younger readers or his "serious" naturalistic works, it is important to consider how Shūsei's works belong to the new urban terrain: foremost as texts to be *consumed* by readers. The Japanese critical practice of distinguishing *jun bungaku* and *tsūzoku shōsetsu* (popular narratives) mirrors my separation of productive from consumed literature. The "objectification" of all things and people through the gaze of *aru ga mama* reveals Shūsei's texts as those that defy easy division into these categories. Other texts written during the early decades of the twentieth century also are part of a rise in literacy that parallels the acceleration of urbanization, but Shūsei's texts address the new reader, a generation of literate people who, unlike earlier readers, did not come from socially and economically privileged families.[24] If earlier Meiji period texts tended to restrict their subjects to students and intellectuals, Shūsei's texts increasingly focused on the working class. Finally, we shall see how it is from an urban geography of textual production that Shūsei narrativizes women, whose subjectivity is accordingly derived from arrangements that may have been every bit as oppressive as in earlier times but, nonetheless, notably different.

As products of a rapidly urbanizing industrial nation, post-Restoration prose narratives would reflect the transformation of a largely rural landscape into a nation reshaped by the contours of city life. This "Westernized" prose might properly be called the second wave of urban literature, for Tokugawa literature was nothing if not a narrative of urban commercial society that catered to a citified audience interested in the urban pleasure quarters. The differences that distinguish these Tokugawa-era texts from later "*shizenshugi* literature" are many, but what concerns

24. See Maeda Ai, *Kindai dokusha no seiritsu*, vol. 2 of *Maeda Ai chosaku shū* (Chikuma shobō, 1989), particularly "Meiji shonen no dokushazō," "On-doku kara kun-doku e: kindai dokusha no seiritsu," and "Taishō goki tsūzoku shōsetsu no tenkai: fujin zasshi no dokusha sō."

me here is the way in which the latter express their location in the urban. "Modern" Japanese texts are marked by their status as signs of changing demographics that make *jōkyō* (migration to Tokyo) a significant social phenomenon in the decades following the Restoration. Accordingly, these prose narratives installed their subjects on the boundaries of a new urban horizon. Stated another way, the "new narratives" (texts shaped in large measure from the currents of Western prosefication that took hold in the decades following the Restoration) took as their major topic of concern the problematization of the subject in specific (private) terms. (The discussion to follow will distinguish the passive subjects of the voyeur-readers' gaze in *gesaku* from the narrated subjects who claim agency in Shūsei's texts.)

As members of an ongoing wave of relocation to the city, writers often encountered urbanity in its myriad manifestations through the gaze of unfamiliarity. The city was many different things to different writers; the intersection of the city as a phenomenon of modern society and textual expression has spawned in recent years a copious outpouring of critical texts that attend to a dizzying range of uses put to the city as it informs readings of literary texts.[25] In the present essay the linkage of city and country is taken to be both a mark of the historical moment inscribed within Shūsei's texts and a strategy of figuration frequently used by Shūsei; I have employed it as a means of contesting *shizenshugi* readings of Shūsei.

Paul Anderer's eloquent examination of Arishima Takeo's writing remains one of the few American texts discussing Japanese literature in these terms. He articulates the purpose of his monograph thusly:

> Arishima sought to rival the prevailingly grounded, place-haunted nature of Japanese fiction, and to do this by upsetting the most basic expectation of a Japanese story: that it will take place in a known and familiar place. . . . The Japanese fictional landscapes which recur in serious literature . . . have common features: they are par-

25. Maeda Ai's work on the semiotics of the city remain the standard in these texts. See, for example, *Toshi kūkan no naka no bungaku* (Chikuma shobō, 1982). Other prominent books include Isoda Kōichi's *Shisō to shite no Tōkyō* (Kokubunsha, 1978), and Okuno Takeo, *Bungaku no genfūkei* (Shūeisha, 1972).

> ticular rural villages or urban neighborhoods or temple grounds—Ashiya, Asakusa, Kiyomizu . . . place names often previously celebrated in Japanese poetry and prose, and which we recognize as semimetaphorical presences within a culturally domesticated homeland.[26]

Anderer's argument cogently captures the proclivity of post-Restoration texts to figurate place in familiar terms, but one cannot link the uses of place with some tradition presumably reaching back in excess of a thousand years. The uses of space in the decades before and after the turn of the century mirror the effects of a society shaken not only by the introduction of Western goods and ideas but by the quickening pace of change. In Anderer's view the inward turn taken by many Japanese writers in the "modern" period displays a fear of engagement with the upheavals that characterized Japan in the grips of accelerated modernization. His observation resonates with the commonplace assessment directed at "naturalists," which has it that they could not feel comfortable in urban life.[27] What Anderer claims was an avoidance of direct engagement with these changes, especially as they rewrite the urban landscape of Tokyo, in my view was in fact a displacement of such confrontation. The ubiquitous appearance of the urban, or of urban–rural tensions, represents a form of mediation enabling writers to come to terms with the radical changes that shape post-Restoration Japan.

The texts of Tokuda Shūsei provide the grounds for contesting the mutually empowering relationship between *shizenshugi* and its practitioners such as Shūsei. It is useful to dismantle this relationship by defamiliarizing the very sign of the "city" that has been an unmistakable, if somewhat marginalized, constituent of Japanese naturalism. Anderer has appropriated the conception of space from Japanese criticism, but he has reified

26. Anderer, *Other Worlds*, 6, 9.

27. See, for example, Arima Tatsuo, *The Failure of Freedom: A Portrait of Modern Japanese Intellectuals* (Cambridge, Mass.: Harvard University Press, 1969), 89. My critical perspective shares rather more with William Sibley, particularly as he takes Arima to task for the deterministic defeatism attributed to so-called naturalist writers. See Sibley, Review of *The Failure of Freedom*, by Tatsuo Arima. *Harvard Journal of Asiatic Studies* 31 (1971): 247–85.

and essentialized the term, forgetting that the city, or its myriad manifestations (urban–rural tension, for example), are thoroughly historicist notions. Recast in the vocabulary of Shūsei criticism, urbanizing Japan gives rise to a catchword designating the spare transcriptive writing attributed to *shizenshugi* writers, particularly to Shūsei. This catchword, which I have called the ideology of *aru ga mama*, symbolizes the objectification of things, events, and people in a narrative practice that unmistakably signals the urban condition. It is in this light that we will read some texts of Tokuda Shūsei, placing him back into the urban–rural landscape from whence he had been wrested by the dehistoricizing rubric of *shizenshugi*.

ARAJOTAI AND *KABI*

In a writing career that spanned fifty years, Tokuda Shūsei wrote fiction as though driven by the same unrelenting rhythm of labor that dictated the lives of the working class about whom he wrote. His texts found their way to newspapers in Hokkaido, Kanazawa (his hometown), and other out-of-the-way regions. An accurate count of his output is not possible, but in 1908 and 1909 alone, during the height of his productivity as an established writer, he produced twenty-nine short stories (*tanpen shōsetsu*) and thirty-eight long prose narratives (*chūhen* and *chōhen shōsetsu*).[28] According to standard literary histories, while Shūsei was well known for his serialized dramas, popular narratives, and translations of Western novels, it was *Arajotai* (New Household, 1908) that signaled his elevation to the rank of serious (naturalist) writer. He himself acknowledged that this piece was written under conditions that allowed him to disregard the usual necessity of stringing along a daily newspaper serial readership.[29] But if critical acclaim greeted *Arajotai*, it was not until *Kabi* (Mold, 1911) began its serial run in the *Asahi shinbun* that Shūsei was recognized as a first-rate writer. In the eyes of most critics, *Kabi* elevated him from a mere producer of popular fic-

28. Tokuda Kazuo, ed., *Tokuda Shūsei shū*, vol. 21 of *Nihon kindai bungaku taikei*, 19.

29. Yoshida Seiichi, *Shizenshugi no kenkyū*, 2: 225. *Arajotai* first appeared in *Kokumin shinbun*.

tion (*tsūzoku shōsetsu*) to the ranks of serious writers such as Tayama Katai and Shimazaki Tōson. While not considered an outright example of popular literature, *Arajotai* still seemed to retain the traces of such writing in the eyes of many critics, and accordingly it has received the subtly dismissive trait of a *sesō shōsetsu*, a period piece. By way of contrast, *Kabi* has been hailed by Japanese critics as a landmark naturalistic text because the characters and events were drawn directly from the author's own life, feelings and events were depicted with detachment and objectivity, and Shūsei avoided traces of sentimentality and narratorial intrusion.

Placed in the discourse of *shizenshugi*, *Arajotai* and *Kabi* stand in developmental relationship to one another, the former depicted as a major step on the way to *Kabi*, which itself has been canonized as the quintessential naturalist text. The reason underlying their inclusion in this study is rather different: Both texts contribute to the construction (a "joint" effort involving the texts in question, literary criticism regarding these texts, the *bundan*, etc.) of a narrative effect designated by the phrase *aru ga mama*. My intention is to discuss these texts in a way that allows us to critique rather than to affirm *shizenshugi* as a fixed unity. In its time, Japanese naturalism was defined by its concern with individuated subjectivity. The commonly employed terms of discussion include natural drive and desire, sexuality, and instinct—those notions that point to a perceiving, sensate subject. Unfortunately, discussions built around such considerations tend to promote an essentialist view of the subject, suppressing the very narrated (constructed) nature of subjectivity. Attention to the rhetorical strategies of *Arajotai* and *Kabi* can help restore that which has been occluded by the installation of the subject as a given.

Among the several rhetorical features common to these two texts and deserving attention, two claim sustained scrutiny here: strategies contributing to the *aru ga mama* effect and the ubiquity of visual markers. Many of the devices used to convey a sense of *aru ga mama* (which is unfailingly associated with Shūsei's work) have been attributed to the demands arising from his working conditions; for example, the use of proleptic sentences (which Gerard Genette defines as "any narrative maneuver that consists of narrating or evolving in advance an event that will take place later")[30] often has been linked to serialization. By examining what has been discursively created as a narrative of *aru ga mama*, we should be able to understand how and what *aru ga mama* signifies in Shūsei's texts and, further, how it contributes to texts that are shaped by the conditions of city life (under capitalism).[31]

As a prelude to our examination of *Arajotai* and *Kabi* together, these untranslated texts deserve brief synopses. *Arajotai* depicts the early years of a newly wedded couple, Shinkichi, a liquor store owner, and his passive and timid wife, Osaku, who live in Arakawa—what was then a faceless, developing new town on the outskirts of Tokyo. Ambitious, hardworking, and anxious to see his business succeed, Shinkichi is eager to find a woman who can help with the day-to-day operation of his shop. Through the help of a go-between he marries Osaku, a gentle and amiable young woman who turns out to be slow-paced and too inept to help with running the store. Shinkichi's diligence is set in relief by another couple, Ono, his smartly dressed hustler friend who ends up in jail, and his free-spirited common law wife, Okuni, who gravitates to Shinkichi's home during Osaku's temporary absence as she visits her mother during her ill-fated pregnancy. At the tale's end, Okuni moves away, Osaku returns to Shinkichi, and the two resume their uneasy life together.

The absence of surnames (except for Ono) suggests the commonplace status given to this couple and the anonymity of their day-to-day life in the city. It also draws attention to the absence of filial ties for this small-time shopkeeper toiling away in the working-class exurbs of Tokyo. Shinkichi is driven by the fear that only hard work, attention to details, frugality, and relentless drive, those qualities prized by the working merchant class, separate him from the likes of Ono, Okuni, Osaku, and her family.

30. Gerard Genette, *Narrative Discourse: An Essay in Method*, trans. Jane Lewin (Ithaca: Cornell University Press, 1980), 40.

31. The post-Restoration serialized prose narrative fits the description of commodity consumption as observed by Terry Lovell: "Capitalist commodity consumption requires the controlled release of pleasures that may be channelled through the purchase of commodities" (*Consuming Fiction* [London: Verso, 1987], 10).

As if to parody the rise-to-success *risshin shusse* tales that were quite popular throughout the middle decades of Meiji, *Arajotai* was written to narrativize concurrent paths taken by those who came to inhabit the city in pursuit of a livelihood. Thus, it charts the rise of a man with modest but nonetheless clear ambitions through a narrative that seems to move serendipitously, subverting any representation of a developmental trajectory of uncomplicated success. *Arajotai* instead chronicles the constraints that guide the lives of a small-time merchant and his wife, around whom hover his petty bourgeois friend who gets caught in shady business deals and a woman who slides informally from one man to another. Only a hard-nosed orderliness, thrift, diligence, and attentiveness to detail can spell survival for a small shopkeeper like Shinkichi. At the most overt level, *Arajotai* is structured around the conflict of petty bourgeois values and a less ordered life of serendipity. It, along with many of Shūsei's other texts, occupies that contradiction between capitalist consumption and capitalist production that marked turn-of-the-century Japan. Shinkichi embodies the productive imperatives of such a society, one that at the same time required those very same producers to suspend the virtues of diligence, thrift, and economy and consume those things that have been so efficiently produced.

Published three years after *Arajotai*, the second text discussed in this section is the highly acclaimed *Kabi*, commonly placed in a trajectory leading to the Taishō *shishōsetsu*. One of the *shishōsetsu*'s central characteristics is illustrated in a criticism leveled by the novelist Mizuno Yoshū at the time of *Kabi*'s serialization that "the characters were not drawn with sufficient clarity and the novel seems to have been written for readers who were already familiar with the persons described."[32] The remark prefigures the standard view that *shishōsetsu* writers wrote with fellow *bundan* members in mind as their audience. *Kabi* captures the enervating social reality that oppressively dogs the lives of people who, in quiet desperation, negotiate their way along the fringes of society. Its title captures the nameless fears that hang over a strained relationship that weathers a near-fatal illness of

32. Keene, *Dawn to the West*, 275.

a first-born son and the death of the protagonist Sasamura's mentor. The narrative begins with a writer, Sasamura, setting up house in Tokyo following an extended journey to western Japan. An old housekeeper-maid helps with the chores, but family illness takes her away to the countryside for a while; her daughter Ogin, who from time to time had already been helping her mother, moves in during her absence. When Ogin's mother returns, Sasamura and Ogin are living together as a couple. Nowhere is there much evidence of passion or even willfulness in this relationship as the two just seem to fall into this arrangement, and registration of Ogin as his wife is somehow left until the time when they register the birth of their child.[33] Life together is tense and difficult, Sasamura feeling resentful, as if he had been tricked into marriage. Soon after the birth of a daughter, he sets out on another journey. The narrative returns to Tokyo, and the couple continue their tension-ridden life together.

ARU GA MAMA AND PROLEPSIS

Earlier I mentioned the well-known connection between the *shishōsetsu* and the *bundan*. Directly attributed to this connection is the treatment of characters as if they were already known to the reader; thus, often there is little clarifying description or placement of characters. The trait cannot be thought as strictly or merely an expression of such relationship; for example, consider the fact that texts like *Kabi* and *Arajotai* appeared in mass circulation newspapers. Let us look more closely at the *aru ga mama* effects, to which belong such practices as treating characters as if prior reference to them had been made or information about them was already known.

Assumed familiarity with characters in a text was noted above as one of the distinguishing marks of the *shishōsetsu*. Noguchi Takehiko gives a compelling text-based "explanation" for the presumed familiarity that graces the pages of Shūsei's texts. He

33. That it was rather common to delay marriage registration until after the birth of a child perhaps attests to the importance of bearing progeny in Japanese society at the time. I am indebted to Miriam Silverberg for this information.

points to the first sentence of *Arajotai*: "Shinkichi ga Osaku o mukaeta no wa Shinkichi ga nijūgo, Osaku ga hatachi no toki, ima kara chōdo yonen mae no fuyu de atta" (It was exactly four winters ago, when Shinkichi was twenty-five and Osaku twenty, that the two were married). Instead of writing *Shinkichi to yū otoko ga*, Shūsei writes *Shinkichi ga*. Noguchi notes that this style, which abruptly introduces an unmodified proper noun, suggests prior appearance or reference, as if the character is already known to the reader. He also points to the following use of *sono* to illustrate Shūsei's assumption of prior familiarity: "Saisho ni okareta Shitaya no ie kara, Omasa ga Kōjimachi no hō e utsutta no wa *sono* toshi no aki no koro de atta" (emphasis added; It was around fall of *that* year when Omasa moved from her first job as a maid in Shitaya to Kōjimachi). Such treatment of characters and moments as already familiar, Noguchi contends, denotes a text that permits the reader to stand in an unmediated relationship to the (world of the) text—a situation that distinguishes the *kindai shōsetsu* from earlier Japanese prose narrative forms.[34]

Noguchi's conclusion is open to question, but I wish to acknowledge the value of his critical perspective, one that avoids the tautology involving *shizenshugi* and writers designated by that rubric. Although he rightly points to the absence of an introductory marker such as *to yū otoko*, he misses the fact that prolepsis itself also signifies prior familiarity. *Arajotai*'s opening is marked by the hallmark of Shūsei's writing: a statement made in a point in time to which the tale will eventually catch up.

> Shinkichi ga Osaku o mukaeta no wa Shinkichi ga nijūgo, Osaku ga hatachi no toki, ima kara chōdo yonen mae no fuyu de atta. Jūyon no toki gosho no rishiden ya nanika de, shōnen no kabin na atama o shigeki sare, Tōkyō e tobidashite kara jūichinen. Arakawa no sake tonya de, wakime mo furazu mechakucha ni hataraita. (93)[35]

34. Noguchi, "'Eibin naru byōsha' no bunpō," 197–98. See also Walter Ong's discussion of familiarity as a fictional technique in "The Writer's Audience Is Always a Fiction," *PMLA* 90 (January 1975): 9–20. I was alerted to this work by Fowler, *The Rhetoric of Confession*, 67–68.

35. All quotations are from *Shūsei zenshū* (Hibonkaku, 1937).

> It was exactly four winters ago, when Shinkichi was twenty-five and Osaku twenty, that the two were married. Eleven years had passed since, at the impressionable age of fourteen, he had been inspired by reading success stories of successful businessmen and had come out to Tokyo, where he threw himself into his work in a wholesale liquor store in Arakawa.

The baseline is "today" (*ima*), which is four years after Shinkichi and Osaku are married; much of the text will be devoted to recounting the events that lead up to this point. The second sentence, which refers back even further (fifteen years before "today"), is not proleptic, for the narrative returns not to the time when Shinkichi was fourteen but just before the moment when the two are married. Interestingly, reading the text to its conclusion, we discover that the narrated tale will only "catch up" about one fourth the way to the *ima* of this opening sentence, ending about a year or so after the two are married. A line at the very end of the tale adds two more years, bringing us to the *ima* of the first sentence: "At the end of fall when the sign celebrating the three-year anniversary of the liquor store opening was hoisted up, Osaku was again with child."

Consider the use of prolepsis in the following passage, which captures the aftermath of the celebration of Osaku's marriage to Shinkichi.

> Ono ga sukoshi tabeyotte kuda o maita kuraide, kuji sugi ni ichido buji ni hiki ageta. Oba to aniki to wa, gotagota no naka de, nagattarashiku aisatsu shite ita ga, deru toki aniki no ashi wa furatsuite ita. Shinkichi gawa no yūjin wa, hitoshikiri nominaoshite kara itoma o tsugeta.
>
> "Aa, hito no konrei de aa sawagu yatsu no ki ga shire nee," to iu yō ni, Shinkichi wa yoi no hiita aoi kao o shite *guttari* to toko ni tsuita.
>
> Ashita me o samasu to, Osaku wa mō okite ita.
>
> (14)

> With no greater mishap than Ono's long-winded prattle, everyone left by a little after nine. Through the din of departure, Osaku's aunt and older brother were overly polite in their farewells; as he left the house, the older brother was unsteady on his feet. After another round of drinking, Shinkichi's close friend made his exit.
>
> As if saying "ah, I can't imagine why someone would go on like

> that at someone else's wedding," Shinkichi plopped on the bedding, the flush of intoxication gone from his face.
>
> Tomorrow when he woke up, Osaku was already up.

The first sentence telling the reader that everyone departed around nine o'clock is a short prolepsis, though we do not realize it until we read the following sentence, which takes us back in time just a few minutes to when the guests had not yet left. The next time shift is equally abrupt, marked by the quotative "Aa, hito no konrei . . ." that shades into represented thought (strictly speaking, it does not have the certainty of represented thought, for it only interprets the look on Shinkichi's face). With this sentence, the narrative has passed the nine o'clock moment of the opening sentence to later in the night. The montage-like abruptness of the temporal juxtapositions takes a different turn in the last sentence of the section, which seems to reflect a shift from the night of the wedding to the next morning through a curiously ungrammatical construction (not uncommon in Japanese): Instead of using a word like *akuruhi* (or some equivalent of the next day or morning), the sentence begins with the Chinese compound *myōcho* or *myōasa*, to which Shūsei appends the *furigana* reading *ashita*, literally "tomorrow." As the literal translation I have provided indicates, the awkward sentence contains two temporal perspectives—the night of the celebration (seen from a moment that would make one say *ashita*) and the following day (*mō okite ita*).

Similar temporal disjunction linked to prolepsis marks the second *shōsetsu*, *Kabi*, which provides a window on four years in the life of a writer named Sasamura and his wife, Ogin.[36] The text begins with a laconic proleptic summation so characteristic of Shūsei's texts.

> Sasamura ga tsuma no nyūseki o sumashita no wa, futari no naka ni umareta yōji no shussan todoke to, kiwadoku onaji kurai de atta. (257)

36. Shūsei's own assertion that, despite its appearance, *Kabi* is more a product of literary imagination than faithful depiction of his own life has not kept it from being endlessly discussed as a close account of the author's own life.

> Ogin was officially registered as Sasamura's legal wife just barely before the registration of their child's birth.

The ensuing narration returns to a point several years earlier when Sasamura has just returned from a trip to western Japan to resettle in Tokyo. It is not until chapter 35 (out of seventy-nine chapters) that the chronology catches up to the time indicated by the opening sentence (registering as a couple). *Kabi* is textured by proleptic temporal dislocations and by the juxtaposition of dialogue and narrative woven between and through these temporal skips. In the following scene from the opening section, Sasamura still lives with an old maidservant (Ogin's mother) who, on short notice, has to return to her native province to care for an ailing relative.

> "I can have my daughter come help out while I'm gone, but I don't know how useful she will be, since she's just a youngster. But as long as you don't mind, since she's just staying with some relatives of mine, doing nothing. . . ." These days, Ogin would show up from time to time in the evening, wearing flashy *yukata* and thick makeup, about which Sasamura had feigned indifference.
>
> "Something has to be done about her appearance. Speak to her about it. The neighbors are going to start talking." Sasamura had discreetly told Miyama about this. Yet, he was not entirely unhappy about her occasional visits to lend a hand around the house. Since Ogin had started to come by, he no longer had to go into the kitchen to pick out his fish, and his meals had shown more variety. He was served fresh pickled vegetables that were new to him, and quite elaborate stews. For Sasamura, who for some time had lived a colorless life, such meals had become the highlight of his day.
>
> "Then I will leave my daughter to help out, . . ." she said, in a way that suggested that she felt it would be quite safe to leave her in the care of this brooding, quiet man.
>
> (266)

The striations of direct discourse, a general statement describing Sasamura's awareness of Ogin, a direct discourse response to the first quotation, and a brief account of Ogin's effect on Sasamura are tightly compressed, requiring close attention to the quickly shifting time periods within which the words belong. Time is not presented in a linear sequence: The words of Ogin's mother are followed by what Genette calls an iterative narrative ("These days. . . ."), an utterance that "takes upon itself several occurrences together of the same event (in other words, once again, several events considered only in terms of their analogy)."[37] The quotation that follows ("Something has to be done. . . .") goes back to a time prior to the words of Ogin's mother, when Sasamura was complaining to a friend about Ogin's appearance. The last sentence of the passage returns to the same moment as that of the opening quotation.

One way to explain such temporal disorganization might be by suggesting that it expresses a specific point of view—in this case, that of Sasamura. The peripatetic movements from direct dialogue uttered at different times to events remembered and so on are not entirely chaotic; rather, they trace the associations that arise in Sasamura's mind. Thus, what might be seen as a device contributing to *aru ga mama* also serves to create a perceiving subject. Another interpretation traces the contours of the text itself. Prolepsis and montage-like time shifts that together thematize the inexorable movement toward the birth of Sasamura's child mentioned in the opening sentence figurate a provisional "destination" for the narrative. As I have stated earlier, prolepsis signals interest not so much in what happens as in how things happen. Once the "destination" (birth of Sasamura's son) has been given, the reader is confronted with a highly disjunctive and meandering narrative that covers much ground before reaching the time and place designated by the proleptic sentence.

If Shūsei's characters wander about, so does the narrative move peripatetically from one time to another. Shūsei's narration signals apparent unconcern with both time and place. With what seems like little forethought, Sasamura will move repeatedly in the course of the story. Chapter 2 begins with the protagonist moving into a newly built rental house in a new town on the outskirts of Tokyo. In the following scene Sasamura settles in with his housekeeper, an old woman introduced by the aunt of a friend.

37. Genette, *Narrative Discourse*, 116.

> Banmeshi ni wa, aomame nado no nitano ga, donburi ni morarete chabudai no ue ni okare, kichōmen ni sōji sareta ranpu no akari mo, fudan yori akarui yō ni omowareta.
>
> Koko ni netomari o shite ita tomodachi to, Sasamura wa botsubotsu hanashi o shinagara, hashi o totte ita.
>
> (260)
>
> For dinner there were cooked beans heaped on a large bowl atop a small dining table, and a lamp that had been fastidiously cleaned seemed to emit a brighter light than usual.
>
> With chopsticks in hand, Sasamura was leisurely talking with a friend who had been sleeping over for some time.

Only incidentally do we discover that this friend has been living with Sasamura since he has moved into his new quarters, but the matter-of-fact narration suggests that this is hardly worth noting. This sort of abrupt revelation is often set up by being preceded by something that is not related in any causal, developmental manner that would point the way to the revelation. A few lines following the quoted section, chapter 3 begins with this line:

> Sasamura no oi ga hitori, inaka kara dete kita koro ni wa uchi ga semai no de, issho ni ita Miyama to iu yūjin wa onaji Nagaya no betsu no uchi ni sumu koto ni natta.
>
> (261)
>
> When Sasamura's nephew had left his home in the countryside to come live with him, his close friend Miyama decided to move to a different unit in the same tenement house because the house was small.

From here, the passage proceeds to outline the circumstances that had brought Miyama to Sasamura's house and how they had lived under the same roof for some time. The information that Miyama has lived with Sasamura was first introduced in the sentence that shows chopsticks in Sasamura's hands. Here, prolepsis is used to signify nonchalance, or *aru ga mama.*

Through a deterministic foretelling by prolepsis, the focus of readerly interest shifts from what happens to how things happen. Such a shift has the effect of putting what happened beyond uncertainty or questioning in a narrative that seems to say "such and such happened—let's now get to how things came about." Genette points to another consequence of prolepsis, a consequence that also contributes to *aru ga mama*: "Anticipation, or temporal prolepsis, is . . . much less frequent than the inverse figure, at least in the Western narrative tradition. . . . The first-person narrative lends itself better than any other to anticipation, by the very fact of its avowedly retrospective character."[38]

Japanese critics have explained Shūsei's use of prolepsis in many ways. The Shūsei scholar Noguchi Fujio argues that such "inverted narration" is used to give depth to descriptions of daily life, and the resulting constant back and forth between past and present is realistic, approximating the jerkiness of life itself, which never feels chronologically straightforward.[39] The backtracking, reminiscence, and sudden chronological twists that characterize Shūsei's narrative give his texts a fullness, says Yoshida Seiichi.[40] A similar point is raised by Shinoda Kōichirō, who claims that prolepsis was employed to avoid the simple, predictable movement of events from one season to the next.[41] Wada Kingo explains it differently: Such temporal complexity, he maintains, is characteristic of popular fiction (*tsūzoku shōsetsu*), a genre in which Shūsei wrote extensively.[42] More recently, Takahashi Toshio has argued that the complex narration constitutes implicit social criticism.[43]

The relationship of prolepsis to *aru ga mama* requires further comment. The effect of reality sought by *aru ga mama*—a sense of the preordained, what Todorov referred to as predestination—conveys the torpor and sameness that stamp everyday life. Reinforcing the sense of unchangeable rhythms of daily life, Shūsei's sentences foreclose the unexpected, the changes, and the different possibilities that might otherwise await the reader. Such prolepsis also enacts recollection or reminiscence; the proleptic statement having been made at point B, the narrative

38. Genette, *Narrative Discourse*, 67.
39. Noguchi Fujio, *Tokuda Shūsei no bungaku*, 19.
40. Yoshida Seiichi, *Shizenshugi*, 2: 232.
41. Shinoda Kōichirō, *Hihyō no kigōgaku* (Miraisha, 1979), 194.
42. Wada, *Shizenshugi bungaku*, 288.
43. Takahashi Toshio, "*Arajotai* o yomu: 'risshi' gensō no yukue," in *Ronkō Tokuda Shūsei*, 7–34.

shifts to an earlier time (point A). A certitude about the events is suggested by such a perspective, unlike narratives that are located in the present and move toward later events along with the reader, who knows only what has transpired up to the point of the narrated present. But, more important, in Shūsei's texts, prolepsis mirrors the clutter of city life. Many more sentences, pages, or chapters with varied little encounters, routines, and nonevents that will occur along the way will intervene before the narrative catches up to the moment prefigured proleptically. These are usually very ordinary matters, but without the constant turnover of such small things in life, there would be only emptiness in a narrative that in effect gives the conclusion first.

The frequency of narrative disruption by prolepsis and spatial and temporal shifting distinguishes Shūsei's work from other post-Restoration writers, but this does not mean that in each one of his texts their occurrence signifies similarly. Nonetheless, several shared functions are discernible. The resulting narrative disjunction reproduces disorderly urban life, while at the same time, by providing foreknowledge of events and by acknowledging readerly awareness, prolepsis infuses certitude within the uncertainties of city life. Prolepsis might be termed the modern, minimalist replacement of a chatty or otherwise obtrusive commenting narrator. Insofar as orderly chronology is temporarily interrupted, such narration imparts an appearance of writerly control over the text and directs attention to the specific details that make up events rather than to the events themselves, which are dispatched in laconic sentences. Prolepsis serves as a sign of presumed familiarity. Shūsei's texts thus demonstrate an interesting phenomenon: Absence (be it narrative self-reference, orderly introduction of hitherto unknown characters, or narrative comment), supplemented by breaks in chronological progression, defines relations between the text and the reader. Shūsei's manifold expressions of narrative disruption must be seen as a strategy for overcoming the conditions governing the production of *kindai shōsetsu*—that is, writing for a large, anonymous readership—and to impart the sense of intimacy between reader and characters demanded by the new form. (At the level of the text as subject, we might remember an earlier statement I made regarding Shūsei as a writer whose production of texts helped engender the production of readers as consumers of narratives.)

ARU GA MAMA AND NARRATIVE PERSPECTIVE

Shūsei's manipulation of perspective deserves the kind of close attention that his prolepsis merits, for it too participates in the construction of *aru ga mama*. Returning to the text of *Arajotai*, the following scene shows the day after Osaku's marriage to Shinkichi, who wakes up and crawls out of bed.

> Toko o hanarete chanoma o deyō to suru to, hyokkori Osaku to deatta. Osaku wa kōshi shiori no fudangi ni akai tasuki o kakete, kao wa heta ni tsuketa keshō ga madarazukutte ita.
>
> "Oya," to itte akai kao o utsumuite shimatta ga, Shinkichi wa nikkori to mo shinaide, sono mama mise e deta. Mise ni wa kinjo no binbō chō kara onna no kodomo ga hitori, akago o obutta shijū bakari no shinabita oyaji ga hitori, sumi ya miso o kai ni kite ita.
>
> Shinkichi wa kozō to issho ni, utte kawatta aisō no yoi kao o shite genki yoku akinai o shita.
>
> (14–15)

> As he got out of bed and was about to leave the living room, he found himself face to face with Osaku. She was wearing a homemade checkered top with red ties to hold up the sleeves, and her clumsiness with makeup was evident in the unevenness of her complexion.
>
> "Oops," she said as she lowered her flushed face, but without pausing Shinkichi went out to the shop with not even a hint of a smile. In the store there was a young girl from the poorer neighborhood and a shriveled-up fortyish old man carrying a baby on his back, here to buy charcoal and miso.
>
> Shinkichi became transformed into the pleasant, solicitous shopkeeper as he joined his help in selling his goods.

In its attention to articles of clothing specified with precision and clarity, the passage resembles *Ken'yūsha* prose, which followed the practice of *gesaku*. (I shall pursue later at greater length the significance of visual cues as an aspect of urban life.) "Not even a hint of a smile," indicates an expectation that belongs either to Osaku or to the narrator; on the other hand, the description of Osaku's poor makeup job suggests Shinkichi's viewpoint. The narrator freely adopts the perspective of different characters who occupy the scene. We find a more detached (subjectless?) narrative perspective in the last sentence, where Shinkichi is shown to be in good spirits, even buoyant, as seen by no one; but, of course, the narrator directs this to the reader's attention, and the deliberate contrast drawn between Shinkichi the shopkeeper and Shinkichi the husband belongs to the narrator. Thus, when we get to this last sentence, we must conclude that the earlier "not even a hint of a smile" could not have been a subversion of the narrator's expectations, for a few lines later the narrator is telling us that Shinkichi is feeling good. Two explanations are possible. The narrator, like the characters, lives moment to moment; its "awareness" is restricted to each scene, given the same purview as that given to the characters. Or, the narrator adopts the perspectives of the characters who occupy a given scene. Rather than observing the convention of having to unify perspective, the narrator constantly shifts, thereby contributing to an "effect" that has been subsumed under the rubric of *aru ga mama. Arajotai* eschews a fixed perspective in favor of frequent shifts, aligning with one character, then another, according to each scene. That such a technique should result in prose narrative uniformly characterized as *aru ga mama* suggests the naturalness of stepping outside one perspective and adopting another in Japanese narration.

Narrative perspective contributes to the distinction given to Shūsei's depiction of women, particularly his practice of focalizing through a female character. Consider the following, somewhat extended passage, which shows an unhappy Osaku six months after her marriage; the only acknowledgment her husband gives comes in the form of harsh criticism. Told that she is worthless in the store, she remains cooped up in the house, knitting in front of the brazier and sitting, lost in thought, before a mirror.

> Isso uchi e kaette, moto no yashiki e hōkō shita hō ga kiraku da na zo to kangaeru koto mo atta. Sono jibun kara Osaku wa yoku kagami

> ni mukatta. Atari ni hito no kage ga mienu to, sotto kagami no ōi o totte, jibun no sugata o utsushite mita. Kami o naoshite, kao e mizuoshiroi nado nutte, shibaraku sono tokoro ni uttori to shite ita. Sō shite kinō no yō ni omou konrei toji no koto ya, sore kara hantoshi amari no tanoshikatta yume o kurikaeshite ita. Jibun no sugata ya, yōki na hanayaka no sono ban no kōkei mo, ariari me ni ukande kuru.
>
> (20)

> There were times when she thought it would be better to return to her family and resume work in the service of her old master. From about this time, Osaku often sat in front of the mirror. When no one else was around, she would remove the cover and look at herself reflected in the mirror. She would fix her hair, apply liquid makeup to her face, and sit absent-mindedly in front of the cosmetic stand. And she would think back to the days that seemed like yesterday when she had just been married, and about the six months of life that now seemed like a dream. Vivid images of herself in the festive scene of their wedding night came back to her.

Relegated to the back of the house, Osaku turns to images of herself in the past that current events and the passage of time have made perhaps more pleasant than they actually were, seeking small comfort in a reflection that casts an image more worthy than the one indicated by her husband's treatment. Shūsei's texts typically depict the absence of dialogic engagement between characters; by using visually perceived surface signs (laughter, eyes) as means of fostering connections, whether they be between characters or between reader and character/narrator, Shūsei's texts posit a reader-viewer in the (meaning-producing) practice we habitually denote with a noun (novel, prose narrative, etc.).

Okuni is initially the live-in friend of Ono, Shinkichi's best friend, but when Ono must spend some time in jail, Okuni swifty insinuates herself into Shinkichi's household during the absence of Osaku, who, during her pregnancy and subsequent miscarriage, stays in the country with her parents. Okuni quickly takes over the management of the house. The *kureta* in *utsuwa nado o katte kureta* (36) denotes Shinkichi's posture of gratitude, showing how at this early stage he sees her in a positive light, particularly as he compares her to the lost, helpless Osaku. Yet, in the next lines, clouds of confusion are introduced. As

Okuni and Shinkichi sit drinking sake to usher in the New Year, they express gratitude for each other's company; in a conversation in which gaps and unsaids say more, the ambivalence and difficulties of human relations at close quarters are revealed.

> Daga, sō yatte asshi no tokoro de hataraite itatte shōganai ne. Asshi wa makoto ni kekkō da keredo, anata ga tsumaranai. . . . Okuni wa shogeta yōna kao o shite dammatte shimatta. Sōshite choko o shita ni oite nan'yara kangaekonda. Sono kao o miru to, "Shinkichi san no kokoro wa watashi ni wa chanto mietōtte iru" to iu yō ni mo mieta. Shinkichi mo ki ga sashita yō ni damatte shimatta.
>
> Shibaraku shite kara onna wa chōshi o mochi-agete mite, "osake wa mō meshiagarimasen ka," to teinei na kuchi o kiku.
>
> (38)

> [Shinkichi:] "But what's the point of staying on and helping around here? It's fine for me, but it's got to be meaningless for you." . . . Looking disappointed, Okuni fell silent. She put down her sake cup and seemed to lose herself in thought. The expression on her face seemed to say "I know exactly what you are thinking." Shinkichi seemed annoyed as he too fell silent.
>
> After a short while, she picked up the decanter and asked very politely, "Will you have some more sake?"

The abrupt shift to solicitous language signals the hidden currents of insecurity that mark their relationship, but Okuni is no stranger to negotiating the often treacherous path of surviving in city life, a path that admits few avenues of self-support for women. She tells Shinkichi that she first came out to Tokyo with a student-type (*shosei-hada no otoko*) and after suffering at his hands for a long while became intimate with Ono. He presented himself as a salaried man (*kaisha-in*), but in fact his circumstances had been far less stable. He would take her to the theater and buy her clothes, she said, but what was absent was any sense of stability and security for the future. The narrator adopts the perspective of Shinkichi, who takes note of the incongruence of the conservatism of Okuni's expressed thoughts and her personality (*gara ni nai jimi na hanashi o shihajimeta* [38]).

In the scene in which Osaku returns to Shinkichi's place after her miscarriage, the narrator overtly assumes only her perspective for the duration of the section, which depicts her alienation from both Shinkichi and Okuni, who in the meantime has become a fixture in this household. The return and the encounter is told entirely from the perspective of Osaku. Osaku has been talking about the presence of Okuni with her sister-in-law, who has brought her back to Shinkichi's place:

> "Omae san wa, yoppodo shikkari shinakucha dame da yo," to itte iru yō ni mo mieru shi, "ano onna ni ya, dōse kanaya shinai," to shitsubō shite iru yō ni mo mieru.
>
> (54)
>
> The look on her [sister's] face seemed to say "you've got to really get a hold of yourself," though it also seemed to say "there's no way you're going to best that woman."

The reader is never told what this sister-in-law's actual feelings about the matter are, and throughout this scene we are told nothing of what Okuni and Shinkichi are feeling. A recurring feature of Shūsei's prose, abrupt phrases intentionally lead the reader astray for an instant, as in the following.

> Heya ni haitte kuru to, Okuni ga sesse to sono tokoira o hakidashite ita. "Bonyari shita kamisan da ne," to yuisō na kao o shite iru.
>
> (55)
>
> When [Osaku] entered the room, Okuni was busily sweeping it out. "What a hopeless wife you are," she seemed about to say.

The quoted words lead us to believe for a second that harsh words have been exchanged, but by the end of the sentence they are shown to be the product of Osaku's or possibly the narrator's imagination. Despite the appearance of *aru ga mama*, Shūsei's text is not, of course, devoid of rhetorical agency, as is revealed by the use of perspectival change calculated to generate certain effects on its readers. More important, we must keep in mind that *aru ga mama* is produced by specific narrative strategies calculated to produce such an effect.

OUTWARD APPEARANCE: THE NEW *FŪKEI*

Yet another trait that contributes to the effect of unmediated "reality" can be seen in the passages quoted above: the preponderance of visual cues such as *yō ni* (appearance), attention to details of dress, and the prominence of eyes (*me*) and vision. The significance of visuality in Shūsei's work is multiple. Foremost in this text, the eye is the source of discrimination—it expresses taste. (*Gesaku* is the most obvious example of a literature built around taste.) In the words of Benjamin, "taste develops with the definite preponderance of commodity production over any other kind of production." As a socio-historical phenomenon, taste as a criterion of selection follows the rise of a group of people who are in a position to consume. But, "as the expertness of a customer declines, the importance of his taste increases—both for him and for the manufacturer."[44] Taste, then, rests on conditions of production and commerce, conditions that are closely interrelated with the development of urban life. At the level of the character, Shinkichi in *Arajotai*, for instance, must rely largely on seeing, on vision; he is handicapped, however, by having to interpret what he sees in the context of urban society, which provides no immediate clues for making sense of what he sees. The irony is that in his initial appraisal of Osaku, he cannot rely on his own visual judgment because he is embarrassed to look at the face of his spouse-to-be. Thus, it is only after the marriage that he is able to apprehend Osaku visually—by noticing her makeup and clothing in carefully calibrated terms.

Vision forms an important part of Noguchi Takehiko's "'Eibin naru byōsha' no bunpō," an essay that takes the *shizenshugi* writer-critic Iwano Hōmei's now-canonized characterization of Shūsei's prose style and shows how this prose realizes the finely detailed, "flat" (*heimen*, denoting level, unadorned) depiction attributed to it. Focusing on Shūsei's use of *metsuki* (the look in someone's eyes), he says that its use enabled Shūsei and other writers associated with *shizenshugi* to describe a character's inner state without the need to attend to the thorny problem of narrator placement while fulfilling the naturalist requirement for unobtrusive narration. Noguchi presents an example from Katai's *Kami* (Hair, 1907) to illustrate the ubiquity of the practice among *shizenshugi* writing:

44. The quotations are from Walter Benjamin, *Charles Baudelaire: A Lyric Poet in the Era of High Capitalism* (London: Verso, 1983), 104, 105.

> "Maa, yokutte yo, ato de hanasu wa," kō yū metsuki o shite, mata otoko no me o jitto mita.[45]
>
> She once again looked intently into his eyes, as if to say, "that's okay, I'll talk about it later."

The main point of Noguchi's essay is to highlight the role *metsuki* plays in promoting the view of "flat description." (Noguchi hints at a more interesting aspect of the issue when he suggests that Shūsei is able to realize an "other" through the dynamics of the gaze—dynamics involving the one observed and the seeing subject; he does not elaborate further. It should be noted that while relationships between viewer and viewed are implicitly unequal, they do not remain statically fixed.) I think, however, that the significance of visuality in Shūsei's texts becomes clearer when considered together with his repeated use of *warau* (laugh) and its variants and of *kao* (face). The appearance of eyes in various forms, including *fuan sō na me no iro ni mieta* (23; eyes that seemed to express uneasiness), appears thoughout *Arajotai* together with words and expressions built upon the ideograph *warau*.

In addition to the ubiquitous *warai* compounds used for matter-of-fact observances such as "Shinkichi wa sabishii warai kata o shita" (9), "Aiso warai o shita" (13), and "'He, he,' to hito no yosasō na waraikata o shita" (55–56), there are more forceful appearances of *warai*, as in the following: "hanasaki de waratta" (44; laughed scornfully), "kushō shita" (49; gave a forced laugh), and "esewarai o shita" (44; laughed affectedly).

In *Kabi*, variants of *warau* are, if anything, even more pronounced. When Ogin starts to drop by to help her mother prepare Sasamura's meals, he praises Ogin's cooking. "'I'm not much of a cook, but my daughter is a bit better. . . .' The mother came forward and smiled agreeably (*aisowarai o shita*), but the daughter did not enter the room" (264). This variant of *warau* is noteworthy, for it allows the narrator to reveal nothing about what Ogin's mother is thinking, a matter that piques our interest retrospectively when Sasamura begins to wonder if he has been brought together with Ogin by design rather than by accident. In another scene, Sasamura admonishes Ogin, who visits Mi-

45. Noguchi, "'Eibin naru byōsha' no bunpō," 195.

yama's sister after Miyama and Sasamura have had a falling out. "'Why do you go over to Miyama's place anyway?' he asked. Ogin smiled and said nothing (*waratte damatte ita*)" (272). In this instance, *warai* reveals Ogin's inarticulateness and her powerlessness in the relationship. In these and many other instances, variations of *warau* serve as the occasion demands: as a rest, a period, an elliptical marker, a substitute for predication such as *omou* or *kanjiru*. By using *warau* to be an outwardly visible sign of a condition requiring further interpretation, this text recreates a space that records communication or noncommunication as it occurs in urban life. There is never any hearty, shared laughter, only the *warai* visible from a vantage point no closer than that of a stranger.

In Shūsei's work, *warai* frequently lacks the force of full predication; more often, it denotes something to be *seen*, visually apprehended. This focus on outwardly visible human expression is reinforced by repeated mention of the face. Thus, we get "Shinkichi to Osaku no kao wa, ichiyo ni hotette, me ga utsukushiku kagayaite ita" (12; Shinkichi and Osaku's faces were both flushed, and their eyes were shining brightly), which depicts the anticipation held by the newly married couple. Strewn throughout his prose are such references to the face as "Osaku wa waraigao o muketa (turned her smiling face)" (15), "Shinkichi wa unzari shita kao o suru (looks disgusted)" (22), and "tsuma no kao o mikonda (read his wife's face)" (25). The face and particularly the eyes provide the means by which characters read each other and the way the reader reads the characters.

Not only is visual perception the means by which one apprehends another person, the very act of seeing itself becomes the subject of the text, as in Ono's reaction to Shinkichi's comment that his own wife is a dud: "Ono wa jirori to Shinkichi no kao o mita" (29; Ono glared at Shinkichi). Ono leaves after the discussion wherein Shinkichi confesses to abusing his wife, and he is left with his own thoughts.

> Ono ga kaette shimau to, Shinkichi wa itsu demo ki no nuketa kao o shite, tsumaranasasō ni kangaekonde iru.
>
> (30)
>
> Once Ono had gone, Shinkichi always sat around looking dispirited and bored, lost in his thoughts.

While at times the narrator informs the reader with the knowledge and authority that is characteristic of omniscience, as the proponderance of these observable signs of feeling and thought indicates, Shūsei's narration invites the effect that we readers are observing without mediation.

In a literal sense, *warau*, unlike *me* and *kao*, is not a physical object; nonetheless, it is a visually observable sign, often transposed into an expression that describes personal affect (e.g., *kushō, aisowarai, sabishii warai*). These three terms, which repeatedly appear in Shūsei's text, foreground the gaze. Seeing replaces knowing as the grounds upon which relationships in the context of urban life take shape. Meaning has been displaced, for it is not the *warai* as an action or behavior that is foregrounded but as a root word for conveying many highly specified and differentiated feelings. The reader is made complicit in the act of interpreting visual cues that the narrator does not comment upon. When Shinkichi argues with Osaku, he replies: "'Baka o itcha ikenei,' Shinkichi wa wazato waraitsuketa" (50; "Cut the crap," Shinkichi said as he forced a laugh). The ironic juxtaposition of *warai* and the intensity and near violence of the suffix *tsuketa* provides an economy of expression (without comment) so prized by admirers of Shūsei's work. Similar as they are, *warau* is used in a way that differs from the other two terms under discussion: It substitutes for other verbs of mundane existence such as *yutta* (said) and *omotta* (thought). Thus, *sabishiku waratta* (23) does not have the full weight of a verb, serving more as a substitute for an adjectival predication such as *sabishikatta*, turning it into a visually apprehended knowledge.

Shūsei's focus on visibly perceived meaning reflects his attention to groups of people less given to articulate verbal expression. In "[Osaku wa] otoko no kao o nagameta" (Osaku looked intently at his face) (25) is revealed the reality that both Shinkichi and Osaku are not verbally expressive. In place of stating how or what Osaku feels, the narrator tells only what is visually observable: "Mezurashiku kao ni tsuya ga dete" (25; For a change her complexion appeared fresh). Observable signs like *warai* are signs of "interiority." When Ono and Shinkichi are talking about how he overestimated Osaku, Shinkichi admits: "'But it must be hard for her too. Three days don't go by without a fight, when she is abused and humiliated. . . . And since the very beginning, I've never treated her decently,' he said with a forced laugh [*sora warai o shita*]" (29).

All too often, the variant forms of "laughter" (*warai*) contradict the sadness, anger, disgust, the emotion that the reader infers. The vocabulary of complex feelings, thoughts, and perceptions is better left to the visible sign of *warai*. Used repeatedly and in so many different ways, it becomes by itself a sign of complexity and nuanced human emotions. The wide-ranging signification given to *warai* is illustrated in a scene in which Sasamura's son returns from the hospital: "The child put his hand on the window ledge and managed to get on his feet, but he couldn't stay up for long. 'He's not quite recovered yet.' Sasamura smiled sadly [*sabishisō ni waratta*]" (417). The *warai* here denotes weary resignation, perhaps to mask the thought that, as he was as a child, his son is frail.

The subtle feelings inscribed in the *warai* represent unprecedented attention to detail. The revealing little smile with a host of possible meanings—twisted, pained, encouraging, resigned—is an indicator of alienated subjects who must read others in these fleeting surface gestures. The shift from a society conceived in filial terms to an increasingly urban society wherein affiliative relations predominate requires new forms of human communication. In Shūsei's texts, the ubiquity of *warau* reveals the paucity of a new vocabulary and of new conventions for depicting these new relations. Far removed from premodern Japanese literature that relied on such culturally shared signifiers as *utamakura* and toponyms to produce emotional effects, Shūsei's prose employs *warau* as a marker of feelings that are given to characters but that remain overtly unstated. Employed repeatedly and for varying significations, *warau* invites the reader to take the next interpretive step. Involvement of the reader opens up the scene of dialogue beyond the boundaries of the text. There is an irony in the fact that such narration contributes to the effect of *aru ga mama*.

The prominence accorded visuality (including the visible act of *warau*) also mirrors consumer-reader relations to the text and the proliferation of reading as a visual act. Shūsei's text prefigures the cultural critic Michel de Certeau, who comments, "reading . . . seems to constitute the consumer, who is conceived of as a voyeur . . . in a 'show biz society.'"[46] Like *gesaku* from an earlier era, voyeuristic interest links reader to text. But in the context of widespread circulation among a mass readership, the relationship between reader (voyeur) and text is not one-sided. The mass or "general" reader imposes a different frame on the reader-text relationship, for in response to such a frame, a text must address different imperatives. The sharpest contrast would be with a diary written to oneself and with documents of increasingly larger readerships. If one of the distinguishing characteristics of the Western realist novel is the solitariness that defines the reader-to-novel relationship, Shūsei's texts belong to a reading environment characterized as a communitarian reader-to-reader-to-narrative. In a city that is rapidly growing, the readership will be dispersed, anonymous, and heterogeneous. As individuals seek to find identity through familiarity and sharedness, one of the ways in which such connection takes place is through reading serialized narratives in mass circulation dailies. Just as the news creates a sense of shared interest, texts such as Shūsei's that appeared in this medium held meaning for a readership seeking alternatives to the filiative ties that many of them left in the countryside. Texts that make real the very conditions of life faced by readers who themselves may have moved from the provinces not so long ago[47] reinforce the values of urban bourgeois lives at the same time that they validate these values to a readership that sees itself in the text. The reader participates in a dispersed yet collective act of reading a text, which, by gazing upon characters and events, appears to present the daily life of the reader her/himself. In that way, such texts help shape "reading subjects." Such a subject is foremost an eruption of urban life, without which the development of a solitary reader, who at the same time is part of an anonymous

46. Michel de Certeau, *The Practice of Everyday Life*, trans. Steven F. Rendall, (Berkeley: University of California Press, 1984), xxi. His quotation is from Guy Debord, *La Société du spectacle* (Paris: Buchet-Chastel, 1967).

47. Henry Smith writes that the "size of the immigrant population surpassed that of the 'native born' in about 1909" ("The Edo-Tokyo Transition: In Search of Common Ground," in *Japan in Transition: From Tokugawa to Meiji*, ed. Marius B. Jansen and Gilbert Rozman [Princeton: Princeton University Press, 1986], 367).

community of other readers, would not have been possible. Shūsei's texts are imbricated in the creation of a constituency for popular culture, which denotes a shared "community" of affiliatively "related" persons.

At many points in human history, and in virtually every nation, written texts have been appropriated for their ability to promote a sense of unity that comes from a shared narrative. (In this regard, myths most readily come to mind.) I am not saying that texts such as *Arajotai* or *Kabi* were exploited by the state for such purposes; indeed other so-called *shizenshugi* texts were often censored by the authorities, generally because they were deemed to be inappropriately explicit in dealing with matters of sexuality.[48] What I am suggesting is that texts such as these constitute expressions of popular culture that not merely reflect but also help shape subjects in increasingly industrialized urban settings. Ironically, Shūsei's text replete with *me*, *kao*, and *warau*, a narrative built around the signs of being seen, is itself not just a passive text that is consumed by its readers.

The ideology of *aru ga mama* is empowered precisely by such an appearance of reflexivity. Unlike either the persons with a salacious twist to their lives (objectives of the voyeur's gaze in *gesaku*) or the solitary intellectual (typically the topic of what has come to be designated *jun bungaku*), Shūsei's narratives appealed to a mass readership by depicting the (virtually) nameless and the ordinary—that is, images of itself. His texts professed the radical notion that subjecthood could belong to everyman. If *genbun'itchi* on the one hand signifies a totalizing discourse convenient for national consolidation, it also stands as an egalitarian sign of language transformation that leveled class and gender-based distinctions. *Arajotai*, *Kabi*, and other texts that bear the stamp of *aru ga mama* signify textual spaces in which everyday life is joined to reading-speaking subjects. Thus, *aru ga mama* bears the signs of a particular social moment in which texts overtly thematize their relation to their social environments. And insofar as they were "speaking subjects," in contrast to the privatized positions characteristic of "naturalist–I-novel" literature, Shūsei's characters are conceived in relation to other

48. See Rubin, *Injurious to Public Morals*.

characters, places, and events—that is, they are dialogic—even though there is little to suggest that these relationships can foster a sense of the social.

FILIATION AND URBAN TEXTUALITY

Earlier I had mentioned how literature of the early decades of the twentieth century reflected the condition of *jōkyō* (moving to Tokyo) that was experienced by the vast majority of those who would come to be counted as residents of Tokyo—including writers. Writing fiction, as the clamor surrounding Natsume Sōseki's defection from academia to pursue a writing career suggests, was a marginal career path. It provided an avenue for those with some education and ability, but who were removed from the limited avenues of realizing personal success, literally to narrate (create) their lives. In the following passage from *Kabi*, Sasamura has returned from a trip to the countryside to see his mother.

> Tears had trickled from Sasamura's eyes as the fresh cool morning breeze brushed against his troubled face, which was pressed close to the train window. . . . Sasamura was deeply moved by his lonely mother living in desolation and poverty and by the kindness with which she had taken in the poor fatherless infant left by his sister.
>
> "Forgive me for not giving you a proper send-off. Who knows when we'll meet again. After seeing you to the gate, I didn't feel like sitting quietly indoors. As I clutched the clothing that you had left, my nose began to bleed, and I felt faint."
>
> Sasamura, who received this letter as soon as he returned to Tokyo, could clearly picture his dazed mother as she walked into the room where, until a short time ago, her son had sat.
>
> "Why can't she be more open while I'm still there? . . ." Several times Sasamura had suggested that his mother move to Tokyo, but she resisted. . . . There were various reasons that made uprooting and moving to Tokyo difficult, but their relationship did not allow them to discuss the matter.
>
> "We used to have a valuable painting, but you've probably already sold it." Sasamura had asked just because of the recollection of the time when, as a child, he had come across a moldy picture book from an old drawer in the dark storeroom.
>
> (365–66)

Sasamura's life in Tokyo is fraught with the tensions and dull torpor of life with a woman he does not love and the burdens of having a sickly child, but it is the old country home that calls forth the deepest emotional pain. The passage is characteristically Shūsei, riddled with rapid temporal and spatial shifts. Disjunctiveness that results from the frequent use of prolepsis, reminiscence, and abrupt changes in venue and time is the signature of Shūsei's work and makes it contrast sharply with the prose of virtually every other Japanese writer of the modern era. The first sentence of the passage quoted above depicts the farewell scene at the train station in the country. The direct discourse that follows at first appears to be words uttered at that very scene, but as the narrative that follows the quotation indicates, the words come from a letter that Sasamura reads after his return to Tokyo. The question that follows ("Why can't she be? . . .") is asked from the same position in Tokyo; the next sentences are iterative, dealing with Sasamura's invitation to his mother to move to Tokyo. The quotation that follows ("We used to . . .") returns to a conversation he has had with her during his visit. In a sentence following the passage quoted above, Sasamura is back on the train returning from the country, where he resolves to send his poor mother some money, "but by the time the train was out of his hometown, the complications of his life in Tokyo had already begun to assault him like the rushing tide" (368).

In writing that on occasion seems to anticipate the experimentation found in modernist prose, Shūsei has taken time and reordered it as if to simulate the peripateticness of city life (to which the narrative nods in the last sentence). Urban life reorders time according to demands different from the rhythms of growing and harvest prevailing in the countryside and from seasonal markers long associated with Japanese literature. The jumpiness of the passage perhaps expresses Sasamura's own sensation or grasp of day-to-day living, but as the segment shows, his experience of life is shaped by his placement in the city. Reshaped into a city subject, he has long lost the ability to communicate with his mother.

This narrative structure of abruptly shifting montage emulates the breezy nonchalance and instability that mark Sasamura's household composition. A far cry from the family (*ie*) promoted by Meiji-era government edicts and didactic tracts, Sasamura's family mirrors the constant mutability that marks city life: His personal associations are affiliative, ever-changing, and replaceable. At various times a friend, brother-in-law, Ogin's father, Sasamura's nephew and parents, Ogin's older cousin, and many others come to live with the couple, and for extended stretches, Sasamura himself leaves the house to escape his stifling marriage and to write. Instead of a narrative that affirms filial lineage, Shūsei's text follows the geography of dislocation, moving about in time and place. Like the people who easily move in and out of Sasamura's life in the city, the narrative writes people linked by association. In the span of a few years covered in *Kabi*, for example, Ogin's father comes to live with the couple, moves to a house a few doors down the street, and returns to the country before moving a few more times. Never close to his son-in-law, Ogin's father only by accident discovers that he is a grandfather.

The Meiji authorities sought to exploit a "procreative, generational urge authorizing filiative relationships"[49] in creating the obedient imperial subject. Figures created by Shūsei found narrative expression by their affiliative relations that could thrive in the "chaos" of time and space reordered to urban rhythms of daily life. Filiation is outright impugned in *Arakure* (discussed below), in which the heroine Oshima is orphaned at an early age and must fend for herself. In *Kabi*, Sasamura and Ogin slide into common law marriage through their association as employer and employee rather than through introduction by a go-between or other means sanctioned by the family. Years after the birth of their child, Sasamura still thinks of Ogin as a kind of mistress, and the narrator's continued use of *onna* (woman) in reference to Ogin graphically underscores the provisional nature of their marriage.[50] Even when Ogin is in labor, she is referred to as *sanpu*—woman in labor (319). When they

49. The quotation is taken from Said's discussion of the loss of the subject in late twentieth-century life. See his *The World, the Text, and the Critic*, 20.

50. When Ogin first suspects that she is pregnant, Sasamura's ambivalence about staying together takes form as a question: "'What does the doctor say?' Feeling somewhat distant, he asked the woman" (294).

are expecting the child, they decide to search for larger quarters. "He went out in search of a house that was set back from traffic" (302)—not only because he seeks quiet for his writing but because he is embarrassed to acknowledge his relationship to her. After they relocate, Sasamura takes a second apartment to separate himself from the domestic space filled by his wife and the newborn.

This interrogation of filiality is reinscribed through the figure of city and country. While both Sasamura and Ogin have only recently come to the city, Ogin cannot shed the markers of an upbringing tied to the countryside. Superstitious and illiterate, Ogin has an appearance and bearing that clearly proclaim her status as recent émigré to the city. Like the protagonist of *Arajotai*, Sasamura occupies a tenuous perch that in any case cannot be called comfortably bourgeois. He is a writer, but not college-educated like most Meiji writers of serious literature who wrote about the new urban intellectual (themselves). *Kabi* depicts the relationship of a couple, recent migrants to Tokyo who are neither urbane nor intellectual (in the sense that signifies a class). Just as Shūsei's narrative strategies can best be characterized as imparting "nonchalance," the very subject of his text signifies the unremarkable. What distinguishes his prose is the thoroughly pedestrian subject that it depicts.

This sense of ordinariness is reinforced by the gestures made to the numbing repetition of city life. Nothing is distinctive about the lower-middle-class neighborhoods that the couple serially inhabit.

> He put his desk in a gloomy four-and-a-half mat room next to the entrance, facing out on the street. Across the street were a little shop selling salted broiled fish and a small liquor store that had just recently opened up in this new town. Diagonally across the way was a small foundry that had been in business for many years. The sound of machinery that came relentlessly from the shop didn't bother Sasamura.
>
> (259–60)

By late Meiji, most residential areas outside the exclusive neighborhoods were dotted with cottage industries (a condition that persists, though in diminished form, to this day), and the sound of mechanical activity was a common one echoing through the neighborhoods of Tokyo. Reference to such small-scale industrial noise occurs with regularity in *Kabi*: "The mechanical sound of the turning machinery that cut through the quiet summer air roused Sasamura from his troubled sleep" (274). There are repeated references to noise made by the nearby foundry: "As he sat next to the brazier, the familiar roaring sound of the foundry ran in his ears. He felt that he was often more distracted when he was in an environment where he could not hear this sound" (310).

Hard and cold as these mechanical sounds are, their repetition nonetheless provides a steady beat for Sasamura's otherwise shapeless life as a writer. While his life is wracked by constant marital tension, the regularity and familiarity of the sounds of machines provide soothing accompaniment to his own work. Ironically, these very sounds that support the writer's work undercut the apparently breezy inattention to "philosophy" or authorial absence supposedly imparted by Shūsei's text, for they refer to the sounds that signal a distant ongoing war.

THE INSCRIPTION OF WAR IN SHŪSEI'S CITY

When narrative ordering, conventions of emplotment, direct narratorial commentary, and other commonly used marks of authorial perspective are absent, frequency of occurrence takes on heightened significance. If we pause to notice, references to war (the Russo-Japanese War) are common in both *Kabi* and in *Arakure* (discussed below as a text markedly different from *Kabi*). One morning *Kabi*'s protagonist Sasamura is awakened by the sound of voices singing a war song (351). The narrator makes no mention of its significance to Sasamura, but several pages later, its association to Sasamura is made clear:

> A friend from Yanaka asked Sasamura, "I heard you were thinking about serving as a war correspondent aboard a battleship. Is that true?"
>
> "That was before I had a child. It's supposedly not dangerous, but it is actual combat. . . ." Sasamura was aware that he was ill-suited for such a job.
>
> (354)

Other references are apparently unrelated to Sasamura. As he is preparing to visit his mother, Ogin borrows an obi from a relative who "about that time . . . was at the front as an army doctor" (363). When Miyama and Sasamura are on their way to see a play, they stop atop a small hill: "For a while they gazed at the smoke from the armory smokestack silently spreading out into the sky" (388). Shortly after Ogin and Sasamura settle in Koishikawa, we find this: "Some days smoke from the armory would invade the yard, the cold wind buffeting coal dust beneath the veranda" (398).

In every instance, references to the war in *Arajotai*, *Kabi*, and even in *Arakure* (where the First World War plays a direct role in the heroine's success) remain unspecified. In *Kabi*, for instance, particular events of the Russo-Japanese War are never raised, and the country with which they are at war is not mentioned. This despite the fact that the Russo-Japanese War was hailed as the earliest sign that Japan could compete against a Western nation, and the sense of national urgency and pride ran high. It is clear that the war is represented according to the significance it had to Sasamura, a young man who has moved from the countryside and settled on the outskirts of Tokyo to make a living as a writer, and to the other characters who appear in the text. The lives of those depicted in this text are relatively untouched by war, and there is no urgent tone demanding national mobilization or other expressions of jingoistic fervor. In *Arakure*, even while the ongoing war provides a steady demand for the heroine Oshima's tailoring services, the incidental mention it receives suggests Oshima as the angle of focalization.

Much like the sounds of machinery that mechanically and repeatedly form the "natural" backdrop to city life, the war too has become a regularized punctuation to quotidian life. Repetition underscores the acceptance of the thing repeated as familiar, as natural, as given. Indeed, such dulling repetition sets the tone to *Kabi*, which my reading takes as a description of urban life and its rhythms. The connection between the mechanical sounds of the cottage industry subcontractors scattered throughout urban Japan and the fierce war going on across the Sea of Japan on the Asian continent can barely be discerned in the dreary urban landscape that Shūsei depicts.

Shūsei's works do not appeal to any shared sense of community that might be invoked through a nation at war with a foreign power; they provide instead a new frame through which to make meaning of life. His texts find validation through the signification of the workaday life in thoroughly unremarkable urban pockets. The city is an analogue for the absent "philosophy," for the lack of direct commentary and perspective that other narrative strategies invoke. Large events like war lose their force, reduced to the interruptions brought by the sounds of machinery directly implicated in the war effort. The mediating "power" of the city, of urban society, reminiscent of the way work is reshaped by industrialization, results in the atomization of subjecthood. The city as it appears in these texts seems to foreclose the gesture of intertextual relations, particularly to Western literature, that often graced the pages of *shizenshugi* texts. Recent textualist criticism has made us acutely aware of literature as it gestures to its own textuality, and a narrative about a writer invites interpretation as a text about writing/telling a story. Instead, *Kabi* displays how the urban narrates a text. City life changed the rules of relations in daily life, allowing propinquity and short and repetitive cycles of exposure rather than familial or village connections to fill social spaces. And, most chillingly, Shūsei's text reveals how the rhythms of urban living suppressed the horror and immediacy of war by familiarizing its traces (the mechanical sounds of machinery) as part of the fabric of everyday urban life.

7

FROM SERICULTURE TO PIECE-WORK

Visualizing the "Rowdy" Subject in Shūsei's *Arakure*

Conventional literary histories represent *Arajotai* as Shūsei's first accomplished "naturalist" work and *Kabi* as the exemplary realization of the tenets associated with this school. Shortly after the work began appearing in serialized form in the *Yomiuri* newspaper, the literary journal *Bungakkai* designated it the "best work of the year."[1] Placed within the explanatory rubric of *shizenshugi*, *Arakure* (1915) has been judged to be similarly "naturalistic" but more "energetic" and "upbeat" than his other works. To explain these assessments, everything from Shūsei's recovery from ill health to a competitive energy directed at the new White Birch society (*Shirakaba-ha*) have been suggested. While *Arakure* has been given a place within *shizenshugi* literature, it is known chiefly as a work that brought recognition to its author for what Shūsei would continue to do for the rest of his career as a writer—depict credible female protagonists with sensitivity. The verdict is mixed with regard to the question of how successful he was in portraying women. The critic Yoshida Seiichi, for example, observed that Oshima, the protagonist in *Arakure*, represented a new type of assertive woman who was neither educated nor intellectually alive but nonetheless sought to carve out a life without having to rely on men.[2] Enomoto Takashi disagrees, claiming that she is little different from other, more obviously dependent female protagonists seen in Shūsei's other

1. Enomoto Takashi, "*Kabi* no seiritsu to sono imi," in *Shizenshugi bungaku* (Yūseidō, 1975), 274.
2. Yoshida, *Shizenshugi*, 2: 680.

texts such as *Ashiato* (Footprints, 1910) and *Tadare* (Festering, 1913).

In the present chapter, I consider matters of gender not as issues of representation (of women) but as they relate to the central concerns of this study: narrative practice, the articulation of subjects, and the very conditions within which these acts take place. In *Arakure* the *aru ga mama* effect-producing devices such as prolepsis and constantly shifting time (as well as the longer cycles of spatial relocation) must be tied to the semiotics that govern the narrativization of Oshima, the "rowdy woman."[3] As we shall see, the discursive creation we call Shūsei (and his work) parts company with most other writers, including those associated with *shizenshugi*, in the very relationship between Shūsei and the reader. Despite overt differences that separate *Arakure* from the texts discussed earlier, like them this piece obtains from the particular conjecture of writer, reader, and worldly conditions that determined the narrativization of *Arajotai* and *Kabi*.

Let us begin with an abbreviated synopsis of this untranslated text. Disliked by her biological mother who abuses her, Oshima is sent away at an early age to be brought up by a childless couple. When she is old enough, Oshima is tricked into marrying Saku (her foster parents' nephew), leading her to run away to her sister's house. A short time later, through arrangements made by her natural father, Oshima becomes the second wife of Tsuru, a canning merchant in Kanda. Upon discovering that Oshima is still legally married to Saku, Tsuru loses interest in keeping up his shop and begins to spend his time drinking and cavorting with women. He goes so far as to accuse Oshima of carrying a baby fathered by another man. Oshima flees once again, this time to the shelter of her natural parents, where, during her stay, she has a miscarriage. Seeking another change, she visits her brother in the mountains northwest of Tokyo. Her stay in the mountains, where she takes in sewing and helps occasionally at a nearby inn, is not long, and she returns to Tokyo, moving in with an aunt in Shitaya, the poor, crowded habitat of

3. I have taken the title, *Arakure*, to refer to the protagonist, Oshima. Donald Keene translates the work as "Wild One."

plebeian sons of Edo and of recent immigrants from the countryside. To earn her keep she begins once again to take in piece work (sewing), and soon she moves in with Onoda to start a small tailoring business. They endure some lean years, moving from one place to another in the poorer sections of the city, but their business begins to pick up as Oshima dons a striking white foreign-style suit and rides bicycles around town to drum up business. The end of this unfinished narrative finds her disgruntled with the slow-moving, unambitious Onoda and attracted to another young man who works for her.

Typically, "naturalist" readings of *Arakure* seek explanation for Oshima's rowdiness in her family background. In line with the discourse of *shizenshugi*, Shūsei had originally titled this text "Yajū no gotoku" (Like a Wild Animal).[4] Shūsei himself had stated that he sought to depict busy people going about their lives, recklessly, with no concern for *giri* (a strong sense of social obligation or duty) or *ninjō* (human understanding and compassion).[5] Presumably, we are to take his statement as willful departure from the cardinal rules of social conduct identified with a premodern era. In a study that is intended to be revisionist in its critique of *shizenshugi* literature but that merely restates its primary tenet, Shinoda Kōichirō argues that these works, unlike earlier *gesaku*, were a literature of desire.[6] We simply would be reaffirming the conventions of Western humanist-realist readings were we to valorize the presence of desire in purely thematic terms. As an indicator of subject positions, desire must be located in the narrative practices of a text; in this instance, it is expressed in the way narrative strategy departs from that followed in the two Shūsei texts discussed earlier.

ARAKURE AND *ARU GA MAMA*

Simply put, in *Arakure* narration does not cater to the imperatives of *aru ga mama* that governed *Arajotai* and *Kabi*. We can

4. Enomoto Takashi, "*Arakure* kō," in *Shizenshugi bungaku* (Yūseidō, 1975), 274.

5. From Tokuda Kazuo, Introduction to *Tokuda Shūsei shū*, vol. 21 of *Nihon kindai bungaku taikei*, 32.

6. See Shinoda Kōichirō, "Nijū no ie: Shūsei o yominaosu," in *Hihyō no kigōgaku* (Miraisha, 1979), 179–98.

identify four particular strategies that bear the burden of this contention: the use of a tale within a tale, composition and presentation suggestive of picture postcard scenes, highly crafted narrative perspective, and what I will refer to as narrative complicity—where the effects of writing subvert thematic intentions and unwittingly reveal a position antithetical to the "content." The first occurs early in the text: Oshima's foster parents work in sericulture, but mystery shrouds the circumstances that have led to their wealth. According to her foster parents, a traveling monk stayed at the house one cold wintry evening, and after he left the next morning they discovered gold coins in the paper mulberry stacked outside. They rushed after the pilgrim, but he was nowhere to be found. From about this time, their fortunes rose precipitously and their business flourished. But at school, Oshima overhears a more sinister account: The pilgrim died from a sudden illness and her foster parents simply kept the money he had been carrying. Oshima is not sure which version to believe, but she feels uneasy in the dark and gloomy room where the pilgrim is said to have stayed.

This tale of mystery is preceded by an account of Oshima's troubled childhood days; the account is laced with strong elements of both folktale and tear-jerker popular fiction.

> One night, led by her father, an old-fashioned man of integrity, she wandered here and there through the open fields to escape the spiteful wrath and cruel punishment of her mother, who intensely disliked Oshima. . . . She remembered how she and her father had come to the edge of a river. Standing there and gazing at the tranquil scene, suddenly she had been seized both by a sense of terror and peace as she silently clung to her father's bony hand.
>
> (4–5)[7]

Other scenes suggest the conventions of popular serials rather than those of so-called serious fiction: "On occasion . . . her mother would press hot tongs against her hands. Oshima would tearfully watch the tongs pressed against her flesh, and the stubbornness which kept her from withdrawing her hand served only to feed her mother's anger" (5).

7. The quotations are taken from *Shūsei zenshū* (Hibonkaku, 1937).

A craftedness that undercuts *aru ga mama* narration can be seen in the text's frequent lapses into description of natural beauty (this characteristic was nowhere present in *Arajotai* or *Kabi*): "Outside, the hues had turned to grey, and the sound of cattle could be heard from nearby ranches. The children who had been playing detective games in the street were now gone, and the stars were shimmering gently in the spring sky" (27). Uneasy about her impending marriage (to Saku, she discovers later), Oshima is presented in a scene suggestive of a picture postcard. "On the day of her wedding she felt restless from the morning. After getting out into the fields still wet with dew and digging up potato roots, she didn't do any work outside. The autumn winds rustled through the stacks of corn and millet that had been cut and left in the fields and overhead a chattering flock of migrating birds flying far into the clear sky" (37). Oshima's restlessness contrasts with the pastoral harvest scene, but unlike the narrative perspective consistently taken in the earlier two Shūsei texts or in other sections of *Arakure*, it is not the protagonist (Oshima) who observes the sky, the birds, or the sounds of harvest, for she is too preoccupied to notice. What is unwittingly revealed in this lyrical interlude is a narrating perspective separate from that of Oshima (or any other character), a perspective that organizes these elements into a picture.

Let us turn to the use of narrative perspective to illustrate yet another way in which *Arakure* shuns the appearance of *aru ga mama*. Shūsei's two earlier texts were marked by what we might call multiple focalization.[8] Instead of being limited to a single viewpoint, perspectives shift, depending upon the characters in the scene being narrated. But in *Arakure*, the focalization remains overwhelmingly fixed, staying throughout most of the narrative with Oshima. When Saku is leering at the sleeping Oshima, we are not told about this until Oshima herself catches him in the act.[9] When Oshima's foster mother takes her on an outing to a shrine, Oshima, still a young child, does not quite realize that her mother is having an affair. The focalization, that is, the angle from which the tale is narrated, remains with

8. I have chosen to follow Gerard Genette's discussion of focalization; see, for example, *Narrative Discourse*, 189–94.

9. See page 10 of the text.

Oshima. Childhood events are somewhat fuzzy, accompanied by such phrases as "the time must have been autumn." But as the descriptive scenes referred to earlier indicate, focalization does not always remain fixed, as the narrator presents his own position. In comments such as "A feeling of self-indulgent (*wagamama*) resistance began to well up" (11), the judgment and the focalization belong to a narrating entity distinct from Oshima. In sum, *Arakure* adopts an independent narrator position not seen as often in *Arajotai* and *Kabi*.

Finally, a more obtrusive act of narrative fabulation reveals itself in *Arakure*. The deception involved in getting Oshima to marry Saku is not merely thematic; it involves the complicity of narration itself. Aoyanagi, a doctor who at one time was having an affair with Oshima's foster mother, Otora, once again begins to pay visits, primarily to set the stage for Oshima's impending marriage to his younger brother. He tells her, "This time around, Oshima, you can't have any more inclination to run away, as my younger brother's a handsome guy" (37). A few lines later, after Oshima is described as unexcited and calm about the prospect of marrying Aoyanagi's brother, a young man she had been acquainted with for years, Aoyanagi teases Oshima and the narrator teases the reader with the following: "As for Sakutarō [*Sakutarō wa to iu to*], having been relieved from his duties, he had gone to the barber and had taken a bath and dressed up. And whenever he saw Oshima [lit., saw her face], he would smile" (37). Such behavior is nothing new, however, as Saku has leered at Oshima ever since he arrived in the household. Oshima is prevailed upon to wear a bride's silk-floss veil, which serves to obstruct her vision, and the reader is surprised by the following revelation: "When [Oshima] changed outfits and reentered the living room, she was confronted by a sea of faces, but it was not until she was led to her seat and comfortably seated that she realized her partner in the nuptial exchange of wine had been Saku" (39). We have come to expect proleptic foreknowledge of events, but instead, by focusing on Oshima's perspective, by teasing us with mention of Saku that in retrospect would suggest the turn of events, and by deliberately keeping from the reader as well as from Oshima the fact that Aoyanagi was involved in a ploy to ensnare her into marrying Saku, the narration is complicit in creating a certain effect (on the reader).

Arakure's narration, which reveals its own status as contrivance, contrasts sharply with earlier works such as *Kabi* and *Arajotai*, which are narrated to appear as if fabulation was absent. Works that most emphatically laid claim to such an absence of artifice, the *shishōsetsu*, exploited the presumption of readerly familiarity with the author's lived life. Despite the persisting characterization of Shūsei as a *shizenshugi* writer (thereby placed in the trajectory leading to the *shishōsetsu*), his prose consistently seeks text-to-reader relationships in very different ways. In place of any presumed congruence between textualized account and the author's lived life, *Arakure* appeals to an anonymous reader and does so through the dictates of commercial appeal.

The narrative strategies outlined above illustrate a shift in the activity of writing texts from an orientation to production to one concerned with consumption. As texts participating in the discourse of *shizenshugi*, *Arajotai* and *Kabi* were written to impart the effects of reality (contributing to *aru ga mama*). (Perhaps unwittingly, they also contribute to the formation of a rational "Western" discourse of reason, centralization, and nation building, insofar as the efforts to articulate and to adopt a "realist" mode of representation are tightly interwoven in the national context of social reconstitution.) A text like *Arakure*, as it stands straddling the divisions between popular fiction and serious texts,[10] reveals, in its overt use of such devices as surprise, the dictates of serial fiction to string along a readership, and a mysterious tale within a tale (the mystery surrounding her foster parents' acquisition of money), an increased attentiveness to the status of the text as commodity. The very title of this text—*Arakure* (in today's vernacular it might come close to "out of control")—signifies a promise made to readers to provide

10. Shūsei himself argued that there was very little difference between *tsūzoku shōsetsu* and serious fiction, illustrating his point by claiming that his "popular" texts attend as much to characterization as to plot (in Yoshida, *Shizenshugi no kenkyū*, 2: 685). But the proponents of the *shizenshugi-shishōsetsu* found cause to devalue all narrative that was fictive, leading to Kume Masao's celebrated contention that even Dostoevsky's *Crime and Punishment* belonged to the lower form of literature that was not rooted in strict adherence to real life.

(within the format of serial form) a particular kind of life. We might say that Oshima is produced from the demands of a promise held out to potential consumer-readers. Just how she is narrated will be the focus of the rest of this chapter.

TEMPORALITY AND THE SUBJECT OF THE GAZE

A text will engender different interpretations for readers at different moments of reading, but whether it be critical opinion in Shūsei's own time or among Japanese critics today, the place of women characters in his text has received close attention.[11] Many of the protagonists in Shūsei's texts were women, and in many cases they were drawn with female audiences in mind. It is not my intention, however, to focus on issues of gender, treating it as an essentialized binarism that endlessly replays the dominance of maleness in its myriad forms over its putative obverse, femaleness. Rather, like the inversion that Karatani employs to counter the essentialism of such discursive effects as naturalism, the modern novel, and the modern, I think it more instructive to examine how the forms of discursive production—narrative—construct such things as "female." My focus, then, will be on the ways in which Oshima is narrated in *Arakure*.[12]

11. For example, Sasaki Hiroshi observes that Shūsei's earlier works (including *Arajotai*, 1908) often depicted weak, ineffective female characters and that, from about *Ashiato* (1910), Shūsei's female characters tended to be strong and distinctive figures (*kosei-teki*; from his "*Arajotai* shiki ron," in *Shizenshugi bungaku* [Yūseidō, 1975], 258). In an essay titled "*Arakure* kō" (271–83) in the same volume, Enomoto Takashi contends that Shūsei never escaped the blinders of a masculinist perspective. Shūsei's son, Tokuda Kazuho, notes that all of Shūsei's prose written around 1909 featured women characters. Throughout Taishō and early Shōwa, Shūsei wrote many pieces for newspapers and women's magazines in order to support his immediate family and his relatives (*Tokuda Shūsei shū*, 26).

12. In *Daughters of the Moon: Wish, Will, and Social Constraint in Fiction by Modern Japanese Women* (Berkeley: University of California Press, 1988), Victoria Vernon discusses the proclivity of male writers such as Tanizaki and Kawabata to idealize and estheticize women. A discussion of a writer like Shūsei would have appropriately complicated issues too facilely dismissed as those of gender in her study. By treating gender as one instance of narrative effect, I have tried to avoid the problems of essentializing common to thematic discussions of the matter. See Lucy North's review of Vernon's book for a thoughtful and insightful consideration of the limits of thematic discussion of feminist criticism in *Harvard Journal of Asiatic Studies* 52 (June 1992): 370–91.

From the perspective of reading, the title *Arakure* (rowdy) sets the text in motion. Although the narrative follows the life of a woman from childhood to mature adulthood, the text, like *Kabi*, stands as a sustained repudiation of a linear, chronological (filial) narration on many levels. Oshima is narrated through motion across the terrain of the countryside and through the dense maze of the city, through an image (a white foreign/European-style suit) fabricated by the protagonist herself in a text fraught with temporal disjunction.

If changes in space furnish the possibility for Oshima to outline her own subjecthood, we must not fail to see how temporality operates as a narrative effect that also serves to affirm Oshima's subjectivity. In the following extended passage that begins chapter 36, Oshima is pregnant with her husband Tsuru's child, when one day her sister visits.

> Visiting for the first time in a long while, Oshima's sister gossiped endlessly about Tsuru-san[13] who was again gone from the store. After prattling on and on about the Uehara's daughter-in-law whom Oshima had no interest in, her sister went home.
>
> Tired from the visit by her sister and her child, Oshima sat leaning against the accounts desk, staring off into space. Enough months had elapsed so that she no longer felt uncomfortable going out to cool off in the evening air in her unlined kimono.
>
> Although Tsuru-san had returned from a trip, there was hardly a day that he would spend actually working on the books in the store. Even when he would stay home, he often stayed upstairs lying around all day. When he was in better spirits, he amused himself singing lewd songs he had never sung before.
>
> "That's awful. Who taught you such songs?" Fidgeting with the material for baby clothing that she had begun to make, she laughed half angrily and half nervously.
>
> "It's not even funny.[14] You're singing about your lover in Hokkaido, aren't you?"
>
> "That's not it at all," he seemed to be thinking as he looked with curiosity at the small underwear that was taking shape.

13. I have retained the polite ending to Tsuru's name because it reveals how the perspective belongs to Oshima.

14. These words also belong to Oshima. I have followed the paragraph breaks found in Shūsei's text.

"By the way, what kind of child do you think we'll have?" Oshima asked of Tsuru-san what had been a nagging question for her.

"The kid won't look like me at all. That you can count on." He laughed through his nose as he turned his back on her.

"That's right, since this is my gift for you." In anger her face turned red. "Even if it's a joke, that's an awful thing to say. The poor child."

"I'm the one to be pitied."

"That's because you can't see your lover, isn't that so?"

They were now both on edge. When Oshima began to cry and push him, Tsuru-san abruptly sprang to his feet and ran out of the house with the folding briefcase he almost never left unattended under his arm. The briefcase held a photograph of the woman and a letter from her.

Even now, Oshima began to feel nervous as she recalled the words of her sister which she had listened to half-heartedly (then) but which (now) seemed ominous. According to her sister, from time to time these letters which stayed locked up in the briefcase never left behind by Tsuru-san would be read in front of Uehara's daughter-in-law.

"That's ridiculous, isn't it?" Partly to inflame Oshima, and in part from jealousy toward the Uehara's in-law with whom Tsuru-san had become so close, her sister carried on like this.

(63–64)

The opening of this passage marks the time as just after Oshima's sister has left after a short visit to gossip. The sentence beginning "Although" ushers in Oshima's memory as she remembers an earlier quarrel with her husband, Tsuru. When she accuses him of thinking about a girlfriend in Hokkaido, the following sentence in the text is a direct quotation—"Dōshite, son'nan ja nai"(That's not it at all)—but the response is swiftly changed by the following "he seemed to be thinking," which reveals Oshima's perspective: Engaged in an argument with him, she anticipates this response, sees it on his face, but doesn't get it. The narrator, for his part, misleads the reader for the duration of the short sentence he places in quotation marks, only to subvert it by framing it as a thought. The deictic "Even now" returns the text to Oshima sitting and thinking about the argument and remembering what her sister had told her. Oshima juxtaposes her sister's words with encounters with her husband to explain and to impart meaning to the latter. Through textualized engagement of different speech events (gossip by Oshima's sister and Oshima's fight with Tsuru), Oshima comes to understand better her relationship to her husband. The temporal dislocations mark Oshima's thinking at "the expense" of, for example, a chronological progression that would provide an apparently more unified perspective for the reader.

Narration that shuns (chronologically ordered) temporality characterizes virtually Shūsei's entire oeuvre. But insofar as every enunciative environment is different (here we are concerned with the environment designated *Arakure*), the effects produced by any given narrative strategy will differ. When such disorder, which is both temporal and spatial in *Arakure*, is presented mostly through Oshima's perspective, the text appears to be foregrounding Oshima's consciousness. And like her peripatetic life, her mind is marked by chaos (*arakure*). Most important, instead of being the object of the (male) gaze, Oshima is the subject of such narrative juxtaposition and time: She brings the different moments together (in order to make sense of her husband). Thus, her status as a subject is fundamentally different from the status of female characters of many other modern era texts, which treat women as *objects* of vision. Diegetic disruption is the strategy Shūsei uses—constantly "displacing" the perspective of the reader.[15]

CITY–COUNTRY AND FIGURATION OF THE OTHER

If temporal dislocation can be said to figurate Oshima's subjecthood, place (or, more accurately, the possibility of movement from one place to another) similarly plays an important role. From its opening lines, *Arakure* narrativizes Oshima rather differently from how she might have been presented in a biographical account that employs the framework of family as a principal determinant of a person. Opening with a proleptic sentence, the predictive depiction that follows it seems to establish her fate.

15. This discussion was inspired by Kaja Silverman, *The Subject of Semiotics* (London: Oxford University Press, 1983), especially 222–36.

> When her foster parents hinted that Oshima was being promised to a man who would come to be her husband, she felt no particular feelings about the matter.
>
> In those days Oshima, who was eighteen, was known as something of a man-hater in her neighborhood. Instead, if she had just taken up sewing or koto lessons like the other daughters of merchants, she could have passed as a pretty eligible daughter of a fine adopted family. But, not very good with her hands, she didn't particularly like quietly being holed up indoors, and from an early age she stayed outdoors in the fields playing with the dirt or planting and harvesting crops with the young men. . . . Oshima liked working with these young men and horsing around with them.
>
> (3)

From the outset, *Arakure* implicitly questions the notion of the family. With characteristic indirection (like the presumption of prior familiarity that marks the introduction of Shūsei's characters) he does not explicitly criticize the family. Instead, the author simply presents us with families whose incompleteness, mutability of household composition, and instability are a far cry from the state's ideological representations of the family as the stable bedrock of Japanese society. In the work under discussion, Shūsei challenges the myths of filiation that assume the subordination of self to the family, particularly for women. As the title suggests, Oshima will not follow the trajectory of wifehood suggested in the opening line of the text. The narrative immediately follows with information regarding her personality traits, which presumably "explain" the subsequent deviation from the presumed norm of life within the narratives of family life. It is precisely such "explanatory" force given to the "natural"—human (animal) drives overcoming socially created determinants such as the family system—that has authorized critics to designate a body of literature as *shizenshugi* (among which many of Shūsei's texts are included).

Such readings, however, fail to see how Oshima is a discursive effect of Japanese modernity. In the section quoted above, the narration tells the reader that Oshima had no strong feelings about the impending marriage plans determined by others; at other points in her peripatetic life, she will exhibit deep affective responses to people and events (e.g., in her marriage to Tsuru).

But whether we look at her affective reactions to various events at different times, or at the apparent absence of them at other times, Oshima is finally far more a discursive product of the (growing) city, a relatively new phenomenon that was only beginning to impose the effects of large-scale concentration of people and social institutions on daily life. Oshima is never depicted in monochrome: Not simply a hard-nosed, driven young woman always at odds with the family and other social systems, she is shown to be weak and virtually helpless at times and at other moments decisive and energetic. The complexity of her figure is thoroughly marked by the city, which allows her the movements that help limn her character, and by a broad range of opportunities and constraints provided by urban society.

The city–country split provides Oshima with a means of reflecting upon her own image. Qualities she judges to be impediments to the realization of personal success (defined in economic terms) are associated with rural Japan. For example, aware that the father of Onoda, Oshima's business partner and lover, is critical of her for not being a model housewife, she says, "He's probably been criticizing me again. How can a country bumpkin [*inakamono*] understand me?" (166).

Her initial reaction to Onoda's father is more visceral: "When Oshima was finally taken there, the sun was beating down on him as he stood tilling the soil on the hillside fields growing horsebeans. When she saw the dirt-covered figure walk out of the field with an empty look on his face, she could barely contain her revulsion" (137). To Onoda's suggestion that they stay a while in the country to make their fortune, she responds: "Absolutely not. Even if you succeed in a little country village like this, it's so limited. You couldn't even brag about it back in Tokyo" (138). Earlier when she flees the city for the mountains, she cannot bring herself to work in a nearby watering hole: "Just the thought that the patrons were mostly local farmers and small-time merchants made her shiver" (89). The more she gets caught up in her own work, the more biting her references to the country become. She is anxious to disassociate herself from the country, connected in her mind with sloth, filth, lack of imagination, and conservatism—qualities that stand in the way of her personal success.

Raised in a new landscape where rural meets urban to create new, faceless, and unfamiliar surroundings, Oshima gives shape to her fears in the figure of "country." She is nonetheless acutely aware of her marginal status: Shuttled between two sets of parents on the outlying regions that are neither rural nor urban, she feels impelled to overcome the ambivalence of her own status. Once her fears have been figured in the spatial notion of countryside, she can then act to transcend its limitations through movement (from countryside to various places in the city) and transgression (bicycling woman in white suit). Active, quick-paced, and with boundless energy, Oshima does not conform to images of passive, obedient, and dutiful women. Earlier I questioned Anderer's contention that modern Japanese writers steered clear of engagement with the turmoil and change signified by urban Japan. Oshima demonstrates some of the particular mediating forms that were assumed by what were unmistakably active confrontations with the "Western" and foreign aspects of a new, city life.

The double-parent structure prefigures the displacement of a narrative concerned with a subject defined in filial terms by a narrated figure who unfolds affiliatively across a network of sites scattered in and out of a growing city. *Arakure* begins on the outer rims of agricultural, unincorporated Tokyo. "It was already dark outside, and through the rising mist one could see the lights of the Yamanote Line and the shimmering lights of nearby houses. The area around the fence surrounding her parents' home which adjoined the tea fields was even more peaceful" (44). The passage marks a specific moment in the development of Tokyo, as Henry Smith's discussion of the conversion of land from leftover *bukechi* (grounds of a samurai's estate) to light agricultural use in the years following the Restoration illustrates.

> A scheme was proposed . . . whereby leftover *bukechi* land would be sold with substantial tax breaks on the condition that it be used for the cultivation of tea and mulberry. The basic idea was to provide the basis for a local tea and silk industry which would generate foreign exports, thereby helping both the national balance of payments and the debilitated economy of the city. A total of 338 hectares, accounting for 8.8% of the former *bukechi*, was actually planted

> in tea and mulberry. . . . Neither crop did very well in Tokyo, and the end result was simply to turn land over at favorable prices to an as yet unidentified group of entrepreneurs.[16]

It will be recalled that Oshima's foster parents work in sericulture on the margins of the city, though it is not clear how they acquired the land they work. But as Smith's notes on such land use remind us, what we subsume under the apparent monolith we call the city is a far-reaching nexus of factors that profoundly influence the lives of those who live in its proximity: bureaucratic policies such as the conversion of *bukechi*, alternations in spatial relations among buildings, temporal cycles contrasting with country time revolving around the sun, changes in human relations that come from sheer numbers, the emergence of new forms and areas of entertainment, and the promotion of the separation of entertainment and play.

In *Bungaku ni okeru genfūkei*, Okuno Takeo restates the by now commonplace view of Japanese naturalist writers as lacking strong or specific attachment to place.[17] Local history is lost as family estates are transformed into anonymous parcels of land designated for the promotion of agricultural policies, as outlying villages lose their identities as rural outposts and as the ever-expanding city incorporates a vast patchwork of towns, cultivated land, and wilderness.[18] The conversion of rural lands to new towns defined by densely clustered populations has stripped them of any shared cultural meaning that may have existed. Much of growing Tokyo must have been just such anonymous space, without the markers of the narratives that link them to past events and people. We must rethink Anderer's observation, quoted earlier, that serious Japanese literature generally confines itself to representations of "a culturally domesticated homeland": "The Japanese fictional landscapes which recur in

16. Henry Smith, "From Edo to Tokyo: The Provincial Interlude," paper presented to Regional Seminar, Center for Japanese Studies, University of California, Berkeley, May 1982. See also his "The Edo-Tokyo Transition: In Search of Common Ground," 359.

17. Okuno, *Bungaku no genfūkei*, 59.

18. Doppo's elegy to such land newly defamiliarized by its very proximity to an ever-growing Tokyo, "Musahino" is a moving testament to the changes wrought by urbanization.

serious literature," he says, "are particular rural villages or urban neighborhoods or temple grounds—Ashiya, Asakusa, Kiyomizu; particular mountains and rivers—Yoshino, Daisen, Sumidagawa, place names often previously celebrated in Japanese poetry and prose, and which we recognize as semimetaphorical presences within a culturally domesticated homeland."[19] Shūsei's prose takes the facelessness of newly transformed borders of the city (once far removed from the city proper, places such as Arakawa or converted daimyō holdings on the western fringes of the city have long been incorporated into Tokyo) and *shitamachi* Tokyo neighborhoods, treating them as colorless backdrops to the unremarkable lives and events depicted. His narration gives rise to a different realist practice of treating place as incidental, much as characters seem marked by the unexceptional. Characters relating not to the signifiers attached to location, they forge their own, unexceptional relations to place. That place is thoroughly substitutable (as even parents seem to be) seems to be the point, mirroring the similar substitutability of affiliative relationships that get displaced continually by Oshima's movement. Whether it serves as a place to have new experiences or as a site of refuge, the city redefines daily life by making filiative and affiliative relations seem replaceable. (Ironically, Oshima must assume a figure of the unusual in order to find a place within the landscape of the ordinary.)

The evolution of such dry-goods stores as Mitsukoshi and Shirokiya's into diversified department stores around the turn of the century, rapid proliferation of cafés a decade or two later, and the lighted streets of the Ginza may have signified progress in the central portions of the capital, but change on a massive scale was also taking place in the outlying areas surrounding Tokyo as well as in the unremarkable corners of Tokyo's densely populated neighborhoods.[20] Shūsei depicts the faceless urban development of Tokyo not so much as the "frontier" regions of "terrifying unknown quantities" as the center of industry and

19. Anderer, *Other Worlds*, 9.

20. An enjoyable overview of transforming Tokyo can be found in Edward Seidensticker's *Low City, High City: Tokyo from Edo to the Earthquake* (New York: Knopf, 1983) and *Tokyo Rising: The City since the Great Earthquake* (New York: Knopf, 1990).

commerce in late Meiji and Taishō Japan. Oshima feels no particular attachment to place, be it the countryside or Tokyo neighborhoods. No longer a primary determinant of a person's identity, place has become faceless and merely instrumental—a space in which one carves out personal success.

During the decades following the Restoration, Japan's confrontation with the foreign would shift. Increasingly, the sense of other would be cast not in terms of Japan and the West—a perception of difference rooted in conceptions of temporal discrepancy—but in the schema of spatial separation (Tokyo and the countryside). Oshima's very peripateticness signifies a "modern" Japan no longer merely a (temporally) backward nation so much as one that would have to create its identity anew. Oshima's very existence signifies the odyssey of an island nation (Oshima) whose task it was to confront questions of subjectivity in the present moment—that is, within the discourse of modernity. *Arakure* is a text that captures the contradictions of the family (as forwarded by state ideologues during the decades following the Restoration) and its new environment—urban, industrializing Japan.

Something of the changing, uncertain tenor is expressed by placing Oshima on the boundaries of Tokyo. Raised in present-day *yamanote* by foster parents, through the intercession of her biological father she marries Tsuru, a canning merchant in the heart of *shitamachi*, Kanda. Over the course of the next several years, she will move back to her parents' home, relocate to the mountains north of Tokyo, and return to the heart of Tokyo, moving several times within the city. None of the specific locales offers memorable signs as places. Like the meaningless repetition of mechanical noise, place is devoid of specified meaning in Shūsei's text. As we have seen earlier, place provides the enabling condition for one of the few choices given to a woman in Oshima's circumstances—mobility. Many of Shūsei's texts and other writers' works tagged *shizenshugi* disturb the notion of the family so painstakingly erected by the post-Restoration authorities; in *Arakure* movement from place to place puts into sharp relief the status of the family in an era of pronounced demographic upheaval and social change. The density of population, differentiated spaces, and entrepreneurial opportunities available to Oshima in metropolitan Tokyo in turn powerfully affect the role and significance played by the family in constituting subjecthood.

The characterization of Tokyo itself as a large cluster of villages is still very much in circulation, but what concerns us here is the particular signification granted the city in *Arakure*. Human relations as they unfold for Oshima may indeed have some of the characteristics of village life, but more important (to continue employing the figure of village), the setting of "villages" is vastly different: Unlike village life, Tokyo subsumes many villages. Oshima can repeatedly experience defeats, but she can also regroup, move to another part of the city, and start anew. The combination of anonymity and opportunity, which come with the critical mass provided by a city like Tokyo, is clearly one of the enabling conditions for a woman responsible for a title such as *arakure* (rowdy). As a woman with limited means, always subject to the greed-driven motivations of her relatives (her natural father is described as interested only in finding Oshima a match that will result in a large inheritance, her foster mother uses her to cover her own infidelity, and, when Oshima visits her brother, he leaves her behind a virtual indentured servant to pay off the debts he has accumulated), there is not much that Oshima can control. Movement is one of the few things she can initiate, however desperate and even unwise the course of action might be. Moving provides a way out of the role of helpless victim. As Oshima tells her sister, "It's not like I'm some kind of geisha or something, I can't be sulking over [Tsuru] forever. I can't stand weak men like him" (73). Unlike Osaku in *Arajotai*, who remains entrapped by the reflected image of her own powerlessness when she sits in front of the makeup table, Oshima is the agent of her own actions, which repeatedly take the course of flight. Oshima has the resilience to successively shed experiences in one place and move on to the next.

The text, however, is not organized as biography; space replaces filial stability in a life wherein serial appearance of place is paradigmatically ordered: one can move, substitute whole sets of relationships, change jobs, and otherwise alter those things that help define a person. Oshima must move from the western outskirts of the city to the *shitamachi* region, not because there is no opportunity in the former but because one escapes filially determined constraints by changing locale. When tricked into marrying Saku or when faced with her next husband Tsuru's excessive drinking and debauchery (he uses the discovery of Oshima's earlier marriage to Saku as an excuse), Oshima does not have the material resources, the filial support, or the social sanction to alter the circumstances. The site of numerous instances where women get exploited, the city is also a labyrinth that provides new beginnings.

Mobility and movement characterize not only Oshima's self-narrativization; they also signify the disfigured family. Thus, Oshima's status as an orphaned child with two sets of parents (neither family being first marriages or otherwise intact and "respectable" families) doubly underscores Oshima's status as a commodity. While to her natural mother Oshima is an object for abuse, her foster mother uses her to cover her own infidelity by taking her along for her trysts. And, as she discovers years after she has left Saku (her tricked marriage to him serving to keep the family fortunes within the family),[21] even had she stayed married to Saku, arrangements had been made to deny her inheritance of her foster parents' estate. (The one family unit that is not set up according to the dictates of greed and material gain is that of her older sister, who had run away from home and chosen a life of poverty for the sake of love and to whom Oshima turns for temporary solace during transitional moments between moves.) Moving is always a response to ills inscribed in the family.

THE SUBJECT IN THE WHITE SUIT

Oshima lived through what was in many respects a turbulent era. By 1911, the cause for women's rights was served by the publication of *Seitō* (Blue Stocking), and the September 1913 edition of the influential magazine *Chūō kōron* was devoted to the "problem of women." It was during the early 1900s that

21. In conversation, Edward Fowler has suggested to me that Saku's name denotes something manufactured, even trumped up, as indeed was his marriage to Oshima.

"social problems" (*shakai mondai*) entered the national vocabulary, almost as a badge of distinction signaling Japan's arrival as a civilized nation. Oshima is never linked to these visible currents of social change that remained confined largely to an educated, elite group of women. She is, however, linked to the war, though there is not a hint of patriotism in her, as the war is merely an ongoing event that advances her own cause. For a woman with Oshima's social standing, financial independence generally meant work serving men as waitress, hostess, and other more compromising pursuits, something Oshima deliberately avoids. Her choices instead follow the climate of the times that the historian Oka Yoshitake finds captured in a book called *On Ambition* written by Sawayanagi Masatarō in 1915.

> No apparent progress has been achieved in the ten years since the war. . . . A series of regrettable circumstances emerged socially, politically, and morally, giving rise to a school of pessimism regarding the future of the empire. . . . Opinion leaders must provide the people with national objectives. As one such objective, Sawayanagi proposes solution of the China problem and, beyond that, the realization of a "greater Asianism" with Japan in the lead. . . . Kayabara Kazan refers to the "degenerate materialism" that characterizes the years following the Russo-Japanese War.[22]

Oshima's single-minded pursuit of success in her tailoring business reflects the world as it was "moving from a 'militaristic' age to a 'commercial' one."[23] The opportunity seized by Oshima is opened up by the economics of a country at war abroad and a nascent feminist movement.

While neither of Oshima's families can be called wealthy, they are both not without some assets. So-called *risshin shusse* narratives still commanded an audience. Although Shūsei's text did not belong to this genre targeted largely for youth, especially boys, *Arakure* may be read as an adult variant of the form, except for a significant difference: Hardly a rags-to-riches-and-fame

22. Oka Yoshitake, "Generational Conflict after the Russo-Japanese War," in *Conflict in Modern Japanese History: The Neglected Tradition*, ed. Najita Tetsuo and J. Victor Koschmann (Princeton: Princeton University Press, 1982), 214–15.

23. Oka, "Generational Conflict," 223.

tale, *Arakure* chronicles the path of a woman who initially appears as if she might inherit fairly comfortable (by the standards of early twentieth-century Japan) family circumstances but who must go on to take matters in her own hands. Even the title, however, suggests that there will never be any stability or steady and inexorable progress to material well-being. Rather, the deployment of successive misfortunes (the belated revelation that Oshima never stood to inherit her foster parents' assets, failed relationships, the "betrayal" by her brother) shares the techniques found in serial tear-jerkers that were a staple of popular fiction.

For Oshima, an uneducated woman in the first decade of the twentieth century, *shusse* would have to be attained outside of socially structured paths. Difference would be the condition from which she would have to make her mark, and it is the powerful image of a striking white foreign (European) suit that enables Oshima to turn difference into a productive asset. Several lean years force Oshima and Onoda to sell their equipment and move in with Onoda's former employer. Following a trip to Onoda's homeland, which gives Oshima ample opportunity to express her antipathy for country life as backward and stagnant, the two set up shop in Hongō, where the business begins to prosper again. Wearing a distinctive white Western-style suit, Oshima bicycles from school to school, soliciting orders for school uniforms. "The figure of Oshima clad in white caught the eyes of the passersby as she rode here and there across the grassy fields until she was veiled by the curtain of dusk. . . . She felt bold and unembarrassed about freely going into places where, had she arrived in Japanese clothing and a stilted *marumage* hairdo, she would never have been able to enter" (182). The theatrical, even cinematic flair with which she performs her work is required of her in a society that provides no room for an ambitious young woman wishing to strike out on her own. In effect, she must write herself into a distinctive narrative that is, like Tsuru's canning business or the new towns that are neither rural nor urban, produced anew in a society that cannot be captured by the static categories of "Western" and "traditional."

Oshima's striking white outfit has multiple meanings. Not a

garment suited for the housewife whose role is limited to family matters, its wearer is marked as urban, self-assured, and flamboyant. Its distinctiveness contrasts sharply with uniforms (first military and, when they have dried up as a source of revenue, school uniforms), upon which she builds her success and which symbolize the regimented life that levels individual variation and militates against the assertion of difference. Her selfhood is built upon the faceless anonymity of the herd, and it must seek definition from the faceless sprawl of the city. The white suit so dramatically etched against an overwhelmingly gray landscape of growing industry, war, and drab exurban growth marks a woman who must be depicted as far more than what Yoshida Seiichi called an eccentric (*fūgawari*) woman.[24]

Much as Oshima would find doors closed to her without her white suit, narrative space was closed to women who were unwilling to transgress the borders of propriety. In popular literature, leading women typically were passive victims, who, in terms of a much overused simile of Meiji writing, "would bend but never break, like bamboo in the fury of strong winds."[25] Some *would* break in the wind, and under the license of lovecrazed madness, many a pulp-novel heroine would finally unleash her wrath on a deserving adversary.[26] Until Oshima is "licensed" by the rubric *fūgawari* (the white dress and bicycle), she must express her impulses in flight (from her real and foster parents, from Tsuru, the Ueharas, the mountains). Her own sense of purpose requires that she cross the line of normality. The white dress signifies how she must work, not only at tailoring but as a "businesswoman," at entertaining her customers.

The price that Oshima must pay to forge a life for herself according to her own desires is to make a spectacle of herself. Early in the text, she is unwittingly the focus of Saku's gaze, and in these earlier references to her physicality, the narrator invites us to look upon an essentially helpless young woman. By the end of the text (*Arakure* was left unfinished), Oshima, the hardworking small-time entrepreneur in the white suit, actively in-

24. Yoshida argues that, rather than examine social issues, Shūsei chose to depict an eccentric woman. In *Shizenshugi no kenkyū*, 2: 684.
25. This passage is from Ozaki Kōyō's *Ninin bikuni irozange*.
26. See Rubin, *Injurious to Public Morals*, 91–93.

vites visual attention to herself. And she uses the resulting self-estrangement to transgress the constraints placed upon a female entrepreneur so that she might shape her own livelihood.[27]

The act of drawing attention to herself as an unconventional woman in the white dress marks the moment when Oshima inserts herself as a commodity in the discourse of capitalism. Here, Oshima mimics the conditions attending the production of a text written for serial consumption (as a commodity) by a large audience in a mass-circulation publication. Oshima participates in a climate of acquisitiveness that is imparted by the early Taishō didactic jingles in wide circulation:

> It is foolish to waste a single day, for it will never come again.
>
> If you care about yourself, get out and work: money doesn't appear out of thin air.
>
> Can there be anybody in this whole wide world who doesn't wish he had something he doesn't?[28]

Here is Irokawa Daikichi's view of the sentiments expressed in these ditties:

> The character of popular thought was undergoing drastic changes, reflecting fundamental shifts in productive relationships in agrarian villages during the Meiji period. . . . Here the "conventional morality" extolling "diligence," "frugality," "harmony" and "filial piety" . . . has become petty and vulgar, telling [people] to accept passively the world and their place in it. The implementation of conventional morality is now seen as an end in itself—the people are to concern themselves only with profit and loss, like *petit bourgeoisie*; they have lost sight of conditions in the larger world round them and no longer have a realistic understanding of their changing situation.
>
> By the 1900s conventional morality had become commonly ac-

27. Laura Mulvey, in "Visual Pleasure and Narrative Cinema," *Screen* 16 (1975): 6–18, identifies two strategies used in film to neutralize anxiety rooted in the lack or absence signified by the female. In Kaja Silverman's discussion of these strategies, "the first . . . involves an interrogation calculated to establish either the female subject's guilt or her illness, while the second negotiates her erotic overinvestment" (*The Subject of Semiotics*, 225).

28. Irokawa Daikichi, *The Culture of the Meiji Period*, ed. and trans. Marius Jansen (Princeton: Princeton University Press, 1985), 192.

> cepted ideas of social deceit. It was no longer an ideology to challenge authority but was incorporated into the ruling ideology. A vicious cycle ensued: the more earnestly ordinary people practiced it, the more they reinforced the existing state structure from below, and the less they could imagine their own extrication from it.[29]

Such an absence of self-reflection characterizes Oshima, who lacks the capacity to contextualize her activities, and in this regard she is similar to many of Shūsei's other characters. On the other hand, as the choice of the title suggests, there is a narrative perspective that stands apart from Oshima. The title signifies the transgression (which is gender-related) that derives from her participation in the discourse of private gain and success, which requires her to forgo self-awareness (and, at one level, considerations of gender). Oshima's shift in status mentioned above from a passive object of the male gaze to an active subject inviting the gaze is important to note, connected as it is to the changing status of subjects and objects in capitalist commodity culture. Such shift in status from object to subject, and the change in status from producer to consumer (Oshima changes from created object to producing subject), is reinforced by the shifts in time and place that narrate the tale, calling into question the fixed signifier status of objects in any sign system.

Arajotai, *Kabi*, and *Arakure* are finally linked in a common narrative that brings exteriority and the everyday together in a way that subverts the central discourse of modern Japanese letters, *shizenshugi*, which sought to validate everyday existence with "interiority." The frequent reliance on external markers such as *warai* and eyes/vision in Shūsei's work signifies people placed within a new environment, where the relations obtained among people and surroundings have shifted. (The shift might be said to anticipate late twentieth-century Japan, where visuality threatens to overcome narrative-textuality, simultaneously marking a move from representation to self-reference.) If, as Karatani argues, Doppo discovered a subjecthood through nature mediated by representational conventions different from earlier ones, in similar terms we might claim that Shūsei's characters find an anonymous subjecthood in a new *fūkei*—the city.

29. Irokawa, *The Culture of the Meiji Period*, 192–93.

The connection of exteriority to the city (in contrast to interiority as a means of coping with one's surroundings) might even be seen as anticipating the conditions of contemporary life that rest on the deliberate displacement of meaning with form.

The Meiji Restoration resulted in the installation of an emperor whose prestige and power were subsequently employed by the government to legitimate a nation configured in patriarchal terms. Our earlier discussion of Tōson's *Hakai* referred to the filiative line of authority that presumably radiated from the emperor at the top or at some originary point (both spatial and temporal forms having been used to represent the system) to families at the base. Texts such as *Hakai* and *Ie* remain captive to a filiative mode of conceptualizing and depicting subjects. In contrast, Shūsei's affiliative texts affirmed new horizontal modes of relationality, where narrativity need no longer be formed in filial, linear terms. Convoluted temporal juxtaposition, the displacement of "traditional" authorities such as *meisho* or the family, uses of urban–rural topography to create a chronotope of the present—such narrative strategies come together to provide a field within which subjects find new possibilities.

8

EPILOGUE

The *Kindai Shōsetsu* and Origuchi Shinobu

The designation of such writers as Tōson, Sōseki, and Shūsei as important figures in *kindai bungaku* stems from their association with a larger discourse of modernization. As standard literary histories have represented them, Japanese literary confrontations with *kindai* unfailingly revolved around the issue of successfully appropriating the individuated subject. In the present study, I have drawn attention to some of the limitations of positivistic conceptions of the subject, notably the consequent suppression of conflict, politics, and history from modern Japanese literary texts. By focusing instead on the way narratives participate in constructing subject positions, we have been able to see how tenuous is the distinction between a text's resistance to and complicity with other interests such as the state vying for control over subjects. In Tōson's case, the representation of social relations in terms of distance from the central city inadvertently promoted the very illusion of horizontality endorsed by the state, in spite of his obvious discomfort with bureaucratic manifestations of the emperor system. My reading of *Neko* revealed in the figure of Sōseki a writer who early in his writing career took issue with the trend toward uniform narrative convention and continued to raise questions regarding the costs of modernity; that *Kokoro* unwittingly participates in the construction of a Japanese modernity serving the acquisitive interests of the state was perhaps unavoidable. Works like Shūsei's *Arajotai*, *Kabi*, and *Arakure* testify to the fabrication of (always new) subjects in a new urban landscape. My reading makes clear, however, how within the concentrated new space of city life, subjects were being created and refashioned not only by obtrusive organs of the nation-state but by the myriad contingencies that define modernity.

The narrative approach pursued here permitted me to identify critical mediations involving the subject, mediations such as the changing ratio of space in the countryside to space in the city, Japan's relations with other nations, and figurative conceptions of social structure (verticality–horizontality). The resulting readings suggest that difference and unrelatedness, not discursive conformity, mark these writers' texts. Even taken together, these works could only prefigure what would be explicitly articulated several decades later with the appearance of Origuchi Shinobu's *Shisha no sho* (Book of the Dead, 1939):[1] In the grand narrative called *kindai bungaku,* the *kindai shōsetsu* had come to assume the position of a unifying *subject.* More correctly, it is the widespread adoption of such a view that Origuchi sought to critique and to contest. A related intention to challenge the centrality of the *kindai shōsetsu* has informed this study's readings of works by writers who, for many different reasons, have been identified as key figures in modern Japanese literature.

Concern about the widespread adoption of what everyone from the "common (wo)man" to government officials has viewed as foreign to Japan—the private subject—has been repeatedly and continually expressed since the Restoration. And indeed, all the texts examined in the current study express in varying ways the private subject as problematic. Among the texts treated here, *Kokoro* came closest to articulating the political nature of conceptualizing subjects in the modern Japanese nation-state. More direct confrontation that would explicitly recognize the central function of textualizing the issue (in the form of the *kindai shōsetsu*) would come a few decades later when Origuchi Shinobu, writing under the pen name Shaku Chōkū, would di-

1. The title owes to Origuchi's reading of the *Egyptian Book of the Dead. Shisha* first appeared in serial form in the literary journal *Nihon hyōron* in 1939. The 1943 Seijisha edition provided commentary in an essay, "Yamakoshi no ama" (The Mountain-Crossing Nun). The text was reissued by Kadokawa shoten in 1947 with an explanatory essay entitled "Yamagoshi no amida zō no ga'in" (The Motif of the Mountain-Crossing Buddha). Subsequently, Origuchi wrote a sequel to *Shisha* entitled "Shisha no sho zokuhen," a short, incomplete draft that never saw publication until it was included in his collected works.

rectly address the discursive links among the subject, the *kindai shōsetsu*, and the nation.

The interrogation of contemporary textuality by this noted scholar of ancient Japanese texts hints at the tensions surrounding *kokubungaku*, the study of "national literature" with clear intent to elevate Japan's native literary heritage, in its relation to *kindai bungaku*, a field whose perspective was more other-directed.[2] In my view, the challenge of modern Japanese literature lies in its defiance of being read in simplistic opposition to native antecedents or to Western sources. *Shisha* acts as a counterpoint to the works considered previously because it underscores the complex mediation (e.g., the subject = the *kindai shōsetsu* = nation) that is present here in the engagement of one culture with another, one era with a distant one. By directly confronting the *kindai shōsetsu*, Origuchi's project permits us to recognize the connections between the private, the social, and the international—connections that, however insistently Japanese critics deny are absent from modern Japanese literature, are inscribed in the very textuality of writing.

SITUATING ORIGUCHI'S *BOOK OF THE DEAD*

Origuchi Shinobu (1887–1953), like his mentor Yanagita Kunio, has been raised to a position of greatness, his status certified by the affixing of *gaku* (study) to his name to denote a distinctive body of knowledge called *Origuchi-gaku*. Despite his considerable talents as a writer, Origuchi has not figured prominently in the discussion of *modern* Japanese literature for a number of reasons: Best known as a scholar who brought ethnology to the study of ancient Japanese literature, he is considered more an ethnologist-folklorist than a literary figure; his major literary scholarship has focused on early Japanese literature; his literary output has been relatively small, confined to a few collections

2. The very rubric *kindai bungaku* relies upon other categories from which it seeks distinction. From the vantage point of today, it stands in serial relation to such other literary eras as *kodai, heian, chūsei, kinsei,* and even *sengo* and *gendai,* two groups with which *kindai bungaku* overlaps. In its own moment, *kindai* signaled its affinities with Western literature, simultaneously marking its difference from *kokubungaku* ("national literature"), a movement inspired by *kokugaku* to install a canon of classical Japanese literature.

of poetry and short prose narratives; the literary works often appear on the surface to be analogous to rewriting baroque music in the modern era; his work does not belong to any of the major literary schools of his time, be they modernism, proletarian literature, or the I-novel. That his oeuvre does not fit the narrow category of "pure" literature (*jun bungaku*) perhaps most directly explains his ambiguous position in the modern Japanese literary scene.

In keeping with the mainstream of modern Japanese letters, the literary and cultural critic Etō Jun criticized Origuchi's *Shisha* for the absence of its author's subjective view. In an essay entitled "Shōsetsu no buntai" (Stylistics of the Novel), Etō stated that "the writing appeared sickly, like that of a somnambulist or a person possessed."[3] The point of departure for my argument is Etō's comment, which rests on subject-centered realist standards underwriting the *kindai shōsetsu*—in my view, precisely the object targeted for criticism by *Shisha*. Origuchi attempts to defamiliarize what had become by the 1930s a new orthodoxy (viz., the *kindai shōsetsu*) by offering a counternarrative capable of recalling the voices of antiquity excluded from the *kindai shōsetsu*. When conventions of Western literary realism entered the discursive field called Japanese literature, they were immediately invested with meanings they could not have had in their "original" contexts. Written to challenge these conventions appropriated from the West, Origuchi's prose narrative *Shisha* confronts the politics of privileging a particular narrative form in a radically different "moment" (that is, early twentieth-century Japan).

Shisha's contestatory stance vis-à-vis the *kindai shōsetsu* can be seen more clearly by introducing Yanagita Kunio's *Tōno monogatari* (Tales of Tōno, 1910) into our discussion. Like his mentor and fellow ethnologist Yanagita Kunio (1875–1962), Origuchi is a revered figure among Japanese scholars, but unlike Yanagita, Origuchi's popularity does not extend to the general public. Methodological differences may in part explain the disparity

3. Etō Jun, *Sakka wa kōdō suru: buntai ni tsuite* (Kawade shobō shinsha, 1988), 99. Etō writes that while historians such as Marx and Hegel were able to unearth the dynamics of history writ large, it is up to writers (*shōsetsuka*) to reveal the concrete figure of man (*gutai-teki na ningen no sugata*).

in public reception accorded the two men,[4] but the distinction that concerns us is graphically revealed in the way these two chose to position their signature prose narrative texts within the field of modern Japanese literature. Yanagita's *Tōno monogatari* is a collection of regional folktales collected from a small mountain village in northern Japan. It is a text that implicitly raises the following question: What does it mean to write a *monogatari*—a narrative form (many earlier *monogatari* are substantially poetry) dating back to tenth-century Japan and considered the representative Japanese literary form—in twentieth-century Japan?

Origuchi had appended an afterword to the first book edition of *Shisha no sho* with a disclaimer that, in spite of the *sho* in the title, the text was not a history but rather a modern prose narrative (*kindai shōsetsu*) written with a "modern perspective" (*kindaikan ni eiji ta*) about antiquity.[5] Such a presentation of *Shisha* prompts a reformulation of the question posed to Yanagita's text: How are we to read a story involving ruminations by a dead man set in eighth-century Japan, a story that could hardly be mistaken for an account of real events? Why designate it a modern prose narrative (*kindai shōsetsu*), thereby alerting the reader to the very field called *kindai shōsetsu* in which *Shisha* was to be located? Finally, what expectations are raised by the author's commentary urging us to read the work as a modern prose narrative—that is, as a work to be taken in the context of its own moment of enunciation?

In an era when the *kindai shōsetsu*, on the strength of its associations with Western literary conventions, had become institutionalized as the mainstream of Japanese letters, writing a fictive narrative that came marked as something other (whether

4. Origuchi's interests would remain close to those of his teacher-friend, while his methods and views would diverge sharply. Widely accepted points of divergence include Origuchi's liking of the sensuous, the demi-monde, and the underside of life in contrast to Yanagita's somewhat sanitized style and interests. But perhaps the most telling difference is in the positivistic orientation of Yanagita in contrast to the perspective of Origuchi, whose studies of antiquity employ textual conventions associated with literary fiction. See Hirosue Tamotsu's Afterword in *Origuchi Shinobu shū*, ed. Hirosue Tamotsu, vol. 22 of *Nihon kindai shisō taikei* (Chikuma shobō, 1975), 367–75.

5. Origuchi, "Yamagoshi amida zō no ga'in," in *Origuchi Shinobu shū*, 328.

monogatari or *sho*) was not an innocent act. Both Origuchi and Yanagita clearly saw how canonization of the modern prose narrative (*kindai shōsetsu*) would result in the same exclusion of voices that developmental histories practiced.[6] They each wrote a text to challenge the installation of the *kindai shōsetsu* as literary orthodoxy in twentieth-century Japan.

Origuchi and Yanagita might properly be placed within a shared critical discourse, but the forms of their voices—their respective narrative strategies for confronting Western forms of representation (be it Western history or the novel)—differ radically. Returning to the two texts mentioned above, for example, the *monogatari* in the title of Yanagita's text simultaneously serves as a pillow word for antiquity, a sign of native identity, and a nostalgic marker; beyond this, the title needs little further explanation. In contrast, the very fact that Origuchi felt it necessary to explain that the title's *sho* did not make the text a history suggests the opacity of a term with no clear associations for the general reader. Origuchi's title requires, and in fact engenders, a narrative act of explanation. Given Origuchi's explicit claim that, contrary to what *sho* suggests, his text was not a history, the reader must pause at the last word of the title, focusing his or her attention on language conceived not simply as a transparent (unproblematic) tool of transmission but as an entity that itself can make claims on the reader's interest.

The choice of *sho* highlights Origuchi's enduring interest in the materiality of language, sound, speech, song, and dance—that is, in narrative conceived as performance. As Origuchi himself has stated, *Shisha* is an enactment of his thoughts about the origins of Japanese literature. The present essay focuses on how

6. The work of the medieval historian Amino Yoshihiko directly interrogates the practice of narrative exclusion. Amino's efforts to recover the histories of nonagrarian people such as wandering entertainers, craftsmen, and mountain dwellers reflects his strong interest in ethnology as the site on which to reclaim those who have been written out of standard developmental histories. See, for example, *Nihon chūsei no hinōgyōmin to tennō* (Iwanami shoten, 1984). H. D. Harootunian, like Amino, implicates methodology as a determinant, asserting that Japanese ethnology (*minzokugaku*) arose in part from a desire to contest a rational and teleological representation of society offered by a statist discourse. See, for example, the Epilogue to H. D. Harootunian, *Things Seen and Unseen*, 407–39.

Shisha "performs," as it must, to contest the institutionalization of a form (the *kindai shōsetsu*) that left no space for prose narratives that did not conform to a strategy of transcriptive representation. *Shisha*'s focus on narrative performance (the signs of orality present in Japanese language) at the expense of Western novelistic traits such as characterization and emplotment does not in itself distinguish this text from many other Japanese texts. My interest lies in examining how *katari* and other elements of the text relate to one another and to extratextual practices of signification to produce a text that challenges the *kindai shōsetsu*.

In the context of twentieth-century Japanese literature, Origuchi found it impossible to avoid conceptualizing the *kindai shōsetsu* through a now familiar opposition to *monogatari*.[7] But at the same time he could not help but conceptualize literature in terms of Western literary standards.[8] In "Minzoku seishin no shudai" (Topics in the Spirit of the Folk, 1928), he noted that Japanese drama and dancing were not subjugated to the West because of their long period of association with the "logic of kami" (*kami no ronri*). To rethink modern prose narrative outside the overdetermined framework of a native–Western binarism, Origuchi provided *Shisha* with a storyteller (*kataribe*)[9] who could effectively problematize the notion of *katari*, a term that differs from the commonly employed English equivalent "narrative" by the orality that is strongly etched in the Japanese language itself. *Kataribe* were storytellers, usually women, who were

7. In the early Meiji period, efforts to install a new subject-centered realist prose narrative were placed in opposition to Tokugawa-era "frivolous tales" (*gesaku*) focused on the demi-monde. Today, the *kindai shōsetsu* continues to be discussed against the *monogatari* and almost never with *gesaku*.

8. Origuchi argues that many so-called Western literary elements were indigenous to traditional Japanese literary forms. See his essay "Shōsetsu gikyoku bungaku ni okeru monogatari yōso," in *Origuchi Shinobu shū*, 193.

9. Origuchi's *kataribe* can be seen as close to the *sybil*, a woman who was "visited by language" when speaking for the gods. As Kittay and Godzich characterize her, "the sybil is but an instance in which we see language take place, where its taking place is thematized as a visitation upon an individual." They continue: "Language happens to her; it takes place by means of her, there, then. . . . And the verbal is believed by virtue of the fact that it takes place that way" (Jeffrey Kittay and Wlad Godzich, *The Emergence of Prose: An Essay in Prosaics* [Minneapolis: University of Minnesota Press, 1987], 9).

retained by a clan or family to transmit events and tales from the past. For Origuchi the *kataribe* embodies the key issues of his project to rethink the naturalization of textual practices (that is, the formal requirements of Western realism) that spell the impossibility of recovering what has been lost to contemporary Japan.

This reading of *Shisha* shows how its competing voices (between the narrator and the *kataribe*) produce a narrative of desire whose object is the subversion of a form (the *kindai shōsetsu*) that Origuchi felt was inadequate to the requirements for proper cultural expression. Contrary to appearances, the protagonist of Origuchi's text is the *kataribe*, a storyteller who mediates the relationship of people to the gods. It is through its focus on this "narrator function"[10] that Origuchi's text raises a question that could not but have strong political overtones in Japan in the late 1930s and 1940s: "Who narrates," or, more pertinently, "who has the right to narrate?" In an environment of increasing state suppression of dissident voices[11] and the emergence of a clear discourse of military expansionism, Origuchi's affirmation of performative narration represents no innocent interrogation of the *kindai shōsetsu*. *Shisha* engages the *kindai shōsetsu* as something that is problematic, not only through its focus on *katari* but through its attention to the figurative possibilities of the notion of threshold. As employed in *Shisha*, the term takes on the dimensions of what Bakhtin called the chronotope of the threshold. Bakhtin coined the term "chronotope" to designate the simultaneity of time and space inherent in any narrative expression. In *Shisha*, thresholds signify the site of transformation, where self encounters "other." In the broadest terms, for Origuchi, Japan itself represents a threshold, the

10. Much as Foucault replaces the term "author" with "author function" to underscore how the notion is socially produced, "function" is used here to denote the meaning that accrues to narration as it appears in its specific context.

11. As Richard Mitchell's *Censorship in Imperial Japan* (Princeton: Princeton University Press, 1983) indicates, writers in post-Imperial Japan faced continuing if altered forms of state restrictions on writing. The contours of writerly restrictions change over the decades, and repression in the late 1930s is shaped by a discourse of global expansionism. See Rubin, *Injurious to Public Morals*, and Silverberg, *Changing Song*, for vivid examples.

place where indigenous native practices like sun worship encounter the foreign religious sign of Buddhism. Origuchi's scholarly explorations are replete with the signs of otherness, finding expression in wandering deities like the *marebito* or in notions of otherworldliness, *tokoyo* (the world beyond). In *Shisha,* Origuchi has refigured the notion of alterity (cast in terms of temporal distance) in the spatial idiom of the threshold and in the juxtaposition of *katari* and narrative.[12]

A notable congruence marks the relationship between Origuchi's scholarly studies and his fictional works. While Origuchi kept the two realms separated by reserving the use of his pen name, Shaku Chōkū, exclusively for literary works, it is an ironic separation, for his "nonfictional" scholarly works exhibit a pronounced proclivity for complex figuration often associated with "fiction." For example, in a seminal essay entitled "Kokubungaku no hassei 3" (The Origins of a National Literature, Part 3),[13] Origuchi's study of *marebito* (wandering god-like figures), *tokoyo,* and *geinō* (entertainment/performance) is developed through a sexually explicit metaphor of the womb. Examining rites of passage in Okinawa and linking them to ancient Japanese practices, Origuchi's narrative moves sequentially from rooms and caves to women and sexuality.[14] His scholarly works have often been characterized as lacking in historical veracity, a criticism that in part represents a reaction to the obtrusiveness of Origuchi's narrative strategy. The criticism also stems from misreading his texts. For example, Murai Osamu argues persuasively that the *marebito* was not a historical figure but rather something created by Origuchi to serve as a method or tool for his folkloric studies.[15] The historical veracity of the *marebito* is

12. It is in recognition of the spirit of critique that animates Origuchi's work that I somewhat ironically apply Bakhtin's reworking of dialectical thinking to Origuchi's project, which opposed the teleology of Western conceptualizations like Marxism.

13. Origuchi Shinobu, "Kokubungaku no hassei 3," *Origuchi Shinobu shū,* 137–71.

14. Origuchi, "Kokubungaku no hassei 3," 160–62.

15. As Komatsu Kazuhiko has indicated, literalist readings have kept critics from separating method from subject of inquiry. See his *Ijinron: Minzoku shakai no shinsei* (Aonisha, 1985), 166–67. For a view that argues against the positivity of the *marebito,* see Murai Osamu, "Marebito no kigen: 'shi' no igata," in *Origuchi Shinobu o yomu* (Gendai kikakushitsu kan, 1981), particularly 240–44.

not as important as the semiotic function given the notion in Origuchi's work.

Among the many concepts that play an important part in Origuchi's studies of ancient literature and appear in *Shisha,* we do not find the *marebito* itself. Instead, the notions of boundary, oral performance, and otherness central to that figure are recast in the form of the storyteller, the *kataribe.* More explicitly, *Shisha* carries out its task of problematizing the modern prose narrative (*kindai shōsetsu*) through the function of *katari.*[16] We shall see how the very plasticity of *katari* implicitly criticizes the closure of written form designated by the *kindai shōsetsu,* which Origuchi claims, with intended irony, to have written.

Before I turn to the text proper, let me briefly examine some of the conditions that govern this reading of *Shisha.* Origuchi has been canonized in the form of two collected works (*zenshū*)[17]—three if one counts as separate a paperback version—and numerous secondary works, including a topical dictionary, the *Origuchi Shinobu jiten.*[18] He claims a volume in Chikuma shobō's *Kindai nihon shisō taikei* and Kadokawa Shoten's *Nihon kindai bungaku taikei* (vol. 46). On the other hand, he is ignored entirely in the Taishō volume of the Chikuma paperback series of literary histories and mentioned only in the chronological table of the Shōwa volume as the coauthor of an essay, "Kokubungaku to gendai bungaku."[19] To the possible reasons mentioned earlier for the banishment of Origuchi to the margins of modern literature, we must add one other—Origuchi's own desire to maintain a distance. The intentional estrangement of *Shisha* from its avowed context of the *kindai shōsetsu* is brought about by multiple associations with both native literary traditions and foreign texts. Origuchi's text borrows from a wide range of earlier materials, employing characters and themes appearing repeatedly in noh plays, *setsuwa,* and various other tales. Perhaps the most obvious is the *yamagoshi amida zō* (image of the mountain-

16. I am indebted to Ryūsawa Takeshi of Heibonsha, Ltd., for alerting me to the importance of orality in Japanese narrative and in Origuchi's work in general.

17. *Origuchi Shinobu zenshū,* 32 vols. (Chūō kōronsha, 1965–68), and *Origuchi Shinobu zenshū nōto hen* (Chūō kōronsha, 1987–88).

18. Nishimura Tōru, *Origuchi Shinobu jiten* (Taishūkan shoten, 1988).

19. Hirano Ken, *Shōwa bungaku shi* (Chikuma shobō, 1963; rev. ed. 1981).

crossing Buddha), which depicts a Buddha setting behind the mountains like the sun. This motif, which has been repeatedly reproduced through paintings and drawings, appealed to Origuchi as an image that situates Buddhism in a Japanese context.[20] *Shisha* also alludes to the many legendary accounts of *chūjō hime*, a motif that appears repeatedly in the literature of the Kamakura period. In this motif a young lady from the Fujiwara clan renounces the world, seeks refuge in Taima Temple, and weaves a mandala as a devotional act. Zeami Motokiyo's "Taima mandara engi" and many other Ashikaga-era texts depict a young lady of noble birth worshiping a material, fleshly Buddha who climbs Nijōzan to weave a lotus-thread mandala in a state of devotional rapture—just as we see in *Shisha*.[21]

Shisha also reproduces themes from Origuchi's earlier texts. *Kami no yome* (The Kami's Bride), serialized in the journal *Hakuchō* in 1922, was based on a dream Origuchi himself had in which he dreamt he was a young maiden yearning to save a man doomed to die.[22] Another earlier prose narrative entitled "Mizu no onna" appears condensed and reworked in the dream sequence of *Shisha* (discussed below). A text that unabashedly announces its ties to narrative practices of the past, *Shisha* proclaims itself at the same time as an intensely personal work.

Among the foreign sources of inspiration, we can trace direct lines to a Chinese classic, *Mu t'ien tzu ch'uan* (The Life of the Emperor Mu), a text that is, like *Shisha*, part history, part fiction, and revolves around a dead person.[23] But the foreign text to which *Shisha* is most overtly connected is the *Egyptian Book of the Dead*, which Origuchi himself explicitly refers to in his own commentary to *Shisha*.[24] The cover of the first book version of *Shisha*,

20. Origuchi wrote an afterword to *Shisha* to inform its readers how much Japanese Buddhism had been altered from its foreign origins by decidedly native expressions such as the mountain-crossing Buddha and the practice of sun contemplation. He refers to a number of devotional practices centering on the sun in "Yamagoshi amida zō no ga'in," 328.

21. See Yamamoto Kenkichi, *Shaku Chōkū*.

22. Fujii Sadakazu, "*Shisha no sho*," *Kokubungaku: kaishaku to kanshō* 44 (September 1979): 81.

23. Kawamura Jirō, "*Shisha no sho* saisetsu: bungaku no ne e no toi," *Bungei* (March 1975): 213.

24. Origuchi, "Yamagoshi amida zō no ga'in," 326.

published by Seijisha in 1943, sports a leather color print of an Egyptian mummy's coffin.[25] *Shisha* deliberately follows the lead of the *Egyptian Book of the Dead* by calling itself a *sho*—notes, or book. It will be recalled that Origuchi felt it necessary to explain his use of this character. The author's very act of drawing multiple associations with this word creates an uncertainty that engenders yet another possibility that takes the form of a question—is it a *monogatari*? Origuchi avoids the word, which too strongly frames a work as fiction. *Shisha no sho* stands somewhere between the fictiveness of *monogatari* and whatever is suggested by a superfluous disclaimer that the text is not a history. Origuchi begins the task of redefining the *kindai shōsetsu* by suggesting what it is not. The *sho* stands at the boundary between the text and the reader, serving not so much as the title as a description of the text.

BETWEEN SCHOLARSHIP AND THE PROSE NARRATIVE

Shisha begins as a young prince (Ōtsu no Ōji),[26] who has been falsely accused of treason and put to death half a century earlier, slowly awakens from his death-sleep. Much of the first half (the entire text runs to twenty-one chapters) is devoted to the process of Ōtsu recovering his memory, remembering his identity, and relating the events leading to his death. We are told that just before the moment of death, he had fallen in love with Mimimonotoji, a young attendant from the southern Fujiwara family. It is the memory of this woman that in effect awakens the dead man's consciousness. In a work conspicuously devoid of any action, Ōtsu exists because he remembers.

The second narrative thread focuses on a young woman of

25. *Shisha* first appeared in serial form in *Nihon hyōron* in 1939. The 1943 Seijisha edition carried background information about the work in an accompanying essay, "Yamakoshi no ama" (The Mountain-Crossing Nun). This Buddha is a familiar iconic image of the devoted pilgrim in search of spiritual purity and enlightenment.

26. The Nihon Roman-ha writer Yasuda Yōjurō has written a homage to this poet, whose work appears in the *Man'yōshū*. See Kawamura Jirō, "*Shisha no sho* ni tsuite," in *Bungei dokuhon Origuchi Shinobu*, new rev. ed. (Kawade shobō, 1982), 121–31.

noble birth (Hime) whom, at the opening of chapter 2, we find sequestered in a tiny hut on the fringes of Taima-dera, sitting in penance for having crossed its threshold. (The act of crossing over overtly mimics the image of the mountain-crossing Buddha that initiates Hime's flight from her sheltered existence in Nara.) In the ensuing chapters we learn more about both the now dead young prince and about Hime, who has wandered into the mountains in pursuit of an image of a Buddha poised above the peaks of Nijōzan that had appeared before her. She sits in an old hut just outside the Taima temple complex, where she hears about the dead man from the mysterious old storyteller (*kataribe*) of Taima. As an act of devotion, she weaves a lotus-thread garment for the Buddha image that appears before her at this hermetic mountain retreat several more times.

A third narrative centers on Ōtomo Yakamochi, the *Man'yōshū* poet who wanders the streets and environs of Nara and who alternately ruminates on the pace of change in eighth-century Nara and on Hime in Nijōzan. Yakamochi and Emi no Oshikatsu,[27] the two characters who are unambiguously rooted in the mundane world, stand in sharp contrast to the shamanistic storyteller, the dead man, and Hime, who, we are told, had seemed destined for work as a priestess, even prior to events narrated in the text.

Shisha's succession of short chapters heralds sudden shifts in time and place without transition. With an abruptness that is imparted by the absence of context, the tale opens with a monologue by the dead man, Ōtsu no Ōji, who is beginning to regain consciousness and remember events that brought him to the mountains of Nijōzan where he now lies buried. The second chapter opens some half a century later, when Hime sits quietly in a hut on the fringes of the Taima temple complex, close to the site where Ōtsu is buried. A few chapters later, the narrative returns to the dead man, who remembers more and more. Another sudden scene shift picks up the third narrative, this one focusing on Ōtomo Yakamochi. We are not concerned with how

27. A sobriquet for Fujiwara no Nakamaro, who rose to power in the Nara period.

cavalier Origuchi was in arranging the scenes[28] but rather with the effects of literary form on the reader. Read against Origuchi's explicit assertion of *Shisha*'s status as a *kindai shōsetsu*, a narrative scheme of calculated disjunction or nonlinear movement signifies constant return to a place or moment previously abandoned and, through a logic of its own, reproduces the acts of longing and return that one also finds in Yokomitsu Riichi's *Ryoshū*, Tanizaki's translation of *Genji*, the nostalgic return of writers associated with the Nihon Roman-ha, and other contemporaneous texts. (While one may be tempted to argue that the content—a tale placed in antiquity—masks a work of modernist experimentation, it should be noted that abrupt spatio-temporal juxtapositioning is not uncommon in Japanese literature.) The displacement of a more "linear" exposition by repetition and return ratifies observations by Hirosue Tamotsu and H. D. Harootunian, who view Origuchi's larger project as eschewing teleological histories in favor of other representational forms.[29] The varied uses of space, particularly the disruption of chronological progression that serves to valorize location, represent a distinctive narrative strategy that challenges linear conceptions of time attributed to Western, teleological representations of reality or fiction. The juxtaposition of dislocated scenes and times is invoked not to further the ends of characterization, for example, but to highlight the act of representation itself.

Origuchi's narrative of multiple returns draws attention to "place" in a text that exacts many uses from it (its expression as threshold being the most significant). The critic Kawamura Jirō

28. Origuchi let it be known in a published roundtable discussion that he switched the first two chapters around in response to a student who had indicated how contemporary readers who read carelessly would not remember what was written pages earlier. The first (serialized) version began with Hime, whereas the first two chapters (Hime sitting in her mountain hut and Ōtsu awakening from his death-sleep) were inverted when the work was reissued in book form (the version discussed here). See Kawamura Jirō, "*Shisha no sho* saisetsu: bungaku no ne e no toi," 214.

29. Sakamoto Tokumatsu makes a similar point when he notes that Origuchi is critical of rationality, which rests on external understanding in opposition to immediate apprehension of the thing itself (Origuchi's *jikkan*). See Sakamoto Tokumatsu, "*Shisha no sho* no kojitsu-sei," in *Origuchi Shinobu: Nihon bungaku kenkyū shiryō sō sho* (Yūseidō, 1972), 282.

argues that in *Shisha* place names are used as pillow words—that is, words that evoke rather than denote.[30] More interesting is his assertion that the protagonist of this tale *is* place. Place names such as Asuka, Yamato no kuni, Nara, Naniwa, and Katashio (river) may indeed be used as signifiers of antiquity (as Kawamura observes), but in my view they also play important roles as *boundaries*. The dead man's burial site lies by the gate and next to the road that slices through the mountains connecting Naniwa (today a part of Osaka) to Asuka (near Nara). If the abrupt shifts in time break up the narrative, it is place that weaves together the strands of this text. Up in the Nijō mountains lies the site where Ōtsu the dead man is buried and where later Hime will come to sit in a small hut and weave her garment in an act of devotion. Near the beginning of the text we witness the dead man Ōtsu regain consciousness, and in the scene that immediately follows, nine men resembling Shintō deities in white garments, white wigs, and traveling garb of the aristocracy, come to the very spot where half a century earlier Ōtsu has been buried. "Yamato ni totte wa Yamato no kuni. Kawauchi [Kōchi] ni totte wa Kawauchi no kuni no ōseki. Nijō no Taimaro no seki" (150;[31] The barrier-gate of Taima-Nijō: for inhabitants of Yamato, it is the gateway to the province of Yamato; for those from Kōchi, it is their gateway). At this site where barriers signify transformation, these nine men prepare to make a final appeal to the spirits (*tamayobi*), when, frightened by a voice coming from deep beneath the ground, they quickly scatter. The voice reverberates from the ground that divides two provinces (Yamato and Kawauchi) and two different eras (the narrative present and fifty years before) but where the boundaries of life and death dissolve. Meanwhile, Hime sits quietly in a small hut not far away, atoning for the transgression of having crossed the threshold of the temple grounds.

Nowhere is the notion of boundary more powerfully articulated than in Origuchi's valorization of the *marebito*, those itinerant figures of alterity who stand in Origuchi's oeuvre as somewhere between *kami* and beggars. As Akasaka Norio has argued,

30. Kawamura, "*Shisha no sho* saisetsu," 219.

31. The text is from *Origuchi Shinobu zenshū*, vol. 24 (Chūō kōronsha, 1975).

marebito point to the tendency for villagers in ancient Japan to limn the separation of insider and outsider. Origuchi, he states, saw it as a way for villagers to come to terms with their own social networks (*kyōdōtai*), at times banishing unwanted folk to itinerancy and invoking them as a means of dealing with the strange and the foreign.[32] In times when Western subjectivism had become virtually naturalized, *Shisha*'s concern with boundaries must be read as an attempt to restore a perspective that would permit a genuine otherness to mark Japan's apprehension of the "modern."

The primary setting of the text, Nijōzan, plays host to various types of encounters with the other. When Hime stands gazing upon the mountains, they engender self-reflection and awareness that have virtually vanished from everyday life. In this light, Nijōzan is not merely background nor even a pillow word conjuring forth associations of antiquity and deities but rather the object of rapturous communion and a place endowed with almost religious significance:[33]

> Nijōzan. Aa kono yama o aogu, yuishiranu muna sawagi. . . . Tabi no iratsume wa, wakime mo furazu, yama ni miitte iru. . . . *Mukashi bito wa, kakujitsu na hyōgen o shiranu.* Daga iwaba—Hirano no sato ni kanjita yorokobi wa, kakoshō ni mukete no mono de ari, ima kono yama o aogimite no odoroki wa, mirai se o omou kokoro odori da, to mo yue yō.[34] [Emphasis added]

> Ahh, the rush of indescribable excitement for Nijō mountain. Nothing could distract the young lady traveler whose gaze remained fixed on these mountains. . . . *The ancients do not have the words for precise expression.* Perhaps the best way to put it is that the joy she felt for her own home village of Hirano were feelings for a life long past, while the emotions stirred by these mountains came from a heart focused on the life to come [afterlife].

32. See Akasaka Norio, "Origuchi Shinobu: marebito tachi no tasogare," in *Kyōkai no hassei* (Sunagoya shobō, 1989), 269–74.

33. The view of mountains as *kami* was deeply rooted in rural life (see Yanagita's *Yama no jinsei* or *Tōno monogatari*). The point is further treated in a discussion linking *Shisha* and Kawabata's *Yama no oto* by Saeki Shōichi, "*Shisha no sho* no jirenma: Nihon no 'watashi' o motomete IV," in *Bungei* (September 1973): 234–47.

34. The text is from *Origuchi Shinobu zenshū*, vol. 24, 164.

Here, contemplation of place offers a means of expressing feelings and clarifies the division of Hime's life into past and future. She has just left behind life in the city (Nara) for the life of a devotee of a nativistic Buddhism. Bakhtin's notion of the chronotope is useful as it draws our attention to the conjunctive use of time and place and clarifies how *Shisha* privileges place over time.[35] Time might keep Hime and the dead man Ōtsu apart, but by leaving the city (Nara) and wandering into the mountains—that is, by occupying the same *space* as the dead man—Hime is able (with the help of the *kataribe*) to overcome the separation. It is also worth noting that the issue of separation through time is unwittingly foregrounded by the narrator's comments that serve to situate the narrator at some remove from "the ancients [who] do not have the words for precise expression." Such precision of expression cannot be taken to be a fault, as it is employed here to contrast with more recent historical moments (whether the narrative present of the text or in Origuchi's own time)—times in which people must depend upon the impossibility of reliance upon the written word for expressing feelings.

The site of these overlapping dramas, Nijōzan is like Japan itself, the place where self encounters an "other." Hime's inexplicable wandering that leads her into the mountains echoes a native Japanese custom of young women becoming possessed and chasing the sun as it sets in the western mountains during the equinox.[36] Here in the heart of Japan, an indigenous folk

35. The emphasis accorded space appears throughout Origuchi's work. Harootunian notes in his discussion of *tokoyo* (land of eternal night) that Origuchi claimed it was closer in meaning to constancy and unchanging than to longevity or eternalness: "He supplied an argument for the primacy of spatiality over temporality, permanence of place over the changes of time" (Harootunian, *Things Seen and Unseen*, 429).

36. Origuchi's professed interest in *geinō* (entertainment), always considered the underside in Japanese society and, not coincidentally, always open to women, is perhaps not unrelated to the "de-gendered" and affirmative value given to spirit possession here. As it occurs in Hime, possession does not take the form of a shocking outburst, although its occurrence in the *kataribe* who, on one occasion, "speaks as if possessed," is frightening to Hime. Hirosue (*Origuchi Shinobu shū*, 384) observes how Origuchi saw *geinō* (entertaining) and *kyōen* (banquets) as the beginnings of folk literature (*minzoku bungaku*). In Origuchi's narrative, these instances of possession reinforce the priority given women in the development of Japanese literature antedating even Heian literature as the originary moment of women's literary production.

custom encounters a foreign spiritual practice (Buddhism) to forge a distinctively shaped new practice. The concern with native–foreign encounter runs throughout Origuchi's work, and in *Shisha* it is presented as the topic of conversation between Yakamochi, the well-known *Man'yōshū* poet, and Emi no Oshikatsu, the powerful nobleman and uncle to Hime. In Nara, the capital, Yakamochi converses with Oshikatsu, known to be excessively interested in appropriating the latest trends from the continent (China). When Oshikatsu reveals in conversation an unexpected preference for things native, Yakamochi is pleased. What are we to make of this treatment of the question of other in tandem with the earlier merging of foreign and native?

In Origuchi, the notion of otherness permits for random (nonsystemic) change beyond the boundaries of the state, officialdom, and Japan as narrativized through writing. Undoubtedly, earlier periods of Japanese history come marked with their peculiar forms for expressing sensitivities toward foreignness or, more specifically, toward China. We must read *Shisha* as a text produced in the geopolitics of 1930s Japan, a time when resistance to the West served to authorize Japanese incursions into the Asian mainland.[37] In Naoki Sakai's discussion of Japanese critiques of modernity in the 1930s and 1940s, he captures the discourse of rising nationalism in the thinking of the Kyoto school philosophers Kosaka Masaaki and Koyama Iwao this way: "The unity of the subject of history, of pluralistic history, is unequivocally equated to that of the nation-state."[38] The discursive currents that appropriate subjectivity in the moment of *Shisha*'s appearance (represented here by Kosaka and Koyama's views) are surely different from those that must have governed the subject in the period depicted in *Shisha*, an era predating the modern nation-state.[39] In Origuchi's text, the notion of the subject is questioned, distanced from reproduction of Western subjects and the Japanese state alike, and finally reaffirmed as an enactment of *katari*.

37. Oshikatsu is associated with China, which signified modernity, though obviously not in the same way that the West would stand for the modern in late 1930s Japan.

38. Sakai, "Modernity and Its Critique," 491.

39. The terms of discussion are indebted to Sakai, "Modernity and Its Critique."

Origuchi's valuation of *katari* and orality should come as no surprise to one who has read his studies of antiquity, in which the notion of threshold underwrites the importance of *katari*. "Kokubungaku no hassei 3" repeatedly mentions the importance of gates (*mon*) as barriers. Such portals were the site of ritual practices such as the clapping of hands (*kashiwade*) at banquets, shrines, and on entering the court. Gates also helped determine the relative stature of itinerant deity messengers (*marebito*), those allowed inside the gate enjoying higher status than those relegated to perform their rituals outside. In Origuchi's texts, gates simultaneously designate a site of performative acts and signify transformation. Critical for our purposes is Origuchi's discussion of *kadobome* (literally, praising at the gate): "Judging from the fact that even today there are places where the word *kuchi* (mouth) is used for *katari* (speaking, reciting, narrating), it is perhaps closer to the truth to see *kadobome* not as a part of *chūmonguchi* (the gateway of the inner walls separating the privileged deity figures from those left out), but as a term denoting *katari* (speaking) at the inner gate."[40] Here, Origuchi directly links oral performance, a form of *katari*, to gates, a sign of transformation.

In *Shisha* Origuchi reworks this narrative linking gates to *katari* into "place" conceived as threshold. What concerns us here is the temporality Bakhtin ascribes to the chronotope of threshold, wherein "[time] is essentially instantaneous; it is as if it has no duration and falls out of the normal course of biographical time."[41] *Shisha* eschews biographical time, employing instead a very different narrative that foregrounds spatiality (place). Origuchi's text attempts to expunge traces of "biographic time" or, to use Etō Jun's words, an "author's subjective view." Instead of a subject-bound temporality ("biographical time"), *Shisha* instates place as the center around which the text is built. Place conceived as threshold does not literally replace subjects (there are, after all, characters, a narrator, and a storyteller in *Shisha*), but the text employs place as the site where meaning is produced (high up in Nijōzan, where a young woman is brought together

40. "Kokubungaku no hassei 3," 141.
41. Bakhtin, *The Dialogic Imagination*, 248.

with a man long gone, the mountain peaks provide the native frame for a Buddhistic image recast as indigenous), much as a realist text is anchored by individuated subjects. The peripatetic shifting of time disorients the reader, but the constancy of place restores a sense of stability.

The valorization of place is not unrelated to daily life, another overarching value that shapes Origuchi's scholarly and literary production. His effort to link *katari* with barriers or gates follows a similar strategy invoking the quotidian as inherently meaningful. Origuchi's writing challenges explanatory narratives of Western thought (linear cause-and-effect rationality and developmental histories, for example) through a tautological designation of everyday Japanese practices as being irreducibly Japanese. Origuchi elides the boundaries that separate ethnology (with its interest in origins) from ethnography (concerned with the present) by studying everyday practices of antiquity. At the same time, he disregards the scholarly convention of separating everyday customary behavior from ceremony, ritual, and other nonpragmatic behaviors.[42] Origuchi's studies of the origins of Japanese literature affirm the connection between quotidian acts of *katari* and different religious expressions—incantations, chants, benedictions (*shukufuku*), and purification sounds (not to mention physical performances such as stomping and dancing).[43] For him, the privileged term in the pairing of *kami* and

42. Jurij Lotman recapitulates this well-established division in "The Poetics of Everyday Behavior," in *The Semiotics of Russian Cultural History*, ed. Alexander D. Nakhimovsky and Alice Stone Nakhimovsky (Ithaca: Cornell University Press, 1985), 67–68.

43. See Konishi Jun'ichi, *The Archaic and Ancient Ages*, vol. 1 of *A History of Japanese Literature*, ed. Earl Miner (Princeton: Princeton University Press, 1984), 95, and Origuchi's 1924 essay, "Kokubungaku no hassei l: Jugen to jojishi to," *Origuchi Shinobu zenshū*, 1: 63–75. Origuchi's connection of *kami* to literature is summarized by Konishi this way: "Incantations, in their later stages, came to contain both narrated (ji) and spoken (kotoba) sections. The narrated section, made up essentially of contents such as those listed above, was well suited for being told in the third person; but because it was told from the god's own standpoint—that is, in the first person—narrative personae were occasionally confused. Narrated sections later came to be exclusively in the third person, and developed into descriptive recitations. Since the spoken section consisted of the god's own direct utterances, it continued to be narrated in the first person" (95–96).

katari is *katari*, validated by its ordinariness and its location in the everyday practices of people's lives.[44]

In a study of Afro-Caribbean narrative and culture, Patrick Taylor has noted that "narrative is a call to order. In its grandest form, narrative is the story of the gods, the myths about their deeds, reenacted in ritual, making possible the regeneration of the natural and social world."[45] The recognition that such ordering creates meaning consistently underwrites Origuchi's project. His scholarly works invert Taylor's relationships of the gods to the social world, however, by centering daily life as the locus of creation. The gods, such as the wandering *marebito*, arise from quotidian needs of farm and village folk. It is not the appropriation of the gods that helps secure meaning and order in *Origuchi-gaku*; such deities are, instead, the *means* for narrative to affirm itself. This is a significant reversal, though not because it simply reclaims agency from deities and gives it to those folk who perform the act of narration. While Origuchi argues that first-person narration originated as expressions of divine perspectives,[46] he does not privilege words by virtue of their association with the gods. In his work, it is always the *practice* of daily life that at once represents and validates Japan as a place of distinction.

Origuchi's elevation of practice comes from an intention to replace the sovereignty of the subject. As we shall see below, for Origuchi, practice denotes an agentless *performance* (be it living, working, singing, or storytelling); put another way, he is drawn to performance because it is an act as much empowered by the viewer as by the performer.[47] *Shisha* eschews a simple recovery

44. It is interesting to note that "mainstream" Japanese literature—or *jun bungaku*—is also closely tied to the quotidian; where Origuchi's work differs radically from such literature is in its rejection of the individuated subject as the focus of literature.

45. Patrick Taylor, *The Narrative of Liberation: Perspectives on Afro-Caribbean Literature, Popular Culture, and Politics* (Ithaca: Cornell University Press, 1989), xii.

46. Konishi, *A History of Japanese Literature*, 1: 95.

47. That Japanese writing tends toward being self-referential and performative is widely acknowledged. See Fowler, *The Rhetoric of Confession*, especially Introduction and Chapter 1.

of antiquity; in this work, the past serves a strategic function—to restore perspective to a present painfully lacking in performance.[48] Performance cannot be preserved for another time; its temporal and spatial coordinates reside in the moment of its articulation.

For Origuchi, it is the singularity of performance as an event that endows Japanese antiquity with an ability to help Japan negotiate its course in the present. *Shisha* is at once an enactment of performance (writing a modern prose narrative in the present) and a defiance of the *kindai shōsetsu* that requires the suppression of its own materiality. In contrast to the *kindai shōsetsu* and its association with temporal development, *Shisha*'s performance designates a spatiality that might even resist the forgetting that time induces.

The association of religious practice with performance comes through a familiar emphasis on the quotidian. The linchpin in Origuchi's mytho-ethnologic studies of Japanese antiquity is the *marebito*,[49] wandering deity spirits from *tokoyo* (distant lands beyond the seas, or Hades) who visit villagers on nights of the Shintō harvest (*niiname*) to ensure abundance. Origuchi traces the development of these itinerant *kami* as follows: villagers' abstract fears taking the form of apparitions; village youth assuming the role of *marebito*; the development of itinerant professionals to serve as deity figures; decreased opportunities for performers in agriculture (harvest rituals), leading to a shift in roles emphasizing entertainment.[50] Literature is the direct descendant of these performance-entertainment events (orational, musical, and physical such as dance), or *geinō*.

In Origuchi's work, daily life, performance, and religious

48. Aeba Takao observes that *Shisha* expresses the feelings and sensibilities of everyday life (*kanjō seikatsu*) of the Man'yōbito. Aeba notes that numerous essays attempting to shed light on the people of the Man'yō period appeared in the 1930s (Aeba Takao, *Hihyō to hyōgen: Kindai Nihon bungaku no watakushi* [Bungei shunjū, 1979], 273).

49. Origuchi ("Kokubungaku no hassei 3," 137) speculates that the term is rooted in the sound *mare* (rare), referring to important guests made more important by the rarity of their visits. Origuchi's essay provides an extended discussion of *marebito*.

50. See Origuchi, "Kokubungaku no hassei 3," 156.

practice are joined by the notion of visitation from afar to coalesce in a chronotope of sound and orality that underwrites all of Japanese writing. The expression *oto o tateru* (found in a *Man'yōshū* poem), he asserts, signifies both the making of sound and of visiting (*otozuru*).[51] In *Shisha* the deity figure *kataribe* repeatedly appears from nowhere to tell Hime stories about Ōtsu; Hime is also visited by the mountain-crossing Buddha image. As a figure with unmistakable signs of religiosity, Hime herself enacts itinerant visitation when she wanders up to the mountain temple complex on Nijōzan. The association of visitation with sound, particularly onomatopoeia, is ubiquitous. The opening scene of the novel finds the dead man stirred from his death-sleep by the sound of dripping water—*shita, shita, shita*.[52] The sounds *kō, kō, kō* prefigure the appearance of the nine figures dressed as *Shintō* deities in the second chapter when the men come to recall the lost spirit of Hime. Chapter 11 begins with the sound of a bird—*hōki, hōki, hōki*. The sound rouses Hime from her reverie as she sits in a hut near Taima-dera and is reminded that *hōki* (a term expressing religious ecstasy) was the very sound that she had heard when copying the Lotus Sutra back in Nara. Here, homophonous sound draws attention to the tenuousness of the boundary separating dream from reality, life from text, and past from present. In these and many other instances linking sound to visitation, the signs of "divinity" are unmistakably if unobtrusively present.

Shisha has been presented as a site in which the interests Origuchi pursued in his scholarship have been reworked. Conceptions of time and place replace the central focus on the subject in *kindai shōsetsu*, permitting in place of the individuated subject a narrative that instead affirms a forgotten antiquity through performance. The remainder of this chapter focuses on the *kataribe*, through which Origuchi focused his efforts to displace the closure of writing embodied by the *kindai shōsetsu*.

51. Origuchi, "Kokubungaku no hassei 3," 142.

52. As Nakagami Kenji notes, onomatopoeia often accompanies the transitions from the dead man scenes back to the real world. See Nakagami Kenji, "Monogatari no keifu: Origuchi Shinobu," *Kokubungaku: kaishaku to kanshō* 28 (December 1983): 16.

THE *KATARIBE*'S NARRATIVE PERFORMANCE

If sound and orality are key notions in Origuchi's extended study of Japanese literature, in *Shisha* they are most fully expressed in the form of the *kataribe*. Usually women, these storytellers were attached to a particular family or village and in some cases were wandering tellers of tales.[53] In *Shisha* the *kataribe* is an old woman who first appears before Hime, sitting quietly in a small hut after having wandered into the mountains of Nijōzan. A shadowy figure whose presence remains virtually hidden until she is suddenly noticed by Hime, the *kataribe* comes forth and tells the young woman about Ōtsu, who now lies buried nearby. The *kataribe*'s oracular account—on several occasions the narrator informs us that she speaks as one possessed, serving merely as a medium for the gods—ends with the prophecy that the most beautiful daughter among the four Fujiwara families will be seen by the dead man as Mimimonotoji, who is the young woman witnessing his last moments as she captures his heart during his last breath.

Repeatedly referred to by the narrator as a decrepit old woman who lives in an age when people no longer pay much attention to such storytellers, the *kataribe* is the embodiment of both narrative form and content. She is at once a character in the narrative and the means by which narrative is generated, links established, traces of the past recovered, and meaning located within performance. The scenes of the dead man regaining consciousness are told by a third-person narrator, but Ōtsu remains hidden from all but the narrator and the *kataribe* who informs Hime about Ōtsu. Through her storytelling the *kataribe* links characters who, to the end, can never occupy the same scene. For that matter, none of the characters inhabit the same time or space; Yakamochi, for example, never sees his niece, Hime, and there is no indication that he is aware of Ōtsu's existence. Ōtsu can be seen by no one and can be heard only by himself. The dead man is an "absent presence" in the work,

53. Origuchi's essays "Kokubungaku no hassei 1, 2, and 3" discuss *kataribe* at length.

mediated by the narrator (to the reader) and by the *kataribe* (to Hime). The absence of this protagonist rebukes and challenges the *kindai shōsetsu*, which Origuchi saw as bereft of soul, a form that centers, in place of soul, a problematic, Western-inspired expression of subjectivity.

The *kataribe* in *Shisha* points to the inscription of desire in narrative. When the dead man regains his consciousness, he is filled with grief, primarily because there is no one to pass on the memory of his existence: "Ore no na wa, daremo tsutaeru mono ga nai. . . . Katari tsutaesaseru hazu no kataribe mo, dekite ita darō ni" (156; There is no one to carry on my name. . . . [By this time] there would have been a family storyteller entrusted with the transmission of my name). His lament for having been denied the opportunity to have a wife and son is an expression of desire to be linked to future generations, to be part of a chain of transmission. Shunning a positivistic identity for characters, self acquires meaning in relationship to its progeny and its ancestors. Most important, meaning exists not so much in living as in having oneself narrated. The self is meaningful not by how it is differentiated from other selves, for example, but by having a place in a narrative of filiation.

If the desire to be narrated is the raison d'être of the dead man, we can argue that narrated desire creates Hime. The *kataribe* echoes the dead man's yearnings by relating the prophecy of a young Fujiwara woman who will respond to the dead man's call. In turn, Hime herself is powerfully drawn to the Buddha-image representation of the dead man. Japanese critics have interpreted *Shisha* as a text representing religious devotion,[54] but such readings ignore a far more "secular" desire dispersed throughout the text, manifesting itself most significantly as narration. If desire sets the entire text into motion, it is finally centered by the blankness of death or, put differently, by the impossibility of locating any object that can fulfill desire. Origuchi's valuation of the notion of direct perception and feeling (*jikkan*) is at once the sign that he recognized the futility of fulfilling desire and the displacement of desire itself.

54. Kajiki Gō, *Origuchi Shinobu no sekai: marebito no sonzai* (Sunagoya shobō, 1982), 368.

Narrated desire leaves its mark in the interaction between the *kataribe* and the narrator. Recent studies of narratology on both sides of the Pacific suggest that what was once dismissed as poor narrative control in Japanese prose can be viewed more fruitfully as properties of the Japanese language.[55] Each occurrence of narrative "irregularities" is, of course, a localized phenomenon signifying matters specific to its moment of expression. In the following scene, Hime has just arrived in the mountains and is surveying the vista before her:

> Kaguyama no minami no suso ni kagayaku kawaraya wa, Daikandaiji ni chigainai. Sore kara sara ni sono minami no, yama to yama to no aida ni, usuku kasunde iru no ga, Askua no mura na no *de arō*. . . . Ano kagerō no tatte iru heigen o, kono ashi de, sumi kara sumi made *aruite mitai*. Kō, sono nyōsho wa omotte iru. [Emphasis added]
>
> (163)

> The tile-roofed structure that shines at the foot of Kagu mountain must be Daikandaiji Temple. Faintly visible below the mountains to the south of it must be the village of Asuka. . . . I would like to thoroughly explore on my own those moors where one can see the heat waves rising. This is what she is thinking.

Whereas the paragraph is framed by the narrator's comment (*Kō sono nyōsho wa omotte iru*), and the sentence-ending forms (*chigainai* and *de arō*) mark the words as plain forms, the desiderative *aruite mitai* belongs to Hime. The abrupt ending of the sentence with *mitai* signifies either the narrator expressing Hime's feelings or a stylistic convention pointing to no identifiable figure. The *arō* can be seen as the narrator's supposition, or it can be attributed to Hime's uncertainty about the exact location of her parents' upbringing, stated in the narrator's voice. As we have seen earlier, ambivalent shifting between dif-

55. Komori Yōichi's studies of Futabatei's *Ukigumo* set the standard for the study of language and agency. See Komori, *Buntai* and *Kōzō*. Many critics tend to view ambiguous subject boundaries as characteristic of Japanese language itself. See Barbara Mito Reed, "Chikamatsu Shūkō: An Inquiry in Narrative Modes in Modern Japanese Fiction," *The Journal of Japanese Studies* 14 (Winter 1988): 59–76. Komori's more historicist project, in contrast, attributes indistinctly drawn boundaries among subjects to the particular moment of narrative development inhabited by Meiji texts.

ferent speaking voices is hardly remarkable in Japanese writing. The language allows us to identify separate voices—Hime voicing her feelings and the narrator showing us the scene. Here the text links Hime's subjective perception to the landscape through a multivoiced narration with inflections indicating shifts in the narrating subject (between the narrator and Hime). Masao Miyoshi's work suggests one way of accounting for such "unstable" voicing: The narrator reveals what Miyoshi calls a "collective we" position that assumes a "public and communal" view of subject positions.[56] Bakhtinian dialogics provides another interpretive accounting where the narrating subject is not conceived as consensual. Instead, the identifiable distinctions among voices correspond to social, political, and perspectival differences. The narrator itself is constituted by different voices and is further inscribed with contest by engaging with other voices, both in the text and outside. In *Shisha*, narratorial gestures to assume communal privilege is undercut by its tense relationship to the *kataribe*.

Although the narrator remains relatively unobtrusive for most of the text, there is sustained drama coming from its encounters with the *kataribe*. The following excerpt shows the *kataribe* about to tell Hime about the dead man.

> Atarashii monogatari ga, issai, kataribe no kuchi no noboranu yo ga kite ita. Keredomo, katakuna na Taima uji no kataribe no furuuba no tame ni, *ware ware* wa ima ichido, kyonen irai no monogatari o shite oite mo yoi de arō. [Emphasis added]
>
> (159)

> The times were here when no more tales would issue forth from the mouths of storytellers. But for the sake of the stubborn old storyteller of the Taima family, let *us* proceed just this once, with an account of events that began last year.

56. In characterizing "middle period" Japanese literature (roughly from the Meiji Restoration to 1970), Miyoshi ("Against the Native Grain," 230) notes: "Transcending the boundaries of the individual's consciousness is the narrator, who is both inside and outside the character. This narrator, however, is not so much an omniscient god as an all-knowing pater familias." It should be noted that Miyoshi's "collective we" does not simply replace the individual as a transcendental subject; rather, it permits the consideration of relations that obtain among text, reader, character, narrator, and so on, rather different from the field of reading that surrounds Western novels.

In this, one of the few places in which the narrator underscores its own presence, it is dismissive of the *kataribe*. In the following scene, which provides a brief historical account of the temple complex in Nijōzan, the narrator intrudes with this judgment: "Although such an account exists, it is merely an old tale that has been handed down by an old *kataribe* of this region. While just a span of what can be called a short period of a hundred years, for lives far removed from the written word, it seems as long ago as antiquity itself" (162). The narrator places the blame on the *kataribe* when things are not clear. If "knowing" is the required condition for narrating or storytelling, this passage shows that matters of the past are worth knowing, and in those matters the *kataribe* knows more than the narrator. Further, the narrator's realm of "knowing" is restricted because it is located in the present (the narrative present, which is in eighth-century Japan, half a century after the death of Ōtsu). While narrative self-reference cannot be claimed as peculiar to modern Japanese prose, the ambivalence imparted by this occasional self-reference seems to be pronounced in post-*genbun'itchi* prose narratives (*Shisha* among them). I am referring not simply to narrative self-referentiality, which appears frequently in *gesaku*, for example, but rather to its occurrence together with "ambivalent narration," which signifies uncertainty in the choice of narrating voice.

To pursue this matter further, let us return for a moment to the narrator's denigrating tone, which signifies the inscription of a perspective (belonging to someone). Paradoxically, the dismissive comments directed toward the *kataribe* do little to discredit her; on the contrary, the effect is to undo, to subvert the role of *narrator* as an effaced, impersonal third person. While the events in *Shisha* go on to validate the *kataribe*'s pronouncements (including her prophecy that a beautiful Fujiwara maiden will be united with a young nobleman who was condemned to death years earlier), the narrator is seen as truculently taking stabs at her credibility, which is, after all, upheld. In effect, the narrator is given a more sharply defined presence as a speaking subject by virtue of its opposition to the *kataribe*. In doing so, the narrator has moved closer to the role played by the *kataribe*, who is at once narrator (of events) and actor in the text. Origuchi invests the *kataribe* with this dual function in order to valorize the performative aspect of narration. The *kataribe* already has a tenuous and anomalous position in day-to-day life. Yet, it is as if the narrator covets the *kataribe*'s substantiality, for she is, after all, both a character in the text and a signifier of performative narration, something that has been systematically written out of the *kindai shōsetsu*, which aspires to transcribe persons and events as if writing was transparent. The narrator's self-referentiality reveals its desire to claim substantiality for itself. Unlike the transparent narration characterizing *kindai shōsetsu*, *katari* is a narrative practice that makes no attempts to suppress its own materiality. In *Shisha*, the narrator's obtrusiveness additionally serves to question a narrative practice (the *kindai shōsetsu*) that threatens to eliminate performance.

TRACING *JIKKAN*

The contentiousness between the narrator and the *kataribe* thematizes another concept crucial to Origuchi's project—direct perception (*jikkan*). Compared to a literate culture, the sense of "long ago" is established much more quickly in a culture reliant on memory. Such difference separates the narrator, who belongs to a literate world, from the *kataribe*, who belongs to the world of what Origuchi calls *jikkan*. As he saw it, unmediated perception, or *jikkan*, had ceased to characterize human exchange, with mediations such as writing taking its place. The clash between narrator and *kataribe* is an expression of the tensions that arise from the paradox of producing a text that attempts to actualize direct experience while relying on the medium of narration. *Jikkan*, like orality or speech, is a signifier of "authentic experience" that stands in sharp contrast to scripted expression.[57] The *kataribe* (in *Shisha* she enables *jikkan* to be ex-

57. H. D. Harootunian represents Origuchi's critical consideration of this dichotomy as manifest in the separation of poetry and prose: "Composition—writing down sentences—suppressed the motive power behind poetry and obscured its links to daily speech, which Origuchi acknowledged was no longer accessible even though its founding source lay in 'words of the gods'" (Harootunian, *Things Seen and Unseen*, 428).

perienced) signifies a space outside of written records, archives, and histories.

By the 1930s, scholarly studies were subject to validation measured in good part by their proximity to an authoritative center represented by Tokyo University. Institutional affiliation mirrors a complex but clearly recognized politics mapping the separation of insider from outsider, the privileged from the less esteemed, in twentieth-century Japan. Origuchi's tenure at Kokugakuin University, and later at Keiō University, situates him outside the center of academic/narrative production. It is not surprising that a text written in such an environment reproduces contestation through a narrative that assumes a decisively different form from that of the reigning elitist discourses and instead disperses (narrative) perspective in order to decenter authority.

A similar relocation of authority to a nonauthoritative site (in this case the listener) underlies the following narratorial lament over changes observed in contemporary (eighth-century) Japan:

> Mō yo no hito no kokoro wa sakashiku narisugite ita. Hitorigatari no monogatari nado ni, shin o uchikonde kiku mono no aru hazu wa nakatta.
>
> (254)
>
> These days people were already far too clever; there was no way anyone would seriously listen to such an old storyteller's tale.

Here, the narrator reveals (as it does consistently) its sympathies to an ancient practice it knows is vanishing. We might posit wistfulness, even desire on the narrator's part, to have at least a listener like Hime; the *kataribe*, in any era, is after all, empowered by the presence of those who will listen. Authority is not something that is fixed; it is to be granted, in this instance through the act of listening. The narrator desires a more substantial engagement with Hime and sees in the *kataribe* and its relation to Hime an interaction that is denied a narrator that must simply present. By its very nature, the *kataribe* performs only under conditions that presume a listener, while a narrator is asked to narrativize as if there were no interlocutor. Speaker and listener-respondent have been wrested from each other in the paradigm of realist literature upon which the *kindai shōsetsu* rests.

By focusing on the "narrator function," *Shisha* situates itself in its own discursive field of the *kindai shōsetsu* at the same time that it defamiliarizes that very discourse. A narrator must establish its own relationships to readers, characters, and other texts in accordance with the requirements of its discursive field. A few decades earlier, writers like Yamada Bimyō, Ozaki Kōyō, Futabatei Shimei, and other early practitioners of modern prose narrative had confronted the same issue of placing the subject, and they did so by experimenting with *genbun'itchi*.[58] The intervening decades had seen the appropriation of Western methodologies to explain and understand scientific and social phenomena. Futabatei and his fellow writers were concerned largely with questions of (subject) representation as strictly a formal matter; by the 1930s, representation was more widely recognized as an ideological battleground as state policy, leftist discourse, strident militarism, and other narratives charting social organization vied for the status of truth. Affirming and situating individuated subjects remained a primary concern, but the question of appropriate linguistic form for presenting the individual subject was displaced by a concern for proper narrative form in which to adequately represent the subject, conceived not as highly individuated but as a member of larger wholes—class, the family, and the nation-state.

Shisha's focus on *katari* and the *kataribe* expresses Origuchi's interest in challenging the conventions of scripted narrative form and its associations with the system writ large. In an afterword to the prose narrative text *Shintokumaru*, Origuchi expressed misgivings about the method of modern history, stating that history is far better served (represented) through novels and plays.[59] For him the value of the past lay not in truths that might be recovered from it but in the *jikkan* possessed by those

58. Masao Miyoshi's discussion of inflections and speaker–listener relations in *Accomplices of Silence: The Modern Japanese Novel* (Berkeley: University of California Press, 1974) remains the best English-language examination of the issue.

59. As Hirosue Tamotsu (*Origuchi Shinobu shū*, 389) observed, Origuchi felt that *jikkan* in the form of a *shōsetsu* could best reveal the traces of antiquity (*kodai*).

who lived in antiquity. Origuchi saw history, like literature, as being a method of representation. But as it became shaped by the teleological approach of Western historiography or of literary realism, it lost its ability to enact the past. Only performative narratives, drama, and poetry could hope to resuscitate Japanese antiquity.

When Origuchi had declared *Shisha* to be not history but a modern prose narrative with a modern perspective, he noted in the same passage that the *kataribe* in *Shisha* was not so much a conscious artifice as something that had materialized on its own.[60] In this way, Origuchi's commentary insistently set up *Shisha* not as a history, nor (despite his statement to the contrary) as a *kindai shōsetsu*, but as the enactment of *jikkan* complemented by "expressivity" (*hassō*). Origuchi hoped to displace the notion of subjectivity with *jikkan* and *hassō*, which signified intuited understanding and expression. By this substitution he shifted the object of privilege from the agent (an individuated subject) to performance (*hassō*) itself.[61]

What Western narrative and epistemological conventions cannot effect, performative narration can realize. Accordingly, *Shisha* invokes the power of visions, reveries, and dreams as a means with which to actualize *jikkan* and *hassō*. Sitting in a hut that has been equipped with a loom, Hime valiantly but unsuccessfully tries to weave fragile lotus threads into a garment for the unclad Buddha image she has seen and perceives as being cold. A nun materializes, and, speaking with the voice of the *kataribe* (this reinscription of the *kataribe* medium serves to attribute *kami* status to her), teaches her the proper technique. When Hime resumes her weaving, she is able to weave the difficult threads without mishap. The chapter (18) ends: "Omoitsumete madoronde iru uchi ni, iratsume no chie ga, hitotsu no iki [threshold] o koeta no de aru" (252; The young maiden was able to break through her trance and reach a new threshold [of awareness]). In these and other repeated lapses into dream-like

60. Origuchi, "Yamagoshi amida zō no ga'in," 328.

61. It is this kind of strategy that led Nakagami Kenji to characterize Origuchi himself as a shamanistic figure (a medium) who merely delivers that which is given to him (Nakagami Kenji, "Monogatari no keifu: Origuchi Shinobu, Part 2, Essay 4," in *Kokubungaku: kaishaku to kyōzai no kenkyū*, 145).

states, Hime realizes a clarity and awareness that eludes her in wakeful states.

In a scene drawn directly from an earlier text entitled "Mizu no onna," Hime dreams that she is walking along a beach, treading on sand that keeps turning into pearls. No matter how often she tries to take some in her hands, they scatter in the wind. When she finally manages to grasp a large, gleaming pearl, a large wave sweeps her into the ocean—the white pearl and her glistening naked body drifting on the surface. She becomes the pearl, which then quickly sinks to the bottom, where it changes into a white coral tree. When she awakens, she associates the dream with the journey that has brought her to the mountains (217–18). Leaving the interpretation of the dream to others,[62] it is worth noting that a sense of ordained transformation runs throughout the dream. Like her reveries, the dream serves as a marker, bringing into sharp relief the meaning of what Hime is confronting in her wakeful state. *Jikkan* represents that crucial field where, against the numbing realities of contemporary life (be it the mid 700s or the 1930s), one must find ways of seeing and re-creating a clarity that can be glimpsed only in snatches of dreams.

In the late 1930s, a period in Japanese history in which writers were turning to the political right and the state permitted little dissent, even Origuchi's narratives authenticating essential Japanese identity came under scrutiny.[63] His endorsement of *jikkan* provided a way to dismiss the strategies of *kindai shōsetsu* writers who sought to narrate individuated subjects, however self-enclosed they tended to remain. *Shisha* stands as an act, a praxis that attempts to produce the intensity and reality of pure experience that has been lost to "quotidian experience"—upon which the *kindai shōsetsu* ostensibly rests. *Shisha* is not "about" the dead man or simply the story of Hime, a young noblewoman who responds to the desire of the dead man as it is communicated through the storyteller (*kataribe*) and in the form of ce-

62. See, for example, Kajiki Gō, *Origuchi Shinobu no sekai*, 377.

63. Saeki Shōichi ("*Shisha no sho* no jiremma," 242) tells us that the authorities forced a softened depiction of the rebellious historical figure, Ōtsu no Ōji. These were the times when Tanizaki, in writing the *Genji*, endured even more obtrusive intervention.

lestial images hovering over mountain peaks. This text narrates the vacancy of modern Japanese life, wherein people can no longer hear or visualize that which is dead and gone. Implicit in the disclaimer accompanying *Shisha* that it is not a history is Origuchi's understanding of the inadequacies of writing conceived of as primarily representational. His distaste for positivistic scholarship steered him clear of the temptations to validate *Shisha* by placing it in reified oppositions to histories, Western literature, or *kindai shōsetsu*. The contingencies of his own moment of enunciation (late 1930s) suggested to Origuchi the futility of offering yet another representation of the past. His was a direct engagement with otherness, through which he hoped to illuminate an antiquity, not as "life as it was, nor even life remembered, but life as it had been forgotten."[64] Not an exercise in nostalgia for the past, *Shisha* was an attempt to speak to the present by creating a version of antiquity. In a time when subjects were expressed in terms of the Western realist subject or of modern nationhood, *Shisha* would write itself around a man long dead, recoverable only through the immediacy of the most performative medium—sound.

I began this epilogue by positioning Origuchi's *Shisha* as a text contesting the widespread presumption that the *kindai shōsetsu* had become the dominant form of *kindai bungaku* by the 1930s. What prompted such a reaction in Origuchi and others of his generation (as well as earlier and succeeding ones) was the practice of literary appraisal that was deeply entrenched in the assumptions of Western realist traditions emphasizing commentary on content and in various ways ratifying the centrality of the private subject conceived in emphatically positivist terms. By reading selected foundational texts of the *kindai shōsetsu* from a perspective that recast subjectivity as both an effect of discursive activity and its agent, I sought to delineate the relations between textuality and "modern Japanese society" that the pre-

64. The phrasing is from Susan Buck-Morss's book on Walter Benjamin: "[Benjamin] retained the notion that the Arcades Project would present collective history as Proust had presented his own—not 'life as it was,' nor even life remembered, but life as it has been 'forgotten'" (*The Dialectics of Seeing: Walter Benjamin and the Arcades Project* [Cambridge: MIT Press, 1989], 39).

vailing Western realist readings tended to suppress. That is, by introducing agency into this consideration of narrative and the subject, texts were necessarily reconceived in terms of the world as it operates in a field of unequally dispersed power. As questions of the individuated Western subject entered the arena of post-Restoration Japanese letters, it became closely linked to the vehicle of its presentation (i.e., the *kindai shōsetsu*), which, like the very notion of the subject, signified modernity in twentieth-century Japan. In some measure, the connections made between the individuated subject, the novel, and a particular socioeconomic system (capitalism) by such writers as Ian Watt and Terry Eagleton, among others, are germane to the Japanese case. Similarly, the ties between writing and nationhood explored by such critics as Benedict Anderson and Homi K. Bhabha would not be exempt as conditions governing modern Japanese textual production. It must be left for future efforts to localize the specific conjuncture of the narration of private subjects and the conditions of nation building on Japanese terrain.

Bibliography

SOURCES IN JAPANESE

(All Japanese-language sources were published in Tokyo.)

Aeba Takao. *Hihyō to hyōgen: Kindai Nihon bungaku no watakushi.* Bungei shunjū, 1979.

Akasaka Norio. "Origuchi Shinobu: marebito tachi no tasogare." In *Kyōkai no hassei.* Sunagoya shobō, 1989.

Amino Yoshihiko. *Nihon chūsei no hinōgyōmin to tennō.* Iwanami shoten, 1984.

Enomoto Takashi. "*Arakuse* kō." In *Shizenshugi bungaku.* Yūseidō, 1975.

———. "*Kabi* no seiritsu to sono imi." In *Shizenshugi bungaku.* Yūseidō, 1975.

Etō Jun. *Natsume Sōseki.* Keisō shobō, 1965.

———. *Natsume Sōseki.* Shinchō bunko, 1979.

———. *Sakka wa kōdō suru: buntai ni tsuite.* Kawade shobō shinsha, 1988.

———. *Sōseki to sono jidai.* 2 vols. Shinchō sensho, 1970.

Fujii Sadakazu. "*Shisha no sho.*" *Kokubungaku: kaishaku to kanshō* 44 (September 1979): 79–81.

Fukae Hiroshi. *Sōseki chōhen shōsetsu no sekai.* Ōfusha, 1982.

Hirano Ken. *Shōwa bungaku shi.* Chikuma shobō, 1963; rev. 1981.

Hiroe Yōko. "*Kabi* no ichi to sono shitsuyō sei." In *Rōnko Tokuda Shūsei,* edited by Kōno Toshirō. Sakufūsha, 1982.

Hirosue Tamotsu. *Saikaku no shōsetsu: jikū ishiki no tenkan o megutte.* Heibonsha sensho, 1982.

———, ed. *Origuchi Shinobu shū.* Vol. 22 of *Nihon kindai shisō taikei.* Chikuma shobō, 1975.

Ishihara Chiaki. "Manazashi to shite no tasha: *Kokoro* ron." *Tōyoko kokubungaku* 17 (March 1985).

———. *Natsume Sōseki: hanten suru tekusuto.* Vol. 14 of *Nihon bungaku kenkyū shiryō shin shū.* Yūseidō, 1990.

Isoda Kōichi. *Shisō to shite no Tōkyō.* Kokubunsha, 1978.

Itahana Junji. "Wagahai wa neko de aru ron." *Nihon bungaku* 31 (November 1982): 1–12.

Itō Sei. "Tōson no hassō to sutairu." In *Shimazaki Tōson zenshū bekkan.* Chikuma shobō, 1983.

———. *Nihon bundan shi.* 24 vols. Kōdansha, 1979.

Kajiki Gō. *Origuchi Shinobu no sekai: marebito no sonzai.* Sunagoya shobō, 1982.

Kamei Hideo. *Kansei no henkaku.* Kōdansha, 1983.

———. *Shintai: kono fushigi naru mono no bungaku.* Renga shobō, 1984.

Kamiyama Mutsumi. *Natsume Sōseki ron josetsu.* Kokubunsha, 1980.

Karatani Kōjin. *Kotoba to higeki.* Daisan bunmeisha, 1989.

———. *Nihon kindai bungaku no kigen.* Kōdansha, 1980.

Kawamura Jirō. "*Shisha no sho* ni tsuite." In *Bungei dokuhon Origuchi Shinobu*, new rev. ed. Kawade shobō, 1982.

———. "*Shisha no sho* saisetsu: bungaku no ne e no toi." *Bungei* 14 (March 1975): 212–23.

Komatsu Kazuhiko. *Ijinron: minzoku shakai no shinsei.* Aonisha, 1985.

Komori Yōichi. *Buntai to shite no monogatari.* Chikuma shobō, 1988.

———. *Kōzō to shite no katari.* Shinyōsha, 1988.

———. "*Ukigumo* no ji no bun: kotoba no bottō to shite no buntai." *Kokugo kokubun kenkyū* 62 (August 1979). Also in *Kōzō to shite no katari.* Shinyōsha, 1988.

Kōno Toshirō, ed. *Ronkō Tokuda Shūsei.* Sakufūsha, 1982.

Maeda Ai. *Kindai dokusha no seiritsu.* Vol. 2 of *Maeda Ai chosaku shū.* Chikuma shobō, 1989.

———. "Meiji risshin shusse shugi no keifu." *Bungaku* 33, no. 4 (April 1965): 10–21.

———. "Neko no kotoba, neko no ronri." In *Kindai Nihon no bungaku kūkan.* Shinyōsha, 1983.

———. *Toshi kūkan no naka no bungaku.* Chikuma shobō, 1982.

Matsumura Tatsuo, ed. *Natsume Sōseki shū.* Vol. 24 of *Nihon kindai bungaku taikei.* Kadokawa shoten, 1971.

Mitani Kuniaki. "Kindai shōsetsu no gensetsu joshō: shōsetsu no 'jikan' to gabuntai aruiwa Kamei Hideo 'Kansei no henkaku' o yomu." *Nihon bungaku* 33 (July 1984): 47–56.

Miyoshi Yukio, Hiraoka Toshio, Hirakawa Sukehiro, Etō Jun, eds. *Sōseki no jidai to shakai.* Vol. 4 of *Kōza Natsume Sōseki.* Yūhikaku, 1982.

Mizutani Akio. "Neko no sekai." In *Natsume Sōseki zenshū bekkan*, edited by Etō Jun and Yoshida Seiichi. Kadokawa shoten, 1975.

Murai Osamu. "Marebito no kigen: 'shi' no igata." In *Origuchi Shinobu o yomu.* Gendai kikakushitsu kan, 1981.

Nakagami Kenji. "Monogatari no keifu: Origuchi Shinobu." In *Kokubungaku: Kaishaku to kanshō* 28 (December 1983): 144–47. A series of Nakagami's articles on Origuchi appear in multiple issues in 1983–84.

Nakamura Mitsuo. *Fūzoku shōsetsu ron.* Kawade shobō, 1954.

Natsume Sōseki. *Sōseki bungaku zenshū.* Vol. 6. Shūeisha, 1983.

———. *Sōseki zenshū*. 16 vols. Iwanami shoten, 1965–67.
Nishimura Tōru. *Origuchi Shinobu jiten*. Taishūkan shoten, 1988.
Noguchi Fujio. *Tokuda Shūsei no bungaku*. Chikuma shobō, 1979.
Noguchi Takehiko. "'Eibin naru byōsha' no bunpō: Tokuda Shūsei no shōsetsu buntai o megutte." *Umi* 13 (August 1981): 192–95.
Okitsu Kaname. *Meiji kaikaki bungaku no kenkyū*. Ōfusha, 1969.
———. *Nihon bungaku to rakugo*. Ōfusha, 1971.
Okuno Takeo. *Bungaku no genfūkei*. Shūeisha, 1972.
Origuchi Shinobu. *Origuchi Shinobu zenshū*. 32 vols. Chūō kōronsha, 1965–68.
———. *Origuchi Shinobu zenshū nōto hen*. Chūō kōronsha, 1987–88.
Ozaki Kōyō. *Ozaki Kōyō shū*. Vol. 18 of *Meiji bungaku zenshū*. Chikuma shobō, 1965.
Ozaki Yoshio. *Sōseki to sokuten kyoshi*. Hobunkan, 1968.
Saeki Shōichi. "*Shisha no sho* no jiremma: Nihon no 'watashi o motomete' IV." *Bungei* 12 (September 1973): 234–47.
Sakamoto Tokumatsu. "*Shisha no sho* no kojitsusei." In *Origuchi Shinobu: Nihon bungaku kenkyū shiryō sō sho*. Yūseidō, 1972.
Sasaki Hiroshi. "*Arajotai* shiki ron." In *Shizenshugi bungaku*. Yūseidō, 1975.
Senuma Shigeki. *Natsume Sōseki*. Tōkyō Daigaku shuppankai, 1970.
Shinoda Kōichirō. "Nijū no ie: Shusei o yominaosu." In *Hihyō no kigōgaku*. Miraisha, 1979.
———. *Shisō to shite no Tōkyō*. Kokubunsha, 1978.
Shinozaki Hideki. "Kabi no kōzu." In *Ronkō Tokuda Shūsei*, edited by Kōno Toshirō. Sakufūsha, 1982.
Sugiyama Yasuhiko. *Sanbun hyōgen no kikō*. San'ichi shobō, 1974.
Takahashi Kuniko, "Tōson no *Kyūshujin* to *Warazōri*." In *Shimazaki Tōson*, edited by Nihon bungaku kenkyū shiryō gisho. Yūseidō, 1971.
Takahashi Toshio. "*Arajotai* o yomu: 'risshi' gensō no yukue." In *Ronkō Tokuda Shūsei*, edited by Kōno Toshiro. Sakufūsha, 1982.
Togawa Shunsuke. *Shimazaki Tōson*. Chikuma shobō, 1979.
Tokuda Kazuo, ed. *Tokuda Shūsei shū*. Vol. 21 of *Nihon kindai bungaku taikei*. Kadokawa shoten, 1973.
Tokuda Shūsei. *Shūsei zenshū*. 15 vols. Hibonkaku, 1936–37.
Wada Kingo. *Shizenshugi bungaku*. Shibundō, 1966.
Yamada Akira, ed. *Shimazaki Tōson shū I*. Vol. 13 of *Nihon kindai bungaku taikei*. Kodakawa shoten, 1971.
Yamamoto Kenkichi. *Shaku Chōkū*. Kadokawa shoten, 1972.
Yanabu Akira. *Hon'yaku no shisō*. Heibonsha sensho, 1977.
———. *Hon'yakugo seiritsu jijō*. Iwanami shinsho, 1982.
Yoshida Rokurō. *Wagahai wa neko de aru ron*. Keisō shobō, 1968.

Yoshida, Seiichi. *Shizenshugi no kenkyū*. 2 vols. Tōkyōdō, 1955.
Yoshimura Yoshio. *Natsume Sōseki*. Shunjūsha, 1980.

SOURCES IN ENGLISH

Altieri, Charles. "An Idea and Ideal of a Literary Canon." *Critical Inquiry* 10 (December 1983): 37–60.

Anderer, Paul. *Other Worlds: Arishima Takeo and the Bounds of Modern Japanese Fiction*. New York: Columbia University Press, 1984.

Anderson, Benedict. *Imagined Communities: Reflections on the Origin and Spread of Nationalism*. London: Verso, 1983.

Anderson, Perry. "Modernity and Revolution." In *Marxism and the Interpretation of Culture*, edited by Cary Nelson and Lawrence Grossberg. Urbana: University of Illinois Press, 1988.

Andrews, William L. "The Novelization of Voice in Early African American Narrative." *PMLA* 105 (January 1990): 23–34.

Arima Tatsuo. *The Failure of Freedom: A Portrait of Modern Japanese Intellectuals*. Cambridge, Mass.: Harvard University Press, 1969.

Auerbach, Erich. *Mimesis: The Representation of Reality in Western Literature*. Princeton: Princeton University Press, 1953.

Bakhtin, Mikhail. *The Dialogic Imagination: Four Essays by M. M. Bakhtin*. Edited by Michael Holquist. Austin: University of Texas Press, 1981.

———. *Problems of Dostoevsky's Poetics*. Edited and translated by Caryl Emerson. Minneapolis: University of Minnesota Press, 1984.

———. *Rabelais and His World*. Translated by Helene Iswolsky. Cambridge, Mass.: MIT Press, 1968.

Banfield, Ann. *Unspeakable Sentences: Narration and Representation in the Language of Fiction*. Boston: Routledge & Kegan Paul, 1982.

Barthes, Roland. "The Death of the Author." In *Image, Music, Text*, translated by Stephen Heath. New York: Hill and Wang, 1977.

———. *Writing Degree Zero*. Translated by Annette Lavers and Colin Smith. New York: Hill and Wang, 1968.

Belsey, Catherine. *Critical Practice*. London: Methuen, 1980.

Benjamin, Walter. *Charles Baudelaire: A Lyric Poet in the Era of High Capitalism*. London: Verso, 1983.

Berman, Marshall. *All That Is Solid Melts Into Air: The Experience of Modernity*. New York: Simon and Schuster, 1982.

Bernstein, Gail Lee, ed. *Recreating Japanese Women, 1600–1945*. Berkeley: University of California Press, 1991.

Bhabha, Homi K., ed. *Nation and Narration*. New York: Routledge, 1990.

Brennan, Timothy. "The National Longing for Form." In *Nation and Narration*, edited by Homi K. Bhabha. New York: Routledge, 1990.

Buck-Morss, Susan. *The Dialectics of Seeing: Walter Benjamin and the Arcades Project*. Cambridge, Mass.: MIT Press, 1989.

Callinicos, Alex. *Making History: Agency, Structure, and Change in Social Theory*. Ithaca: Cornell University Press, 1988.

Carroll, David. *The Subject in Question: The Languages of Theory and the Strategies of Fiction*. Chicago: University of Chicago Press, 1982.

Chambers, Ross. *Story and Situation: Narrative Seduction and the Power of Fiction*. Minneapolis: University of Minnesota Press, 1984.

Dale, Peter. *The Myth of Japanese Uniqueness*. New York: St. Martin's Press, 1986.

de Bary, Brett. "Karatani Kōjin's *Origins of Modern Japanese Literature*." *South Atlantic Quarterly* 87 (Summer 1988): 591–613.

de Certeau, Michel. *The Practice of Everyday Life*. Translated by Steven F. Rendall. Berkeley: University of California Press, 1984.

Doi Takeo. *The Psychological World of Natsume Sōseki*. Cambridge, Mass.: Harvard University Press, 1976.

Dower, John D., ed. *Origins of the Modern Japanese State: Selected Writings of E. H. Norman*. New York: Pantheon Books, 1975.

During, Simon. "Literature—Nationalism's Other? The Case for Revision." In *Nation and Narration*, edited by Homi K. Bhabha. New York: Routledge, 1990.

Ebersole, Gary. *Ritual Poetry and the Politics of Death in Early Japan*. Princeton: Princeton University Press, 1989.

Field, Norma. *The Splendor of Longing in the "Tale of Genji."* Princeton: Princeton University Press, 1987.

Foucault, Michel. "Language to Infinity." In *Language, Counter-Memory, Practice: Selected Essays and Interviews by Michel Foucault*, edited by Donald F. Bouchard. Ithaca: Cornell University Press, 1977.

———. "What Is an Author?" In *Textual Strategies*, edited by Joshua Harari. Ithaca: Cornell University Press, 1979.

Fowler, Edward. *The Rhetoric of Confession:* Shishōsetsu *in Early Twentieth-Century Japanese Fiction*. Berkeley: University of California Press, 1988.

Frow, John. *Marxism and Literary History*. Cambridge, Mass.: Harvard University Press, 1986.

Fujii, James A. "The Subject in Meiji Prose Narratives." Ph.D. diss., University of Chicago, 1986.

Gates, Henry Louis, Jr. *The Signifying Monkey: A Theory of African-American Literary Criticism*. New York: Oxford University Press, 1988.

Gellner, Ernest. *Nations and Nationalism.* Oxford: Basil Blackwell, 1983.

Genette, Gerard. *Narrative Discourse: An Essay in Method.* Translated by Jane Lewin. Ithaca: Cornell University Press, 1980.

Gluck, Carol. *Japan's Modern Myths: Ideology in the Late Meiji Period.* Princeton: Princeton University Press, 1986.

Harootunian, H. D. "Between Politics and Culture: Authority and the Ambiguities of Intellectual Choice in Imperial Japan." In *Japan in Crisis: Essays on Taisho Democracy*, edited by Bernard S. Silberman and H. D. Harootunian. Princeton: Princeton University Press, 1974.

———. "Disciplinizing Native Knowledge and Producing Place: Yanagita Kunio, Origuchi Shinobu, Takata Yasuma." In *Culture and Identity: Japanese Intellectuals during the Interwar Years*, edited by J. Thomas Rimer. Princeton: Princeton University Press, 1990.

———. "Ideology as Conflict." In *Conflict in Modern Japanese History: The Neglected Tradition*, edited by Tetsuo Najita and J. Victor Koschmann. Princeton: Princeton University Press, 1982.

———. "Late Tokugawa Culture and Thought." In *The Nineteenth Century*, edited by Marius B. Jansen. Vol. 5 of *Cambridge History of Japan.* Cambridge: Cambridge University Press, 1989.

———. *Things Seen and Unseen: Discourse and Ideology in Tokugawa Nativism.* Chicago: University of Chicago Press, 1988.

Harvey, David. *The Condition of Postmodernity: An Enquiry into the Origins of Cultural Change.* Cambridge: Basil Blackwell, 1990.

Havens, Thomas R. H. *Farm and Nation in Modern Japan: Agrarian Nationalism, 1870–1940.* Princeton: Princeton University Press, 1974.

Hirschkop, Ken. "A Response to the Forum on Mikhail Bakhtin." In *Bakhtin: Essays and Dialogues on His Work*, edited by Gary Saul Morson. Chicago: University of Chicago Press, 1986.

Hirschkop, Ken, and David Shepherd, eds. *Bakhtin and Cultural Theory.* Manchester: Manchester University Press, 1989.

Irokawa Daikichi. *The Culture of the Meiji Period.* Edited and translated by Marius Jansen. Princeton: Princeton University Press, 1985.

Ivy, Marilyn. "Critical Texts, Mass Artifacts: The Consumption of Knowledge in Postmodern Japan." *South Atlantic Quarterly* 87 (Summer 1988): 419–44.

Jameson, Fredric. *Marxism and Form.* Princeton: Princeton University Press, 1971.

———. "Third World Literature in the Era of Multinational Capitalism."*Social Text* 15 (Fall 1986): 65–88.

Jay, Paul. *Being in the Text: Self-Representation from Wordsworth to Roland Barthes.* Ithaca: Cornell University Press, 1984.

Keene, Donald. *Dawn to the West: Japanese Literature of the Modern Era.* New York: Holt, Rinehart, and Winston, 1984.

Kermode, Frank. "Institutional Control of Interpretation." *Salmagundi* 43 (Winter 1979): 72–86.

Kinmonth, Earl. *The Self-Made Man in Meiji Japanese Thought.* Berkeley: University of California Press, 1981.

Kittay, Jeffrey, and Wlad Godzich. *The Emergence of Prose: An Essay in Prosaics.* Minneapolis: University of Minnesota Press, 1987.

Konishi Jun'ichi. *The Archaic and Ancient Ages.* Vol. 1 of *A History of Japanese Literature,* edited by Earl Miner. Princeton: Princeton University Press, 1984.

Kristeva, Julia. "Word, Dialogue, and Novel." In *Desire in Language: A Semiotic Approach to Literature and Art.* New York: Columbia University Press, 1980.

Kumakura, Chiyuki. "Interpersonal Speaker: The Point of View in Japanese Narrative." Paper presented at a colloquium, Center for Japanese Studies, University of California, Berkeley, May 5, 1986.

LaCapra, Dominick. "Bakhtin, Marxism, and the Carnivalesque." In *Rethinking Intellectual History: Texts, Contexts, Language.* Ithaca: Cornell University Press, 1983.

Layoun, Mary. *Travels of a Genre: The Modern Novel and Ideology.* Princeton: Princeton University Press, 1990.

Lifton, Robert J., Shūichi Katō, and Michael R. Reich. *Six Lives, Six Deaths: Portraits from Modern Japan.* New Haven: Yale University Press, 1979.

Lord, Albert B. *The Singer of Tales.* Cambridge, Mass.: Harvard University Press, 1960.

Lotman, Jurij. "The Poetics of Everyday Behavior." In *The Semiotics of Russian Cultural History,* edited by Alexander D. Nakhimovsky and Alice Stone Nakhimovsky. Ithaca: Cornell University Press, 1985.

Lovell, Terry. *Consuming Fiction.* London: Verso, 1987.

Marx, Karl. "The German Ideology." In *The Marx-Engels Reader,* edited by Robert C. Tucker. New York: Norton, 1978.

Mitchell, Richard. *Censorship in Imperial Japan.* Princeton: Princeton University Press, 1983.

Mitchell, W. J. T., ed. *On Narrative.* Chicago: University of Chicago Press, 1980.

Miyoshi, Masao. *Accomplices of Silence: The Modern Japanese Novel.* Berkeley: University of California Press, 1974.

———. "Against the Native Grain: The Japanese Novel and the 'Postmodern' West." *South Atlantic Quarterly* 87 (Summer 1988): 525–50.

———. "Against the Native Grain: Reading the Japanese Novel in

America." In *Critical Issues in East Asian Literature: Report on an International Conference on East Asian Literature.* Seoul: International Cultural Society of Korea, 1983.

Moi, Toril. *Sexual, Textual Politics.* London: Methuen, 1985.

Morson, Gary Saul, ed. *Bakhtin: Essays and Dialogues on His Work.* Chicago: University of Chicago Press, 1986.

Myers, Ramon H., and Mark R. Peattie. *The Japanese Colonial Empire, 1895–1945.* Princeton: Princeton University Press, 1984.

Najita, Tetsuo, and H.D. Harootunian. "Japanese Revolt against the West: Political and Cultural Criticism in the Twentieth Century." In *The Twentieth Century,* edited by Peter Duus. Vol. 6 of *The Cambridge History of Japan.* Cambridge: Cambridge University Press, 1988.

Ohmann, Richard. "The Shaping of a Canon: U.S. Fiction, 1960–1975." *Critical Inquiry* 10 (September 1983): 199–223.

Oka Yoshitake. "Generational Conflict after the Russo-Japanese War." In *Conflict in Modern Japanese History: The Neglected Tradition,* edited by Tetsuo Najita and J. Victor Koschmann. Princeton: Princeton University Press, 1982.

Okada, Richard. *Figures of Resistance: Poetry, Narrating, and the Politics of Fiction in "The Tale of Genji" and Other Mid-Heian Texts.* Durham, N.C.: Duke University Press, 1991.

Ong, Walter. *Orality and Literacy.* New York: Methuen, 1982.

Pechey, Graham. "Bakhtin, Marxism, and Post-Structuralism." In *Literature, Politics, and Theory,* edited by Frances Barker, Peter Hulme, Margaret Iversen, and Diana Loxley. New York: Methuen, 1986.

Pechter, Edward. "The New Historicism and Its Discontents: Politicizing Renaissance Drama." In *PMLA* 102 (May 1987): 292–303.

Pecora, Vincent. *Self and Form in Modern Narrative.* Baltimore: The Johns Hopkins University Press, 1989.

Pollack, David. "Framing the Self: The Philosophical Dimensions of Human Nature in *Kokoro.*" *Monumenta Nipponica* 43 (Winter 1988): 417–27.

Reed, Barbara Mito. "Chikamatsu Shūkō: An Inquiry in Narrative Modes in Modern Japanese Fiction." *Journal of Japanese Studies* 14 (Winter 1988): 59–76.

———. "Language, Narrative, Structure, and the 'Shōsetsu.'" Ph.D. diss., Princeton University, 1985.

Rimmon-Kenan, Shlomith. *Narrative Fiction: Contemporary Poetics.* New York: Methuen, 1983.

Rubin, Jay. *Injurious to Public Morals.* Seattle: University of Washington Press, 1984.

Ryan, Marleigh Grayer. *Japan's First Modern Novel: Ukigumo of Futabatei Shimei.* New York: Columbia University Press, 1967.

Said, Edward. *Beginnings: Intention and Method.* New York: Basic Books, 1975.

———. "Representing the Colonized: Anthropology's Interlocutors." *Critical Inquiry* 15 (Winter 1989): 205–25.

———. *The World, the Text, and the Critic.* Cambridge, Mass.: Harvard University Press, 1983.

Sakai, Naoki. "Modernity and Its Critique: The Problem of Universalism and Particularism." *South Atlantic Quarterly* 87 (Summer 1988): 475–504.

———. "Voices of the Past: The Discourse on Language in Eighteenth-Century Japan." Ph.D. diss., University of Chicago, 1983.

Seidensticker, Edward. *Low City, High City: Tokyo from Edo to the Earthquake.* New York: Knopf, 1983.

———. *Tokyo Rising: The City since the Great Earthquake.* New York: Knopf, 1990.

Shimazaki Toson. *Before the Dawn.* Translated by William Naff. Honolulu: University of Hawaii Press, 1987.

Sibley, William F. "Naturalism in Japanese Literature." *Harvard Journal of Asiatic Studies* 28 (1968): 157–69.

———. Review of Tatsuo Arima, *The Failure of Freedom. Harvard Journal of Asiatic Studies* 31 (1971): 247–85.

Silverberg, Miriam. *Changing Song: The Marxist Manifestos of Nakano Shigeharu.* Princeton: Princeton University Press, 1990.

Silverman, Kaja. *The Subject of Semiotics.* London: Oxford University Press, 1983.

Smith, Henry D., II. "The Edo-Tokyo Transition: In Search of Common Ground." In *Japan in Transition: From Tokugawa to Meiji*, edited by Marius B. Jansen and Gilbert Rozman. Princeton: Princeton University Press, 1986.

———. "From Edo to Tokyo: The Provincial Interlude." Paper presented to Regional Seminar, Center for Japanese Studies, University of California, Berkeley, May 1982.

Smith, Paul. *Discerning the Subject.* Minneapolis: University of Minnesota Press, 1988.

Sommer, Doris. "Irresistible Romance: The Foundational Fictions of Latin America." In *Nation and Narration*, edited by Homi K. Bhabha. New York: Routledge, 1990.

Spivak, Gayatri. "The Post-Modern Condition: The End of Politics?" In *The Post-Colonial Critic: Interviews, Strategies, Dialogues*, edited by Sarah Harasym. New York: Routledge, 1990.

———. "Subaltern Studies: Deconstructing Historiography." In *In Other Worlds: Essays in Cultural Politics.* New York: Routledge, 1988.

Stewart, Susan. "Shouts on the Street: Bakhtin's Anti-Linguistics." In

Bakhtin: Essays and Dialogue on His Work, edited by Gary Saul Morson. Chicago: University of Chicago Press, 1986.

Taylor, Patrick. *The Narrative of Liberation: Perspectives on Afro-Caribbean Literature, Popular Culture, and Politics*. Ithaca: Cornell University Press, 1989.

Todorov, Tzvetan. *Mikhail Bakhtin: The Dialogical Principle*. Minneapolis: University of Minnesota Press, 1984.

Tomashevsky, Boris. "Sterne's *Tristram Shandy*: Stylistic Commentary." In *Russian Formalist Criticism: Four Essays*, edited by Lee T. Lemon and Marion J. Reis. Lincoln: University of Nebraska Press, 1965.

Torrance, Richard Edgar. "Tokuda Shūsei and the Representation of Shomin Life." Ph.D. diss., Yale University, 1989.

Twine, Nanette. "The Genbunitchi Movement: Its Origins, Development, and Conclusion." *Monumenta Nipponica* 33 (Autumn 1978): 332–56.

Vernon, Victoria. *Daughters of the Moon: Wish, Will, and Social Constraint in Fiction by Modern Japanese Women*. Berkeley: University of California Press, 1988.

Volosinov, V. N. "Discourse in Life and Discourse in Poetry: Questions of Sociological Poetics." In *Bakhtin School Papers*, edited by Ann Shukman, translated by John Richmond. Oxford: Holdan Books, Ltd., 1983.

———. *Marxism and the Philosophy of Language*. Trans. by Ladislav Matejka and I. R. Titunik. New York: Seminar Press, 1973.

Walker, Cheryl. "Feminist Literary Criticism and the Author." *Critical Inquiry* 16 (Spring 1990): 551–71.

Walker, Janet. *The Japanese Novel of the Meiji Period and the Ideal of Individualism*. Princeton: Princeton University Press, 1979.

Ward, Cynthia. "What They Told Buchi Emecheta: Oral Subjectivity and the Joys of 'Otherhood.'" *PMLA* 105 (January 1990): 83–97.

Watt, Ian. *The Rise of the Novel*. Berkeley: University of California Press, 1957.

White, Hayden. *Metahistory: The Historical Imagination in Nineteenth-Century Europe*. Baltimore: The Johns Hopkins University Press, 1973.

———. "The Value of Narrativity in the Representation of Reality." In *The Content of the Form: Narrative Discourse and Historical Representation*. Baltimore: The Johns Hopkins University Press, 1987.

Wolfe, Alan. *Suicidal Narrative in Modern Japan: The Case of Dazai Osamu*. Princeton: Princeton University Press, 1990.

Young, Robert. *White Mythologies: Writing History and the West*. London: Routledge, 1990.

Index